William Henry Lyon

A Study of the Sects

William Henry Lyon

A Study of the Sects

ISBN/EAN: 9783337825867

Printed in Europe, USA, Canada, Australia, Japan

Cover: Foto ©Lupo / pixelio.de

More available books at **www.hansebooks.com**

A

STUDY OF THE SECTS.

BY

WILLIAM H. LYON.

One God and Father of all, who is above all, and through all, and in you all. — EPHESIANS iv. 6.

Fourth Edition.
WITH AN INDEX.

BOSTON:
UNITARIAN SUNDAY-SCHOOL SOCIETY,
25 BEACON STREET.
1892.

PREFACE.

This manual has been prepared at the request of the Unitarian Sunday-School Society for the use of the older classes in the schools to which that valuable body ministers. It may also be found useful to adult readers. Its aim is to present on the one hand a just and sympathetic account of the history and beliefs of the various bodies considered, and on the other hand to show plainly wherein Unitarians differ from them; to counteract the bigotry and conceit from which Unitarians have by no means freed themselves, and at the same time to show how weak and inconsistent is the position of those Unitarians who are anxious to have it understood that there is not, after all, much difference between them and their Evangelical brethren. The fundamental idea of this book is that the difference between the two parties is as great as that between the Evangelicals and the Catholics, or would be if our Orthodox friends would stand still long enough to be photographed distinctly. The study of this subject and the consultations I have had with various representative men have surprised me by revealing the state of confusion and change in which all beliefs except those of the Roman Catholics now exist. Few of those who claim to hold the faith of their fathers are aware how far they have drifted from that faith, or what chameleon powers words have to assimilate themselves to the mental environment of succeeding generations.

Realizing the danger of misrepresenting the beliefs of others, I have submitted, so far as I could, the various chapters to revision by prominent members or friends of the sects treated in them, and have in every case accepted the corrections made. This is true of the chapters on the Jews, Roman Catholics (doctrine only), Episcopalians, Congregationalists, Baptists, Methodists, Friends, Universalists, Unitarians, and Spiritualists. I am thus indebted to the Rev. Messrs. RAPHAEL LASKER, RICHARD NEAGLE, L. W. SALTONSTALL, A. L. PLUMB, D.D., R. J. ADAMS, Bishop R. S. FOSTER, D.D., C. C. HUSSEY, E. L. REXFORD, D.D., GRINDALL REYNOLDS, and M. J. SAVAGE.

The entire chapter on the Society for Ethical Culture was written by Mr. W. M. SALTER, and the doctrinal part of the one on the New Church by the Rev. J. K. SMYTH. I am also greatly indebted to the Rev. H. G. SPAULDING, Secretary of the Sunday-School Society, for many suggestions and much aid in putting the book through the press, and to the unknown but acute and learned proof-readers of the University Press for valuable corrections in both form and matter.

The word *sect* is used in no invidious sense, but as a convenient term for the parts into which the Christian body is actually divided or dissected. The words *Evangelical*, *Orthodox*, and the like are employed in their popular sense, without any concession of their literal truth; nor must the word *Liberal* be construed as implying that the only liberality in religion is to be found in the bodies so named.

PREFACE.

The manifold nature of the subject has involved an amount of labor not likely to be appreciated by any one who has not attempted something of the same kind. Yet the necessity of giving to it only the fragments of a busy life may well have left it lacking in unity as well as mistaken on single points. As I review the extent of ground covered and the number of questions answered which have puzzled the saints and the ages, I fear to draw upon myself the latter half of the judgment pronounced upon Whewell, that "science was his forte, and omniscience his foible." Still more do I tremble at my temerity in daring to state the belief of Unitarians, which I have done against my wish and at the request of the Society which publishes the manual. Yet some such book seems to be needed, — is certainly demanded; and this may serve till a better one takes its place.

W. H. LYON.

THE STUDY OF ALL SOULS CHURCH,
ROXBURY, May 1, 1891.

NOTE TO SECOND EDITION.

The only change of importance in this edition is in the remarks on the Society for Ethical Culture, pp. 180, 181. While I am grateful for the unexpectedly cordial reception which this book has found with both the religious and the secular press, I am sure there must be errors which a more careful reading might have detected. I shall be sincerely grateful for any corrections which may be suggested to me.

W. H. L.

ROXBURY, Sept. 16, 1891.

CONTENTS.

Part I.—THE JEWS.

Part II.—THE CHRISTIANS.

CHAPTER	PAGE
I. Doctrines held by Christians	13

1. Creeds, 13. — 2. Source of Authority, 17. — 3. God, 22. — 4. Jesus, 24. — 5. Human Nature, 29. — 6. Salvation, 33. — 7. The Future Life, 39. — 8. The Church and the Sacraments, 45.

II. The Roman Catholics	52
III. The Old Catholics	62
IV. The Eastern Church	64
V. The Protestants	69

Section I. — The Evangelical Protestant Sects.

1. The Lutherans, 77. — 2. The Reformed Church, 82. — 3. The Episcopalians, 85. — 4. The Reformed Episcopalians, 96. — 5. The Presbyterians, 99. — 6. The Congregationalists, 109. — 7. The Baptists, 119. — 8. The Moravians, 125. — 9. The Methodists, 127. — 10. The Salvation Army, 135.

Section II. — Certain other Protestant Sects.

1. The Anti-Sectarian Sects, 137. — 2. The Friends, 140. — 3. The New Church, 147. — 4. The Adventists, 154.

Section III. — The Liberal Protestant Sects.

1. The Universalists, 158. — 2. The Unitarians, 163.

Part III.

SECTS NOT CALLING THEMSELVES CHRISTIAN.

1. The Society for Ethical Culture, 179. — 2. The Spiritualists, 181. — 3. The Mormons, 187.

A STUDY OF THE SECTS.

PART I.

THE JEWS.

WHOSE is the adoption, and the glory, and the covenants, and the giving of the law, and the service of God, and the promises; whose are the fathers, and of whom is Christ as concerning the flesh. — ROMANS ix. 4, 5.

Name. — The Jews were originally called by others *Hebrews*, or "those who came over," because Abram and his family came over the Euphrates down into Canaan (Gen. xii. 5). They called themselves *Children of Israel*, after Jacob, or Israel (Gen. xxxii. 28), from whose sons or grandsons the Twelve Tribes were said to have descended. After the Captivity they were called *Jews*, a name at first given to the Tribe of Judah, who formed the chief part of those who were carried into exile at Babylon, and who returned to found the nation as we know it.

History. — The word *Jew* is applied to a nation and to a religion. Until the last century all Jews by birth were Jews by religion also, but since that time a rapid divergence in beliefs has taken place. It is the religion which we have especially to consider.

The Jews belong to that branch of the human race called the Semitic, of which the Arabs, Assyrians, and Phœnicians were also members. They are therefore of different descent from most of the nations among whom they dwell, who are of the Aryan family, — a difference which has probably had something to do with their isolation. From the Semitic races have come three of the great religions, — Judaism, Christianity, and Mohammedanism.

The history of the Jewish religion may be divided roughly into three periods, *formation, affirmation,* and *reformation;* or, according to their distinctive marks, *sacrificial, Scriptural,* and *rational.*

The period of formation extends from the beginning to the return from exile. The family of Abram came down from Ur of the Chaldees to Canaan, and, migrating thence, grew to a tribe, and settled upon the borders of Egypt, from which they were led out by Moses, who made Jehovah, or Jahweh, their distinctive God, and gave them as law the "Ten Commandments" and a few ceremonial precepts. Coming back into Canaan, their religion was much corrupted and confused by contact with the worship of other gods, whose existence they acknowledged, though they claimed Jehovah as the most powerful. Worship consisted almost entirely of sacrifices, offered during their wandering-time in the Tabernacle, but after David had made Jerusalem the fixed capital, in the Temple. Toward the latter part of the period a remarkable class of men, the Hebrew Protestants, arose, called "prophets," or "spokesmen," — in their own tongue, "seers," — who strove to hold the people to the worship of Jehovah only, and to make that worship consist of a just and pure life as well as of ceremonies. These elements were still contending when the Exile ended the national existence.

When the Jews, comparatively few in number, returned (B. C. 536), they were marvellously changed. Their religion gathered less and less around the altar, but more and more around the Book. Separated from their Temple and its sacrifices, they had still many of their sacred writings; and their zeal had centred in the minute study of these. The Temple was rebuilt, indeed, and the sacrifices restored on a magnificent scale; but *synagogues,* or meeting-houses, rose all over the land, in which the reading and exposition of the Law and the Prophets became the centre of interest; and by the side of the priests and Levites, who conducted the sacrificial worship, rose the scribes, lawyers, rabbis, etc., who were students of the sacred books, and the Pharisees, Sadducees, Zealots, etc., who were divided on their application. Idolatry had disappeared forever; and Jehovah became to all, not merely the most powerful national god, but the only God of the world. As His chosen and peculiar people, the Jews proudly withdrew from all unnecessary intercourse with the "Gentiles," or nations, and forbade intermarriage with them; while as a consolation for political subjection to them, they clung tenaciously to their belief in a Messiah, or "anointed one" of God, who should subdue the nations, and make His people the masters and teachers of the world. There had also crept in or been developed a belief in immortality, in angels and devils, and in the divergent destiny of the good and the wicked, which to most meant respectively Jews and Gentiles.

The appearance of Jesus made no appreciable difference in this religion, except to intensify it under the persecution by his later followers. Christianity became a religion of the Gentiles. The destruction of the Temple with Jerusalem, in 70 A.D., not only dispersed the surviving Jews over the world, but put an end to the sacrificial side of their religion. It lived henceforth only in the synagogue and the home, and only as a religion according to the Scriptures. The Books became a bond between the dispersed and persecuted communities, and received a wonderful but morbid microscopic study. The comments of various revered rabbis were collected into a second work, called the *Talmud*, which became almost as sacred as the original books. The first part of this, the *Mischna*, or commentary on the text, was finished about A.D. 200; and the second, the *Gemara*, or commentary on the first part, about A.D. 400. To keep the text of the Law pure through all copying, there grew up the *Masora*, or study of the form, under the care of learned men called Masorites. The shameful persecution of the Jews during the Middle Ages, their pathetic fidelity to each other and to their religion, and the development of their national characteristics should be carefully read, but does not belong here.

The third period, the reformative or rational, came on slowly, and has become distinct only in the last hundred years. The Reformation brought the Jews little mercy at first, though the revived prominence of the Bible led to the study of Hebrew, but the growth of kindlier sentiments and broader views in general have gradually freed the Jews from all political disabilities, and set the national talents free for a development which has been no less than wonderful. But the change in their religion, thus opened to the influences of modern thought, has been as great. The majority of the more intelligent have thrown off the yoke of the Talmud, and a large and increasing part treat even the Law in a free, rationalizing way, agreeing with the most radical of the Gentile scholars in the treatment of the questions of inspiration, miracle, and the like. Though the national consciousness and loyalty are still marvellously strong, they are melting at their outward edges; and the race may in time be amalgamated with the rest of mankind.

Doctrine. — As the Jews own no authority above the individual congregation, they have no common formal creed. The variations in their belief are very great, ranging from the extreme "orthodox," who have kept the faith almost if not quite intact, to the extreme "reformed," who are hardly to be distinguished from rationalistic theists or even agnostics. Converts to Christianity are extremely rare.

The distinctive doctrines of the Jews in Jesus' day were the one God, the "chosen people," the Messiah, and the divine origin and authority of their sacred books, especially the Pentateuch, or Law. Of these, the lofty and pure though severe and cold idea of God has been held against modern trinitarianism, as against ancient polytheism. That the Jews are His chosen and favored people, destined to rule the world, is a belief that is rapidly dying, though still held by the more ignorant in the Old World. It survives, however, in an almost universal pride of race and of its history, which shows itself especially in refusal to marry with "Gentiles," and even to be buried in the same cemetery with them. The expectation of a Messiah, or political and religious leader, who shall be sent by God to gather His people into Palestine again to begin their rule of the world, has even more completely disappeared. The "Mosaic" Law, though treated by many "reformed" Jews with great latitude of interpretation and practice, has still a great hold upon the race as a whole. It is always read at public worship, partly in Hebrew. The Sabbath is observed upon the seventh day of the week, beginning at sunset on Friday and ending at sunset on Saturday, but generally only as a day of public worship, to the men usually nominal. The commandment to do no work on that day is found by all but extreme orthodox Jews impossible to obey in Christian lands. It is proposed to change the Sabbath to Sunday. Circumcision is commonly practised. The distinction between "clean" and "unclean" meats (Lev. xi.) is still regarded, at least in the home; and the only flesh eaten is that killed by men approved by the rabbis, so that the blood ("which is the life") is surely drained out. A most remarkable change, however, is the entire abolition, or rather silent abandonment, of the sacrificial system, once the centre of public worship, but made impossible by the banishment of the Jews from their own land and its Temple, and their scattered and persecuted condition. On the other hand, belief in immortality and its corollaries, which have been noticed as added to the ancient beliefs before Jesus' day, are still retained. Of course, the denial of Jesus' Messiahship carries with it denial of all the theology which has grown up around it in most Christian creeds, — the incarnation, atonement, etc., as well as the authority of the New Testament.

The modern Jew holds his public worship in "synagogues," or "temples." It is liturgical, consisting of prayers, some very ancient, but varying in different books; reading from the Law and from the Prophets, which are divided into lessons for the purpose; a sermon, and a benediction. The worshipping body is called a "congregation," and consists nominally only of men who are heads of families, ten at least being necessary, and is governed by trustees with president, etc., like most corporations. In very "orthodox" synagogues, the women sit apart in a gallery, which is sometimes latticed. There is usually a Sabbath-school.

Various religious festivals are observed, as the New Moon; the New Year (about September 6); the Passover (in March or April, like our Easter); Pentecost, or Feast of Weeks (May), commemorating the giving of the Law from Mount Sinai; the Feast of Booths, or Tabernacles; and Purim (March), which celebrates the Jewish victory recounted in the Book of Esther.

The debt of Christianity to Judaism is seldom fully appreciated. It was the hardy stock into which the graft that was to overshadow the world was set. That the Jews did not appreciate Jesus when he came is no more strange or culpable than the resistance of Roman Catholicism to Protestantism, of Lutheranism to Calvinism, of Calvinism to Methodism, or of the old faith generally to the new one that is born from it. A frank study of the Hebrew prophets also shows how little resemblance Jesus bore to the Messiah actually predicted by them, though it reveals how much affinity often exists between his teaching and theirs upon the nature of religion.

From Judaism Christianity inherited the conception of a pure and single God; the belief in immortality; the custom of preaching as a part of worship, and indeed the general elements of public service; the Sabbath; the Ten Commandments; and many of its finest precepts, as some of the Beatitudes. The defects of Judaism which Christianity filled up were the cold separation of God from His creation, and especially from the human soul, and the separation of religion from the common duties and affections of life. The God of the Hebrews was far superior to the sensual gods of the nations around them and to the half-human gods of even the classic nations. Though severe, He was holy and reverend, and far above such deeds as the Greeks and Romans attributed to their deities. The Christian idea of His Fatherhood, by which His own life was conceived to be in the souls of men, inheriting this nobility of conception, has brought God near to men without degrading Him or making Him common; and the Christian idea that "the true *liturgy* and undefiled before God the Father" is daily acts of love and self-respect, has made religion a warm and living thing. As we shall see, however, the popular Christianity, in concentrating worship upon Jesus, has again set God at a distance as a stern and implacable King, while it has degraded religion often into a repetition of Jewish ritualism and ceremonial pettiness.

The treatment of the Jews by "Christians" is one of the worst stains upon mediæval and modern history, as it has been in direct violation of the spirit and even of the precepts of him who said, "Father, forgive them, for they *know not* what they do." The vitality of the Hebrew stock through all persecutions and the brilliancy of its modern sprouting and blooming are evidence of the vigor of the stem into which Christianity was grafted. The peculiarities at which Christians are so incensed are largely the result of the treatment they have given; but if, as seems likely, there is to be an amalgamation of life, if not of belief, both will be gainers.

In secular life the Jews are remarkable for their aversion to trades and agriculture (a great change from their ancient ways, and due to their exclusion from guilds and the like during the Middle Ages) and their aptness for financial and mercantile life. They have many brilliant representatives in literature, art, and music, — such as Mendelssohn, Heine, Disraeli, the Rothschilds, and many others of note. Their home-life is very pure and domestic. They care for their own poor most generously, and are remarkable for their general health — due to "Mosaic" precepts largely — and freedom from intemperance and crime.

To Unitarians the reformed Jews especially are intellectually akin by their emphasis upon the unity of God, upon the spirit rather than the letter of the Bible, and upon character rather than creed, as well as by the rapid progress they are making toward a purer and more rational theistic religion. Between many Jews of this type and many Unitarians there is warm sympathy. Between the "orthodox," or ritualistic, Jews and the Unitarians the resemblance is only superficial, and the agreement as to the one God only arithmetical.

Statistics. — There are reckoned to be about 7,000,000 Jews in the world, the largest number in any one country being 2,552,000 in Russia. They are rapidly increasing in the United States from immigration, nearly 125,000 having come between 1885 and 1889, most of them from Russia and Poland; and there are probably in this country over half a million in all.

QUESTIONS.

By what different names have the Jews been known? When did these names arise? What do they mean? Into what periods is their religious history divided? What kind of a religion had they in the first period? What is a sacrifice? Do we make sacrifices now? What is there in common between theirs and ours? Who were the prophets? Can you name any? What did they teach? What do you know about the Exile? What changes had come over the re igion? What do you call the second period? What were "the Scriptures" to the Jews? Do they believe in the New Testament? Why not? What other books did the Jews study? What can you tell about the persecutions of them? Were they just? Are they continued to-day in any form? What is the third period? What is its characteristic? What do you mean by "rationalism"? Name any distinguished Jews of our day. What do you think of the Jews you know? How far are Christians to blame for anything that is disagreeable in them?

Is there unity of belief among modern Jews? Why not? What is the basis of doctrine? How does the Hebrew Bible differ from ours? What variation of opinion about it exists among them? As to God, are they Unitarian or Trinitarian? How do they regard Jesus? Do they expect any other Messiah? What do they think about future destiny? What is their Sabbath? What can you say of their worship? What festivals do they hold? What peculiar views have they as to food? As to burial? Marriage? How are their congregations organized? What are their meeting-houses called? What part do women take in worship?

REFERENCES.

The best handbook is *The History of the Religion of Israel*, by Crawford H. Toy, Unitarian Sunday-School Society. See also *Encyclopædia Britannica*, articles "Israel" and "Jews." Stanley's picturesque *Lectures on the Jewish Church*, 3 vols., end at the Christian Era; Milman's *History of the Jews*, 3 vols., brings the story nearly to the present day; J. K. Hosmer's *The Story of the Jews* gives interesting sketches of mediæval and modern Jewish history and biography. For a most graphic epitome of mediæval Judaism and the reform movement, see *North American Review*, vol. cxxv., two articles by Prof. Felix Adler; also, from the Jewish point of view, *Outlines of Jewish History*, by Lady Magnus. Solomon Schindler's *Messianic Expectations and Modern Judaism*, and *Dissolving Views in the History of Judaism*, are from the extreme "reformed" standing-point.

For the relation between the two religions, see Prof. C. H. Toy's *Judaism and Christianity: a Sketch of the Progress of Thought from the Old Testament to the New*.

A STUDY OF THE SECTS. 9

PART II.
THE CHRISTIANS.

REFERENCES ON THE GENERAL SUBJECT.

The best mere abstract is J. H. Allen's *Outline of Christian History*, Unitarian Sunday-School Society. The best short history is Prof. G. P. Fisher's *History of the Christian Church*. If but one book can be bought, it should be this or the first volume of Prof. Philip Schaff's *The Creeds of Christendom*. The latter contains the "History of Creeds," with a valuable comparison of the doctrines of the great branches of the Church; vol. ii. contains the "Greek and Latin Creeds," and vol. iii. the "Evangelical Creeds." For charming accounts of the rise of the sects which began in England, see Green's *Short History of the English People*, and Brooke Herford's *Story of Religion in England*. The cyclopædias of McClintock and Strong and of Schaff-Herzog, Blunt's *Dictionary of Sects, Heresies, and Schisms*; Lyman Abbott's *Dictionary of Religious Knowledge*; many articles in the Encyclopædia Britannica ; the histories of Neander, Milman, Schaff, Gieseler. and Baur, and for doctrine Hagenbach's and Shedd's, — are also valuable. See also Dorchester's *Christianity in the United States.* A very valuable bibliography, both on the general subject and on special periods and movements, is at the end of Fisher.

By this shall all men know that ye are my disciples, if ye have love one to another. — JOHN xiii. 35.

Name. — The name "Christian" was not used till several years after the death of Jesus, and then at Antioch (Acts xi. 26), a heathen city, and probably as a nickname. Before that his followers were called "disciples," "brethren," "believers," "saints" by themselves, and "Nazarenes" or "Galileans" by others. The word "Christian" is derived from the title "Christ," which is a Greek translation or equivalent of the Hebrew word *Messiah*, or "anointed one," given to Jesus as the true realization of the Jewish national expectation of a divinely sent deliverer and teacher.

History. — The history of Christianity properly begins with the first preaching of its founder, Jesus, who having been born probably about 4 B.C., became known to the public about A.D. 26 or 27. Rejected by the religious authorities of his nation, he soon began to preach in the open air; but after a career the length of which is variously estimated from one to three years, he was crucified by the Roman authorities at the demand of the Jews, probably in March, A.D. 30.

Hardly a score of years had passed when a division took place among his followers which it is very important to notice. It was the division between *ritual* and *spiritual* religion. We have found it between the Hebrew priests and prophets, and it runs through all Christian history. The first Christians were little more than a small Jewish sect, clinging to the laws of Moses and worshipping in the Temple. They differed from the other Jews mainly in the belief that the Messiah had come and that Jesus was he. The persecution which arose after the preaching and death of Stephen drove them from Jerusalem, scattered them among the Gentiles, and brought them into contact with wider and higher thought. A more spiritual Christianity was the fruit of this union; and it embodied itself first in Saul, or Paul, who denied the necessity of the observance of the Mosaic Law, — an external matter, "dead works," — and based Christianity upon *faith*, an act of the soul. Bitter dissension arose, ending at last in a compromise (see Paul's story in Galatians). But the two kinds of religion remained, and can be traced down to our own day. Mosaic Christianity, or the Christianity of Peter, died away; but its spirit passed into the more splendid ritual and priesthood of the Roman Catholic Church, whose head is claimed to be Saint Peter. Spiritual Christianity, or the Christianity of Paul, though it gained the victory at first, disappeared under Catholicism during the Middle Ages, to emerge in the Protestant Reformation, whose motto, "The just shall live by faith," and whose general spirit came from the Epistles of Paul. The same fundamental difference may be traced between Protestant sects, and between parties in those sects, from the Anglican ritualist to the silent "Quaker."

The first great division in the *body* of Christianity was the secession, or excommunication, of the Eastern Church, in 1051, which was due more to national than to doctrinal causes. Then Western Christianity divided, in the sixteenth century, into Catholic and Protestant. These three great branches must be now considered separately.

Government. — In government, Christians may be divided into *episcopal*, or those under the authority of bishops; *synodical*, or those controlled by representative bodies; and *congregational*, or those who own no human power above the individual church, or congregation. The first class is by far the most numerous, including Roman and Greek Catholics, most Methodists, the Episcopalians, and the Moravians. The second class includes Lutherans, Presbyterians, Reformed, many Methodists, and smaller sects. The third class includes Baptists, Congregationalists, Christians, Friends, Adventists, and Unitarians.

Another division might be made into those who do and those who do not believe in one visible church. The first of these classes would include the first two of the previous division, the second of these would coincide with the third.

Statistics. — There are in the world about 452,000,000 Christians, as against 340,000,000 Buddhists, 201,000,000 Mohammedans, 175,000,000 Brahmins, 80,000,000 Confucians, 14,000,000 Shintos, 7,000,000 Jews, and — if the entire population of the globe be reckoned as 1,434,000,000 — 165,000,000 "heathens." Less than one third of humanity is thus Christian.

Of the 452,000,000 Christians, 210,000,000 are Roman Catholic, 92,000,000 Greek, and 150,000,000 Protestant.

Who are entitled to the name "Christian" is a much vexed question. In popular usage it signifies anything that is good. Many sects deny it to all who do not hold their interpretation of Christianity. If the question were settled by votes, the Roman Catholics would have the plurality; but if it were decided by the common meaning of such adjectives, Christian would mean agreeing with Christ in the main points of his teaching. A Darwinian or an Hegelian is not one who believes every word that Darwin or Hegel has said, but one who accepts the main principles of the scientist or philosopher, or at least his characteristic principle. Unitarians maintain that they are Christians because they believe in the main principles of the teaching of Jesus, — as the unity and spiritual nature of God, His fatherhood to all men, the duty of men to love Him and each other, the sure reward of goodness and punishment of wickedness, and the life after death. Whether these beliefs were original with him or not, they were by him made effectual upon the world, — especially upon those from whom we are descended as to religion. Certainly to be a Christian does not compel acceptance of what Paul said, or what the writer of the Fourth Gospel said, or what any one else said who seems to have added to the original utterances of Jesus, or reported or interpreted them in a way which seems now to have been wrong. In a more interior and spiritual sense, to be a Christian is to live the life of love which was the characteristic of Jesus. This is the definition which he himself is said to have given to discipleship.

QUESTIONS.

What was the origin of the name "Christian"? What does it mean? What sort of Christians were the first disciples? Ought we to wish for a restoration of "primitive Christianity"? Who changed this? What did he teach? What is the fundamental division of religion? What other manifestations of spiritual Christianity besides that of Paul? What was the first great division in the body of Christendom? How did Western Christianity divide? How does this division stand to-day? What was the first division of Protestantism? How is Protestantism commonly divided to-day? What is the meaning of these names? Under which would you put the Presbyterians? Universalists? Episcopalians? Methodists? Friends? Unitarians? What are the three sources of authority? How are Christians divided as to government? How in numbers? Are Christians or heathens the more numerous? What difference of opinion exists as to the meaning of the name Christian? What should guide us? Are Unitarians Christians? Can one doubt the miraculous birth or resurrection and be a Christian? Why? What did Jesus say of discipleship to himself? Which is the deeper likeness, that of belief or that of character?

CHAPTER I.
DOCTRINES HELD BY CHRISTIANS.

REFERENCES FOR THE DOCTRINES IN GENERAL.

THE points of agreement and disagreement between the larger divisions of Christendom are summed up in Schaff, vol. i. pp. 919-930. For exposition at greater length, see Hagenbach's *History of Doctrines*; Shedd's *History of Christian Doctrine*; E. H. Hall's *Orthodoxy and Heresy in the Christian Church*; and articles in McClintock and Strong, Schaff-Herzog, Britannica, and other cyclopædias. Calvin's *Institutes of the Christian Religion* and the works of the leading theologians of the various sects — as Pond, Hovey, Foster, Wesley, etc. — are also useful. For liberal Anglican views, see Haweis's *Thoughts for the Times*, Stanley's *Christian Institutions*, and Momerie's sermons. For Unitarian opinions, see Hedge's *Reason in Religion*, Clarke's *Truths and Errors of Orthodoxy* and his *Ideas of the Apostle Paul*, G. E. Ellis's *Half-Century of Unitarian Controversy*, the tracts of the American Unitarian Association, and the published sermons of Channing, Dewey, Clarke, Chadwick, Savage, and others.

---

1. CREEDS.

Our little systems have their day;
They have their day and cease to be;
They are but broken lights of thee,
And thou, O Lord, art more than they. — *Tennyson.*

The word "creed" is derived from the Latin *credo*, "I believe," and is used to designate a formal statement, usually authoritative, of belief on religious subjects. All Christian bodies have creeds except the Friends, the Unitarians, the Disciples of Christ, the "Christians," the Christian Union, and some smaller sects. The Methodists have no formal creed, but a virtual one in certain standards which are regarded as authoritative. The Congregationalists and Baptists, with other congregational bodies, hold to the right of each church to formulate its own statement of faith. Many Unitarian churches have "covenants," or other statements of belief and purpose; but they are often of no practical use, and are never intended to express exhaustively or to limit in any way the belief of the signer.

THE FIRST CREEDS.

NATHANAEL'S (John i. 49). — "Rabbi, thou art the Son of God; thou art the King of Israel."

PETER'S (Matt. xvi. 16). — "Thou art the Christ, the Son of the living God."

PAUL AND SILAS'S (Acts xvi. 31). — "Believe on the Lord Jesus Christ, and thou shalt be saved."

THE THREE GENERAL CREEDS.

These are either formally or tacitly acknowledged in the Greek, Latin, and Evangelical Protestant Churches.

I. **The Apostles' Creed.** — This name came from the legend that the creed was composed by the twelve Apostles, each contributing a clause, or article, beginning with Peter. This was believed till two hundred years ago. It is now certain that the creed first took shape at the end of the fourth century in the Western Church, attained its present form at the end of the fifth century, if not later, and was formally adopted in the eighth. For an interesting table showing its growth, and also for many statements of belief between it and those in the New Testament, see Schaff, vol. ii., pp. 11-40.

"I believe in God the Father Almighty, Maker of heaven and earth.

"And in Jesus Christ, His only begotten Son, our Lord, who was conceived by the Holy Ghost, born of the Virgin Mary, suffered under Pontius Pilate, was crucified, dead, and buried; he descended into hell; the third day he rose again from the dead; he ascended into heaven, and sitteth at the right hand of God the Father Almighty; from thence he shall come to judge the quick and the dead.

"I believe in the Holy Ghost, the holy catholic Church, the communion of saints, the forgiveness of sins, the resurrection of the body, and the life everlasting. Amen."

QUESTIONS.

Is there any Trinity here? Any deity of Christ? Inspiration of the Scriptures? Atonement? Predestination? Eternal torment? How do you account for the lack of these important doctrines in so early a creed? What does the word *catholic* mean? The *resurrection* of the *body?* How much of this creed can a Unitarian accept?

II. **The Nicene Creed.** — This is so called from the Council of Nicæa, in Asia Minor, by which its first form was adopted as a decision against the Arians, 325. The clauses after "I believe in the Holy Ghost" were added later, and formally adopted by the Council of Chalcedon in 381. The words, "and the Son," were illegally added by a Western Council in 589, and became a cause of division between the Eastern and Western Churches. The circumstances amid which the creed arose naturally led to stress on the divinity of Jesus and of the Holy Ghost. It was a Greek, or Eastern, as the Apostles' was a Latin, or Western, creed.

"I believe in one God the Father Almighty, Maker of heaven and earth, and of all things visible and invisible.

"And in one Lord Jesus Christ, the only-begotten Son of God, begotten of the Father before all worlds, God of God, Light of Light, very God of very God, begotten, not made, being of one substance with the Father; by whom all things were made; who for us men and for our salvation came down from heaven, and was incarnate by the Holy Ghost of the Virgin Mary, and was made man, and was crucified also for us under Pontius Pilate; he suffered and was buried; and the third day he rose again, according to the Scriptures, and ascended into heaven, and sitteth on the right hand of the Father; and he shall come again with glory to judge both the quick and the dead; whose kingdom shall have no end.

"And I believe in the Holy Ghost, the Lord and Giver of Life, who proceedeth from the Father and the Son; who with the Father and the Son together is worshipped and glorified; who spake by the Prophets. And I believe in one Catholic and Apostolic Church; I acknowledge one Baptism for the remission of sins; and I look for the resurrection of the dead, and the life of the world to come. Amen."

III. **The Athanasian Creed.** — This name arose from the belief that the creed was composed by Athanasius, the defender of the divinity of Christ at the Council of Nicæa, 325. But it is now certain that the creed did not appear till the close of the eighth century. It was of Latin origin, and is much used in the Roman Church. The Church of England ordains its use on thirteen festival days in place of the Apostles' Creed; but it is much disliked. The American Episcopalians omitted it from their Prayer-Book; but it is proposed to restore it for use four times a year. It is too long and tedious to give in full, but a few clauses will show its tone: —

"1. Whosoever will be saved: before all things it is necessary that he hold the Catholic Faith:

"2. Which faith except every one do keep whole and undefiled: without doubt he shall perish everlastingly.

"3. And the Catholic Faith is this: That we worship one God in Trinity, and Trinity in Unity;

"4. Neither confounding the Persons: nor dividing the Substance.

. . . . . .

"15. So the Father is God: the Son is God: and the Holy Ghost is God.

"16. And yet they are not three Gods: but one God.

. . . . . .

"29. Furthermore it is necessary to everlasting salvation: that he also believe rightly the Incarnation of our Lord Jesus Christ.

"30. For the right Faith is, that we believe and confess: that our Lord Jesus Christ, the Son of God, is God and Man:

"31. God, of the Substance of the Father; begotten before the worlds: and Man, of the Substance of his Mother, born in the world.

"32. Perfect God: and perfect Man, of a reasonable soul and human flesh subsisting.

"33. Equal to the Father, as touching his Godhead: and inferior to the Father as touching his Manhood.

. . . . . .

"37. For as the reasonable soul and flesh is one man; so God and Man is one Christ."

REFERENCES.

The first chapter of Schaff's work states the arguments for creeds. For the creeds themselves, see the whole work. A summary of them forms the last chapter In Shedd. Good essays in Stanley's *Christian Institutions*, chaps. 12 and 14. A little book of fine spirit is Phillips Brooks's *Toleration*. The Unitarian view is given in Dr. Channing's *The System of Exclusion and Denunciation in Religion* (American Unitarian Association Tract 122 in First Series), and *Extracts from a Letter on Creeds*, and in most statements of Unitarian belief.

---

2. THE SOURCE OF AUTHORITY.

> Out from the heart of Nature rolled
> The burdens of the Bible old;
> . . . . .
> The word unto the prophet spoken
> Was writ on tables yet unbroken;
> The word by seers or sibyls told
> In groves of oak or fanes of gold
> Still floats upon the morning wind,
> Still whispers to the willing mind. — *Emerson.*

All Christians rely upon human reason to some extent. But the reason finds limits beyond which it cannot go, — subjects upon which it is not competent to decide. It must then ask whether there is any authority higher than itself which can decide for it, and to the decision of which it will bow even when it cannot understand that decision, or when it shrinks from it. The Roman Catholic and the Evangelical Protestant answer this question in the affirmative. The Roman Catholic maintains that God has established upon the earth an institution called the Church, whose function is to instruct men upon those religious subjects which lie beyond their own ken and yet are of vital importance. This Church was founded by Jesus Christ, who was God the Son, who proved his divine nature and office by his miracles, and who constantly guides and instructs his Church. Moreover, by this Church the revelations made to various men before and at the time of Christ have been gathered, protected, guaranteed, and are interpreted. "We indeed devoutly receive the whole Bible as the word of God," said Cardinal Newman; "but we receive it on the authority of the Church; and the Church has defined very little as to the aspects under which it comes from God and the limits of its inspiration. . . . Not the Bible, but the Church, is to him [the Catholic the oracle of revelation. Though the whole Scripture were miraculously removed from the world as if it had never been, grievous as the calamity would be, he would still have enough motives and objects for his faith. Whereas to the Protestant the question of Scripture is one of life and death."

The Reformers swept the authority of the Church entirely out of their religious system, and, though after some wavering and confusion, established the Bible in its place as the sole "oracle of revelation." They were driven, by the necessity of opposing to the supernatural Church an authority of equal divineness and infallibility, to make the most extreme claims for the inspiration of the Bible, even declaring the Hebrew vowel-points to be of divine origin. Luther held views which even now would be called lax. Calvin, however, drew the lines closer; and the Westminster Confession asserted that "the whole counsel of God . . . is either expressly set down in Scripture, or by good and necessary consequence may be deduced from Scripture: unto which nothing at any time is to be added, whether by new revelations of the Spirit or traditions of men." The Bible became to the Puritan his guide, not only in religion, but in affairs of State and in the most private matters. In place of the Church as interpreter, the Protestant put the Holy Spirit. Reason might decide upon the credentials of the Scriptures, but the appreciation of their inner and saving meaning could come only by "the inward illumination of the Spirit of God." In the view of Calvinists this illumination could come only to the elect, and indeed was one proof of their election.

The Unitarian joins with other Protestants in decisively rejecting the authority of the Church. That Jesus founded any such institution as this pretentious ritualistic organization seems too absurd to need refutation. Its history is the answer to its claims.

As to the Bible, Unitarians have varied somewhat in their estimate of its authority. The early Protestant view was determined largely by the accompanying view of the corruption and helplessness of human nature, reason included. As this false view has retired, the reason has come to the front, and claimed greater rights. But the first Unitarians in New England were, or thought they were, as firm believers in the authority of Scripture as their Trinitarian opponents. Yet, for the most part unconsciously, they had adopted principles of interpretation which were at war with the old view. Both these facts are seen in these words of Dr. Channing : " Whatever doctrines seem to us to be clearly taught in the Scriptures we receive without reserve " (*Unitarian Christianity*) ; " All those interpretations of the Gospel which strike the mind at once as inconsistent with a righteous government of the universe, which require of man what is disproportionate to his nature, or which shock any clear conviction which our experience has furnished, cannot be viewed with too jealous an eye " (*Preaching Christ*). In the latter passage lie the germs of that reliance upon reason and conscience, and that freedom from unreasonable and unmoral subjection to mere textual authority, which have borne fruit in Parker, Emerson, and the majority of the Unitarian teachers of to-day. They recognize the inspiration of the Bible, but look upon revelation as progressive, according to the increasing capacity of men to receive the truth. Many passages in the Bible seem to them of supreme and unsurpassed value to the soul. Yet they look upon inspiration as not confined to any period, but as acting still, revealing both new depths in the old truths and new views of the divine nature and action. The sole criterion of truth, when it cannot be fully demonstrated by the reason, is satisfaction of the intellectual, moral, and spiritual needs of human life. What seems beyond the reach of reason and conscience and contrary to the deepest instincts of the soul was not intended to be known, or is not yet ready for human use. In this belief in the continuance of inspiration the Unitarian feels himself justified by the last words of Jesus to his disciples : " I have many things to tell you, but ye cannot bear them now. Howbeit, when he, the Spirit of truth is come, he will guide you into all truth." In reality, however, all Protestants qualify Scripture by the use of their own reason. It is simply a question of degree and often of frankness.

Moreover, the old Protestant view of the infallibility of Scripture is not warranted by Scripture itself. It rose out of the exigencies of controversy. A few simple facts, admitted by all, are decisive : (1) The Bible never speaks of itself as a whole. This is to be expected from the fact that it was a gradual growth, an aggregation of books, generally having no relation one with another nor even so much as referring to one another. The word "Scripture," as used in the New Testament, refers to the Old Testament, the New not yet having been collected. The infallibility of the Bible, therefore, *is not and cannot be a doctrine asserted in the Bible.* (2) Nor do the separate books claim divine warrant, with the exception of a few of the prophetical writings and some sayings of Paul. The inspiration of Genesis, for instance, has been thrust upon it; it claims no divine authority for itself. (3) Most of the books of the Bible are anonymous. The authorship named in their titles is the guess of the translators, not the assertion of the writers. (4) We have no guarantee that the books of the Bible have come down to us unharmed. The original manuscripts have all disappeared; and the oldest copy of any part of the New Testament does not date back of 300. Had God meant us to rely upon words, He would have made those words certain beyond doubt. (5) Jesus never wrote a word of his Gospel, and made no provision whatever for having it written. That he should have left it to the oral teaching of his disciples for a generation, then to be committed to four varying accounts, all of uncertain authorship, is inconceivable upon the old theory of the value of texts.

No one who comprehends the real weight of these simple facts, which are generally hidden in a cloud of petty arguments, can hold to the old theory of the Bible; yet whoever reads the Bible, not in a state of suspended intellectual animation, but with soul awake to the light of God on its mountain summits, will see that it is indeed "The Book."

QUESTIONS.

How do Christians agree as to the use of reason? Who acknowledge an authority beyond its limits? What is the Catholic doctrine of authority? of the interpretation of Scripture? How far could the Catholic dispense with the Bible? What was the position of the Reformers toward the Church? toward the Bible? What was Luther's view? Calvin's? that of the Westminster Confession? What was the Protestant principle of interpretation? the Calvinist?
What does the Unitarian say of the Church? What view of human nature modifies his view of reason? How did the first Unitarians use the Bible? What change has come? What is the view of inspiration now common among Unitarians? What do they say of what lies beyond human ken? What is their sole criterion of truth? What words of Jesus foreshadow the continuance of inspiration? Was the old Protestant view of Scripture warranted by the Bible itself? How did it arise? Does the Bible ever speak of itself as a whole? Why? What follows from this as to the doctrine of Biblical infallibility? What do the separate books claim for themselves? What must be said of their authorship? What guarantee have we of their preservation? What did Jesus write? Why? Do Unitarians still speak of the Bible as "The Book"? Why? Of what use is the Bible to you? What parts do you like most to read? What has been its influence upon the world?

REFERENCES.

The Catholic view of authority may be found in Newman's *Apologia pro mea Vita*, which all Protestants should read. The early Protestant position is stated in Calvin's *Institutes*, book I., chaps. vi.-x., and in chapter i. of the Westminster Confession. For a striking illustration of the change which has come over many of the descendants of the Puritans, see *What is the Bible?* by Prof. G. T. Ladd. For the Unitarian views, see Dr. Channing's sermons on "Unitarian Christianity," "Preaching Christ," and "The Church;" Andrews Norton's *Evidences of the Genuineness of the Bible;* Theodore Parker's *A Discourse of Matters pertaining to Religion*, books iv. and v.; J. W. Chadwick's *The Bible of To-day*; J. T. Sunderland's *What is the Bible?* M. J. Savage's *Beliefs about the Bible;* F. H. Hedge's *Ways of the Spirit;* and James Martineau's *Authority in Religion*, especially book ii., in which the Catholic and Protestant positions are very fairly stated. For shorter statements, see American Unitarian Association Tracts, Fourth Series, Nos. 69 and 80, and J. F. Clarke's tract among the "Miscellaneous."

3. GOD.

> O Source divine, and Life of all,
> The Fount of being's wondrous sea!
> Thy depth would every heart appall
> That saw not Love supreme in thee. — *Sterling.*

All Christians believe that there is but one God, and that He is infinitely powerful, wise, and loving. All Christians except Unitarians, Universalists, "Christians," and the "Hicksite" Friends, believe also in a Trinity within this unity. The common doctrine of the Trinity is thus defined in the Athanasian Creed: "We worship one God in Trinity, and Trinity in Unity; neither confounding the Persons nor dividing the Substance. For there is one Person of the Father, another of the Son, and another of the Holy Ghost. But the Godhead of the Father, of the Son, and of the Holy Ghost is all one: the Glory equal, the Majesty co-eternal."

This doctrine is nowhere distinctly stated in the Bible. The word "Trinity" does not occur at all, nor any word corresponding to it. This all admit. The texts which have been quoted in favor of the dogma from the Old Testament deserve no consideration whatever. In the New Testament one text has stated it (1 John v. 7, 8); but this has long been known to be spurious, and is omitted from the Revised Version. The strongest text remaining is Matt. xxviii. 19, 20; but as many Trinitarians admit (Meyer, McClintock), no equality or divinity or unity of substance is here expressed any more than in the common phrase, "Peter and James and John." The fact that no distinct and decisive proclamation of so new and startling a doctrine is anywhere made in the New Testament is conclusive against its truth. The Catholic theologians frankly say that the Trinity is one of the doctrines which only the Holy Spirit, acting through the *Church*, not the individual's judgment, can find in the Scriptures.

It was only gradually that the doctrine took shape, and probably by contact with Greek, and especially Alexandrian, philosophy. It is not in the Apostles' Creed. Its strongest support came from the growing belief in the deity of Jesus, which is considered under another head. The Greek word *trias*, or "triad," which does not necessarily involve unity of substance, does not occur till after 170; and the Latin word *trinitas* is not found till Tertullian wrote, after 200. A strong Unitarian party (that is, asserting the integrity of the Father's essence or substance) existed in the Church till after the Council of Nicæa, in 325, pronounced for the deity of Christ. The deity of the Holy Spirit seems never to have been very much discussed or very strongly asserted until the Athanasian Creed appeared. The Nicene Creed was changed without authority in 589, so that the Spirit was said to proceed "from the Father *and the Son*," — an addition which was one of the causes of the secession, or excommunication, of the Greek Church.

The Trinity remained the universal doctrine until the Reformation, when it was questioned, among others, by Michael Servetus and by Lælius and Faustus Socinus. The tendency among modern Trinitarians is to assert the doctrine as a revealed fact, without attempt to explain it. Such explanations have often brought to light great differences of opinion, amounting in many cases to tritheism on the one hand and utter destruction of the equality on the other. The modern Unitarians, of course, deny the doctrine of the Trinity in any and every sense.

QUESTIONS.

On what are all Christians agreed as to God? Who do not believe in the Trinity? Try to state that doctrine. Where is it stated in the Bible? Where was it ever stated? What is the strongest text now? What does it really mean? What do you infer from the lack of clear statement? How did the doctrine arise? What is the most important element in it? How soon do any words alleged to denote it appear? When was it officially adopted? When was the deity of the Holy Spirit asserted? What unwarranted thing was done? Who denied the doctrine at the Reformation? What is the tendency of modern Trinitarians? What do the Unitarians think of the doctrine? May not God act in many ways? Must we restrict them to three? But do manifestations imply persons? Do you think the doctrine would have any influence on you, if you could believe it?

(For references, see under next head.)

4. JESUS.

O Love! O Life! our faith and sight
  Thy presence maketh one;
As through transfigured clouds of white
  We trace the noonday sun, —

So, to our mortal eyes subdued,
  Flesh-veiled, but not concealed,
We know in thee the fatherhood
  And heart of God revealed. — *Whittier.*

The rank and office of Jesus form the core of Christian doctrine. The point of separation between the first Christians and Judaism was as to whether he was the Messiah or not; in the belief in his deity centres the whole system of Roman, Greek, and Evangelical Protestant doctrine; and, rightly understood, the idea of " God in Christ " is also the heart of the Unitarian faith.

It is impossible to go into the full discussion of Scriptural texts; but a few main points must be briefly stated: (1) The Jews, who studied their Bible (Old Testament) with most devoted and minute care, never dreamed that the Messiah there predicted was to be Jehovah himself. He was either a personification of the righteous part of Israel or, later, a prophet or king divinely sent, endowed, and guided, but like all other prophets and kings, — like Moses, Elijah, and David, — a man. (2) Those who heard Jesus never understood him to claim to be God except once (John x. 33), when Jesus promptly disclaimed the title in any other sense than as it had been given to the ancient Hebrew judges; that is, as representative of God. No one who understands how holy, inaccessible, and separate from humanity the Jews held God to be can fail to see that the claim of Jesus to be identical with Him would have roused too great a tumult to have escaped record, and would have been made the centre of the accusations against him. The one case cited, to any one who understands the nature of the Fourth Gospel, is under suspicion. (3) Moreover, it must be remembered that Jesus, as a Jew, was brought up Unitarian, and any such enormous change in his view of God or of himself must have been made the very heart of his teaching. On the contrary, the first three, or Synoptic, Gospels contain not a single clear enunciation of this tremendous assumption; but they do contain sayings of Jesus which imply his subordination to God, as Matt. xix. 17, xxvi. 39-42, xxvii. 46. There is no reason why he should *disclaim* deity, for without some clear assertion of it by himself no Jew would have suspected it. His appearance and life were human; and nothing short of irresistible proof, which is made impossible by these naive utterances, can lead us to think he was anything else. (4) The Fourth Gospel is evidently not so much a narrative as a philosophy of Jesus. The Jesus who speaks there is not the Jesus of the Synoptics, but a dramatic personification of the writer's ideal, — often beautiful and rich in spiritual suggestion, but not drawn from life. But even there, while many passages, especially those which come from the author himself, as the first verses of the first chapter, point to an exaltation of Jesus' nature above the human, there is no such equality with the Father as the creeds assert, while on every page there are words ascribed to Jesus himself which most clearly imply his subordination (v. 19, 30; vii. 16; viii. 28, etc. As for x. 30, see xvii. 21). (5) The first preaching after Jesus' death set him forth as a prophet (Acts ii. 22, iii. 22, xvii. 31). (6) Paul spiritualized his idea of Jesus, as he did every other point in Christian belief, — as baptism and the resurrection, — and undoubtedly assigned to Jesus a supernatural mission and endowment, but never deity.

In short, the nearer we get to the words of Jesus himself, the less we hear of any exaltation of him above the rank of a prophet of God.

It is when Christianity moves away from Judaism, with its utter separation of God from man, into the atmosphere of the classic world, where the line between gods and men was always vague, and where it had seemed easy to deify even the Roman emperors, — it is then that Jesus mounts rapidly to Deity. The remnants of primitive Christianity, as the Ebionites, retained the original belief in Jesus' humanity; but Greek and Latin Christianity drew from Greek and Latin philosophy and theology abundant sustenance for the deification of their Master. First, however, must come a long struggle, which reached its climax in the debate between Arius, a presbyter of Alexandria, and Athanasius, a deacon in the same city. Arius maintained that Christ was a being above humanity, but created by God out of *different* substance from His own. The Semi-Arians held him to be of *similar* substance, but created and subordinate. Athanasius asserted him to be of the *same* substance and equal in rank. The Emperor Constantine assembled at Nicæa, in Asia Minor, the first "œcumenical" (or world) council in 325, at which the Athanasian view prevailed; and Arianism, though widely spread, died away. Then followed a long controversy over the exact nature of the union between the human and the divine. Apollinaris, Bishop of Laodicea, denied the *humanity* of Christ, as Arius had denied his *divinity*, making the divine Reason, or "Logos," take the place of the human spirit. The Council of Alexandria (362) decided that the two natures, divine and human, *co-existed* in Christ. Then Nestorius, Bishop of Constantinople, denied any closer union than this co-existence, and claimed that it happened only after the birth of Christ, so that to call Mary "Mother of God" was absurd. The supernatural union of the two natures was proclaimed by the first Council of Ephesus, in 431. But Eutyches, of Constantinople, fell into error on the opposite side from Nestorius, uniting the two natures so closely that the human was lost in the divine. The Fourth Council, at Chalcedon, decided that the two natures were united in one person, without confusion, change, division, or separation, or loss of properties by either; but the Monophysite or one-nature party were still active, and were crushed at the Council of Constantinople in 553. Then came the question whether there were two *wills* in the two natures, the Monothelite party contending for but one; but the Council of Constantinople in 680 affirmed the two wills, the divine following the human. The "Monophysites" and "Nestorians" still exist, however, as sects in the Eastern Church.

So trimmed and cut back, the doctrine remained throughout the Middle Ages. The great Reformers made no change in it, and it passed over into 'Evangelical' Protestantism. But Michael Servetus, in 1531, taught a human Christ, and Lælius and Faustus

Socinus (d. 1562 and 1604), founded a large, wealthy, and intellectual sect in Poland on the doctrine that Christ was a human teacher, but deified after death for his holiness, and therefore to be worshipped. In England the subordination of Christ was made the centre of a separate sect by Lindsey and others, and in the United States by Channing and his co-workers. Beginning with Arianism, the view of Unitarians has gone on more or less frankly to pure humanitarianism.

The doctrine of the deity of Jesus has been of great service to many by bringing to their minds and hearts a God whom they could easily conceive and so love. That the infinite and unapproachable Jehovah should have come to this suffering and sinful earth, should have taken upon Himself the human form, and submitted Himself to human temptation and suffering, touches the heart by its apparent love and self-abnegation. The broader truth which underlies this we are to see later; but the love of God is taught to many minds more clearly by this one apparently exceptional case than by the more diffuse though truer conception which is now growing upon the human mind. On the other hand, however, it is as certain that the deification of Jesus has thrust the one true God into the background, robbed Him of His love and compassion, which are transferred to the Christ, made Him an implacable and exacting judge, and narrowed and lowered the whole conception of Deity. As the human intellect grew still feebler, even Christ was thrust in his turn into the background; his love and compassion were transferred to the Virgin Mary, or to the saints, who seemed nearer and more easily apprehensible than the superhuman Christ. The alternative is one which often meets the student of theology, — between warmth and truth; between adaptability to immediate need, and exact and conscientious conception.

But Unitarians also hold to the incarnation of God in Jesus. They differ from Evangelicals in denying that it was *only* in him, and that it ceased with him. They believe, and it is the very heart of their religion, that God is not only immanent in the physical universe, the One Power working by Eternal Law, but that he dwells in every human being, the giver of all light to the mind, all love to the heart, all life to the spirit. The difference between men in this respect is one of degree, not of nature. The glory of Jesus is not only his superiority in degree, but his clear consciousness of his sonship, and his announcement of it to the world. "Alone in all history, he estimated the greatness of man.

One man was true to what is in you and me. He saw that God incarnates Himself in man, and evermore goes forth anew to take possession of His world." Hence flows whatever is distinctive in Unitarianism, as the doctrines of the dignity of human nature, the internal authority, the eternal hope.

QUESTIONS.

What place does the belief about Jesus hold in Christianity? How can you illustrate this? What was the Jewish expectation of the Messiah? What view of Jesus had those who heard him? Was he ever accused of claiming to be God? What was his answer? What else can you say of the passage? What do the Synoptic Gospels say of Jesus? The Fourth Gospel? The first Christian sermons? Paul? When does the doctrine of his deity begin to take shape? Under what influences? What did the remnant of the original Christians hold? When did the debate reach its climax? Who were the two champions? Define Arianism, Semi-Arianism, the Athanasian doctrine. How was the debate settled? What was Apollinarianism? Nestorianism? Eutychianism? The Monophysite view? The Monothelite? How does all this impress you?

How did the Reformers stand? Who first taught a human Christ? What was Socinianism? Who started modern Unitarianism? What is this now?

What good has the doctrine of the deity of Christ done? What harm? What has happened to the worship of God? To that of Christ? What are the two points between which religious ideas vibrate? What is the Unitarian attitude toward Jesus? What is the difference between him and other men? How is our belief in the incarnation of God in humanity related to our religious beliefs? What difference has Jesus made to human history? What is he to you now? Examine your belief frankly.

REFERENCES.

The most remarkable book on the Trinitarian side is the late Canon Liddon's *The Divinity of our Lord*, the Bampton Lectures for 1866. The history of the doctrine may be found in Hagenbach or Shedd, and from the Unitarian side, in Lamson's *History of the First Three Centuries*, and Priestley's *History of the Corruptions of Christianity*. Liddon was answered by "A Clergyman of the Church of England" (who maintained that the doctrine is not to be found in the Bible by the unaided reason, but is taught on the authority of the Church) and by Dr. Vance Smith. Singular views of the Trinity may be found in Stanley's *Christian Institutions*, and Robertson's Sermons, Series III. No 4. The tracts and books of the American Unitarian Association, especially Norton's *Statement of Reasons*, give Unitarian views, often of the old-fashioned textual kind; but broader ground is occupied in Hedge's *Reason in Religion* (pp. 227-247), *Channing* (pp. 302-328, A. U. A. edition), Emerson's *Divinity School Address*, and best of all, Martineau's *Authority in Religion*, book iv. chap. ii. The Council of Nicæa is described most picturesquely in Stanley's *History of the Eastern Church.*

---

5. HUMAN NATURE.

> It is not ours to separate
> The tangled skein of will and fate,
> . . . . .
> And between choice and Providence
> Divide the circle of events.
> But He who knows our frame is just,
> Merciful, and compassionate;
> And full of sweet assurances,
> And hope for all, the language is,
> That He remembereth we are dust! — *Whittier.*

All Christians except the Liberals believe that God created Adam and Eve in a state of innocence, but needing probation. The serpent (by most supposed to be an embodiment of Satan), was therefore allowed to tempt them to disobedience. They yielded to the temptation, and in consequence of this "fall" sin obtained an irresistible power over them. Shame, labor, pain, the pangs of childbirth, and death entered into their lives, and they were thrust out of the Garden of Eden in disgrace. These consequences of their sin have fallen upon their descendants, so that all are helpless in the bonds of inherited corruption. All that they do or can do is worthless and even abhorrent in the divine eyes, and unless some aid can be secured from a source external to themselves, they are doomed to eternal punishment. This innate tendency to evil is called "original sin;" the helpless state into which man is brought by it, "total depravity;" and the process by which guilt is attributed to him, "imputation."

This view of man rests almost entirely upon the second and third chapters of Genesis, and upon the interpretation which Paul gave to them in his Epistle to the Romans, especially v. 12-19. Belief in it, therefore, must depend largely upon the opinion held of the authority of the Scriptures. But the following points must be considered: (1) This view of human nature finds no support from the *words of Jesus*. He never mentions Adam, Eve, or Eden, or refers to the story of the Fall in any way. Nor does he imply that the souls he addresses are not able to respond. The doctrine of total depravity is never referred to in any manner. (2) Genesis claims no divine warrant for its statements. They are frankly and naïvely written like any other history. That these chapters have been made the basis of a tremendous system of theology is not the fault of their authors. (3) No part of the Bible has been so squarely contradicted by modern discoveries as its opening chapters. If they are simply, as they seem, the statement of the belief of their day, or of their writers, this is not strange. If any one persists in taking them for a divinely inspired statement of infallible truth, he must choose between them and the almost universally accepted views of modern men of science. That pain and death were in the world before man came, being the common heritage of all sentient life; that man was not made directly of the dust of the earth, but, at least physically, developed from lower orders of animals; that the human race did not spring from a single pair; that there is no trace of a primeval innocence and a subsequent fall, but that all signs point to a gradual ascent from a savage condition; besides the minor points that woman was not made from the rib of man, and that the serpent never went upright or on legs, — all these views steadily gain ground, and relegate the story of Genesis to the realm of poetry, from which indeed it may have first come. Add to them the discrepancies between the two stories of the Creation (Gen i., ii. 1-3, and ii. 4-25), and the remarkably few references to either of them in the rest of the Bible except those of Paul, and we have abundant reason for doubt as to the literal accuracy of this account of the origin of man. As to the inferences of Paul from the original story, our view of them will depend, first, upon the value we set upon doctrines asserted by a follower which the Master did not teach, — a follower, too, who had never seen him; secondly, upon our idea of Paul's purpose in these words, — whether he meant to speak dogmatically and with authority, or whether he was speaking rhetorically, in the enthusiasm of his gratitude to Jesus. The Epistles were *letters*, and their style is not formal or exact, or even always correct. They were evidently not meant as doctrinal treatises (see Matthew Arnold's "St. Paul and Protestantism"). Yet it is on Paul's letters, not on the Gospels, that the popular view of human nature is based.

The doctrine of man's nature was worked out by the practical Western or Latin part of the early Church, as the doctrine of Christ's nature was by the speculative Eastern or Greek part. The general belief at first was in the inherited or Adamic *corruption* (not *guilt*) of man, and his ability to co-operate with the Holy Spirit in regeneration. Pelagius, a British monk, precipitated discussion by asserting, about 405, that man inherited nothing from Adam, neither original guilt, which was impossible, nor innate corruption, nor physical consequences, as pain and death, which were in the world before Adam. Every man was born free and unbiassed. Augustine in 412 maintained that man inherited not only inborn corruption, but guilt; that he was helpless, and could be saved only by the absolute power of God. This view at first gained the complete ascendency, and Pelagianism never had any considerable footing. But Augustinianism gradually softened into Semi-Pelagianism, which was very much the original doctrine of inherited corruption and the power of co-operation. This has remained the doctrine of the Roman Church, as fixed by the Council of Trent after the Reformation. This Church, though it has not pronounced authoritatively upon this point, holds that righteousness was not a natural quality of man at Creation, but was a supernatural addition, lost again at the Fall. Man's corruption is therefore a negative thing, — disorder and helplessness from loss of a leader, not a positive wilful rebellion.

"Augustinianism asserts that man is morally *dead*: Semi-Pelagianism, that he is morally *sick*; Pelagianism, that he is morally *well*."

The three views were revived at or after the Reformation. Calvin (1536) revived Augustinianism, Socinus (about 1590), Pelagianism, and Arminius (1589), Semi-Pelagianism. Calvin was followed by most Protestants of his century, — Presbyterians,

Congregationalists, Baptists, etc., — Socinus by the early Unitarians, and Arminius practically by the Church of England (the Romanists being already of the same mind), and formally by the Methodists in the eighteenth century. Since then Calvinism has largely died away and Arminianism now has decidedly the supremacy. Pure Pelagianism is made impossible by the facts of habit and heredity. No one would maintain that we come into the world without bias or corruption, amounting often to serious crippling, if not to helplessness. But that men are *guilty* of what they did not originate and cannot help, and deserve God's wrath and extreme penalty, is a doctrine which shows no sign of return. That there is original or hereditary *misfortune*, or moral *disease*, is more clearly seen, but original or hereditary *sin* is an obsolete phrase. That infants are guilty and under divine wrath and punishment, as Augustine and Calvin taught, is a doctrine that no one now can be found to own, scarcely to remember.

QUESTIONS.

What is the doctrine of man's nature called ? What is the common belief of Christians ? What is "original sin" ? "Total depravity" ? "Imputation" ? What are the Scriptural bases of this view ? What was Jesus' position ? What is true of the infallibility of Genesis ? What has modern science to say of Genesis ? Of pain and death ? Of man's origin ? Of his first condition ? Of woman's creation ? Of the serpent ? What differences can you find between the two stories of the Creation ? What shall we say of doctrines of Paul not given by Jesus ? Of Paul's style ? Of his idea of his letters ? Is the popular doctrine based on Jesus or on Paul ? Where was the anthropology of the Early Church worked out ? What was at first believed ? What did Pelagius teach ? Augustine ? The Semi-Pelagians ? How have these been revived in Reformation times ? What does the Roman Church teach ? What is the situation now ? What have science and philosophy to say upon the question ? Wherein do they agree with Calvin ? Wherein do they disagree ? Who believes in the guilt and damnation of infants ? Look into your own life. Does it seem to you that you have any bias toward good or evil ? Whence come your impulses ? Are you entirely free to do as you like ? Can you sympathize with Paul in Rom. vii. 15-25 ? Is sin ever the consequence of an irresistible disease ? How about inebriety ? How much power has heredity ? Habit ? Circumstances ? Are you Arminian, Socinian, or Calvinist ? Do you know any thorough Calvinists ? Can one be such and be happy ?

REFERENCES.

For the Catholic view, see Addis and Arnold. For the Calvinistic, besides Calvin's *Institutes*, see Jonathan Edwards's *A careful and strict Inquiry into the Prevailing Notions of the Freedom of the Will*, *The Great Christian Doctrine of Original Sin Defended*, and many of his sermons, especially *Sinners in the Hands of an Angry God*. For a milder view, see the discussion between Channing and Moses Stuart, and Horace Bushnell's *Nature and the Supernatural*. For the Unitarian view, see Dewey's sermons *On Human Nature* and *On Human Life*; Hedge's *Reason in Religion*, book i. chap. vii.; Martineau's *A Study of Religion*, book iii. chap. ii.; M. J. Savage's *Beliefs about Man*; *Human Nature not Ruined but Incomplete*, by C. C. Everett (American Unitarian Association Tract, No. 3, in Fourth Series).

6. SALVATION.

Feeble, helpless, how shall I
Learn to live and learn to die?
Who, O God, my guide shall be?
Who shall lead thy child to thee?

Blessed Father, gracious One,
Thou hast sent thy holy Son.
He will give the light I need;
He my trembling steps will lead. — *Furness*.

All Christians agree that the life and death of Jesus mark the chief epoch in the moral history of humanity, and that he has done more than any one else to bring about an atonement between God and man. Here, however, begin great differences of view, in harmony with the various views of human nature. Liberals, believing human nature to be essentially sound, though weak and stumbling, define atonement according to the original meaning of the word, as meaning *at-one-ment*, or leading the divine and the human will to be at one. They make this consist in the action of Jesus upon *man*, not upon God. They believe that God is always seeking to enter the world of humanity, — pressing upward through humanity to ever higher forms of spiritual life, as through the world of Nature into ever higher forms of physical life. It is the blindness, weakness, and selfishness of men that need to be overcome; and this Jesus has helped men to do by the power of his truth and his personality through the natural laws which are always at work in the moral and spiritual world.

Other Christians, including both Catholics and Protestants, consider the atonement as working upon the wrath or offended justice of God. It is He who has been reconciled to man, not man to Him. This has been effected by a compact between God the Father and God the Son, the latter agreeing to leave his heavenly home and bliss, to take upon himself human form and human nature, to be tempted, persecuted, and put to death upon the disgraceful cross, that so God may be moved to forgive the sins of men; since they, being corrupt, can do nothing to earn that forgiveness for themselves. The atonement is thus a supernatural matter, out of the range of ordinary moral and spiritual laws, as it is beyond the comprehension of human reason. To explain *how* it satisfies the justice of God there have been many theories. The two most generally held in modern times are that of the *vicarious* atonement, or substitution of Jesus' sufferings for those due from mankind, their sin being *imputed* to him and his righteousness to them; and the *governmental* theory,—that a great example was needed to show mankind the enormity of its sin, and to vindicate the divine justice by a punishment proportionate to the offence. The former view was adopted by the Calvinists, the latter by the Arminians. It is needless to say that to the Liberal both seem to be inconsistent with any true conception of justice. If man has sinned, it is man who must be punished; and no substitution of the innocent for the guilty, and no exhibition of an innocent "example," is justifiable. As to the support from Scripture, it may be said in general: (1) That the prophecies in the Old Testament are too vague or too contradictory to be made the basis of any such doctrines. (2) That they find no favor in the words of Jesus. Had we only the Gospels, no one would ever have dreamed of such theories. (3) That the Epistles were written by men who were fresh from Judaism, and unable to break away yet from the Jewish idea of sacrifice. The Epistle to the Hebrews shows the process of transition. Jesus is compared to the sacrificial victims on the Temple altar. This leads to language which Jesus never used, and which must be most liberally, not literally, construed. (4) When reconciliation between God and man is spoken of, it is almost invariably man who is said to have been reconciled to God (Rom. xi. 15; 2 Cor. v. 18-20; Col. i. 21).

Predestination. — But for whom was the atonement intended? The Arminians (including Romanists, Anglicans, Methodists) say *for all men*. It was a "*universal* atonement." The Calvinists say that it was only for the *elect*. All men are alike guilty and helpless; but God chooses to save some and let the rest go on to their merited doom. The former act is called "predestination," or fixing destiny beforehand; the latter, "preterition," or passing by. To the elect God gives faith and keeps them in holiness, so that they can never fall away ("perseverance of the saints"). The non-elect, including all the heathen and perhaps many children, strive they never so much, cannot attain to salvation. This doctrine is the heart of Calvinism as our Puritan forefathers held it, and is still nominally held by the Presbyterians and some among the Baptists and the Congregationalists, but is rapidly fading away. The Liberal, of course, positively rejects it. That there is predestination in this life cannot be denied. What we call the "force of circumstances," including the era and place of our birth, our surroundings, physical and moral, and the myriad influences which play upon us continually and mould us more than our own will, is largely but another name for what theology calls the sovereignty of God. How deeply this affects our inner life it is hard to say; but that it affects us in most important ways we cannot help seeing. The scientific doctrines of heredity and the power of environment are but other ways of stating this. The predestination of this life troubles the thoughtful mind with an unavoidable sense of injustice. The only escape from this is to look upon the present life as a stage of probation. When we begin it, we have no character, no merits or demerits, upon which divine justice could be exercised. God has a right, therefore, to use us for His own ends. But the opportunities and trials of this use bring out our latent moral powers, and we may believe that the character thus developed will be regarded in the life to come. The common doctrine of predestination, by extending the disregard of human character into the eternal future, cuts off this refuge of the sense of justice, and prolongs what we can understand if it is a temporary arrangement for judicial ends, into eternal selfishness and cruelty. All attempts to reconcile this doctrine with anything which we can call goodness, and can worship as worthy of our adoration, must fail. Its effect upon the moral life would be profoundly discouraging, so far as it were really believed.

The Arminian believes that the atonement was for all mankind. The human will is free to accept or reject the offer of pardon and restoration. This was the message of "free grace" which Methodism brought to a Calvinistic Protestantism, and is virtually the belief of Catholics and Episcopalians.

Conversion. — The atonement is appropriated by the individual through faith, by which great souls have meant a personal union with Christ, but which commonly degenerates into assent to creeds or ceremonies. To faith the Catholic adds reception of the sacraments of the Church, by which grace is conveyed to the partaker. By most Protestants this faith is expected to come during some sudden and peculiar crisis of religious experience, in which the sinner comes "under conviction of sin," realizes that he is "lost," seeks for help, and finds it with joy in a burst of "faith in the atoning merits of Jesus." To bring on this crisis, "revivals," or times of intense emotional excitement, are stimulated, during which, under the appeals of fervent preachers and the contagion of crowded congregations, people are supposed to be especially visited by the Holy Spirit. These "awakenings" are not as frequent as they were, and seem better fitted for people of crude than for those of developed natures. They fall in with the Evangelical view in general, — that the spiritual life proceeds by miracles, special interventions of divine power, since human nature is of itself helpless in its corruption. The Liberal, however, denying this corruption and helplessness, looks rather for gradual development than for crises, and relies more upon steady culture under constant influences than upon revolutions under sudden attacks from without. In this he is joined by Catholics and Episcopalians, and by an increasing number of other Protestants.

Justification. — The first effect of faith is "justification," by which the Catholic means *making* just, and the "Orthodox" Protestant *reckoning as* just. The conditions of justification, according to the Catholic view, are baptism and, at the age of reason, faith in God and love of God. By baptism the supernatural gift of righteousness, which was lost at the Fall of Adam, is restored to the recipient, fed by the other sacraments of the Church — especially the Eucharist — and by constant exercise of faith and love. The Protestant, however, denies that any rite can be the supernatural channel of divine grace, and makes faith alone the condition of acceptance with God, and justification a judicial declaration of mercy, by which the sinner's past is forgiven and washed away, and he is accepted for Christ's sake as already righteous.

Sanctification. — This seems to be with the Catholic identical with or a continuation of justification. The Protestant, however, makes it the process by which the remains of original sin, the habits and tendencies inherited from a sinful past, having now become involuntary and as it were external to the soul, are gradually eradicated. If the sinful soul be considered diseased, conversion is the crisis, justification the doctor's verdict that he has passed the crisis favorably, and sanctification the gradual convalescence under careful nursing and (says the Arminian) the recuperative power of his own system. The Calvinist, as we have seen, holds that the "elect" are kept from backsliding by divine power. The Methodist believes that it is possible for the soul to attain such purity of motive that however the old Adam may yet hover about the outside of one's life, one may be "perfect" in spirit. There has been in both these cases a danger of underrating the value of moral laws to those who are saved by faith, — a danger called "Antinomianism," by which some have been led into what mankind in general have considered and punished as ordinary wickedness.

Among Liberal Christians the terms "justification" and "sanctification," with many others, have passed out of use with the theology from which they sprang. All the truth which they covered is now included in the thought of that divine education which is constantly going on in the earnest soul through the various experiences of life. The care of God for the soul is seen by the Liberal, not merely in those influences which are called religious, or in those times and places which are considered sacred, but in every joy or sorrow, success or defeat, by which the mind is enlightened, the sympathies broadened, the faith of the soul awakened and trained, and the beauty of holiness made manifest. This may come sometimes in shocks which open the eyes suddenly, but generally through the experiences of every day.

QUESTIONS.

Upon what do all Christians agree as to the effect of Jesus' life and death upon human welfare? What difference is there between the Liberal and other views of the atonement? Which needs to be reconciled, God or man? What is the "Orthodox" theory of the atonement? What two explanations of the *mode* are given? What parties hold these? What does the Liberal answer to them? What can be said of the Old Testament texts cited to support them? What does Jesus say about them? How can you explain the strange language of the Epistles in many cases? Who is reconciled, according to the New Testament?

What difference of view exists as to the *extent* of the atonement? What is election? predestination? preterition? perseverance of the saints? What becomes of the heathen? of infants? Who still hold this view? Is there any predestination? What is the scientific principle of heredity? of environment? How does this differ from the theological doctrine of predestination? What is the Arminian belief?

How does man avail himself of the atonement? What difference exists between the Catholics and the Protestants as to this? What is the Protestant theory of conversion? What is a revival? From what deeper theory of "Orthodoxy" does its idea of conversion spring? What is the Liberal view? On what grounds is it held?

What does justification mean to the Catholic? to the Protestant? What are the conditions in each case? What is sanctification? What difference here between Catholic and Protestant? How far does the Calvinist carry sanctification? the Methodist? What is the difference between the two views? What is Antinomianism? What is the Liberal view of salvation in general? What do you think of revivals? of the conversions which you have known?

REFERENCES.

For Unitarian views, see C. H. Toy's *Judaism and Christianity*, chap. iv.; F. H. Hedge's *Reason in Religion*, book ii. chaps. vi. vii. and viii.; Martineau's *The Seat of Authority in Religion*, pp. 450 490; E. H. Sears's *Regeneration*; J. F. Clarke's *Christian Doctrine of the Forgiveness of Sins*; American Unitarian Association Tract, Fourth Series, No. 4, *The Atonement in Connection with the Death of Christ*, by F. H. Hedge, D. D., LL. D., also Nos. 16 and 18; S. J. Barrows's *Doom of the Majority*; Dewey's *Works*, pp. 373-381; J. H. Allen's *Ten Discourses on Orthodoxy*, chap. v.; J. F. Clarke's *Manual of Unitarian Belief*, and *Ideas of the Apostle Paul*, chaps. viii. xiii. xv. xvi.

The Calvinistic doctrines are given in Charles Hodge's *Systematic Theology*, and A. A. Hodge's *Outlines of Theology*; the Arminian, in Wilbur Fisk's *The Calvinistic Controversy*; the present Congregationalist, in R. W. Dale's *The Atonement*; a milder form, in J. McLeod Campbell's *The Nature of the Atonement*, and Horace Bushnell's *Vicarious Sacrifice* and *Forgiveness and Law*; the Catholic, in H. W. Oxenham's *The Catholic Doctrine of the Atonement*. The history of predestination is well condensed in the Encyclopædia Britannica, article, "Predestination." For the doctr'ne, see J. B. Mozley's *Augustinian Doctrine of Predestination*, and J. T. G. Shedd's *Discourses and Essays*. See, also, J. H. Newman's *Lectures on the Doctrine of Justification*.

---

7. THE FUTURE LIFE.

I know not where His islands lift
Their fronded palms in air,
I only know I cannot drift
Beyond His love and care. — *Whittier.*

All Christians, except the few who hold to the annihilation of the wicked, believe in the eternal continuance of every human life. One of the most striking consequences of Christianity at first was the calmness, and even joy, with which its disciples looked upon death. The inscriptions in the catacombs bear witness to this. But when the Catholic Church began to invoke the terrors of the Judgment, to force submission to its demands, and when later the Protestants rivalled it in working upon the imagination, a morbid fear of death, such as the heathen world never knew, fell upon Christendom. The Catholic Church is able to still this fear in those who die under its protection. Orthodox Protestantism cannot always lull the dread which it has roused, and is responsible for much needless mental suffering. Unitarians, Universalists, and Swedenborgians probably die with much more calmness; and the same is true of the better class of Spiritualists.

The reason for this difference is that the Catholic Church is able to impress the imagination of its members with the belief that it is mightier even than mighty death, and holds the keys of heaven and hell. As between the Evangelical and the Liberal Protestant, the latter maintains that death is a purely physical event, common to all living things, and not a moral crisis. It was not a penalty in the beginning, and has no relation to the moral condition now. The soul goes on hereafter from the point where it was at death. But the common belief among the Orthodox is that death was originally the punishment of Adam's sin, and that it marks for every man the end of his probation. After it there is no hope of essential change. In this they are joined by the Roman Catholic and Greek Churches. The Catholic, however, holds the doctrine of purgatory, — a region where sins not mortal are expiated, or *purged* away, and penances not finished before death are worked out. But those convicted of mortal sins, including wilful unbelief, have no chance after death. The Reformers rejected the doctrine of purgatory; but there have always been a few among Evangelical Protestants — represented now by the "Andover School" of the Congregationalists — who have held to "probation after death" for those who have had no opportunity of hearing the Gospel preached in this world. But the Evangelicals are practically united in believing that the destiny of *all* is fixed at death, and that those who have not saving faith in Christ, whether they have heard of him or not, including the heathen, are doomed to eternal misery.

The great drama of the future life, in the belief of the early Christians, consisted of four acts, — the "second advent" of Christ, the millennium, the last judgment, and the eternal continuance of the fate then assigned.

The first Christians believed that Jesus would come again before his generation had passed away. (See remarks under "Second Adventists.") Less is said of the fate of unbelievers than of the joyful union of believers with their returned Master. This belief died away with remarkable quietness; but the expectation of Christ's sudden return in judgment has at times flamed up with great fervor, — as in the year 1000, at the time of the Reformation, and in this century among the "Millerites." It is commonly held among Evangelicals that the second advent cannot be foretold with any definiteness, but that it may happen at any time. Practically, however, the belief seems dead.

As to the fate of the soul between death and judgment, little is commonly said, and the belief is very vague. Apparently it is commonly held that the soul remains with the body in the grave in an unconscious state.

The Christians of the first two or three centuries believed that the second coming of Christ would be followed by the resurrection of believers, and their happy reign with him upon the earth for a thousand years, or *millennium* (Rev. xx.). This belief faded away, but has been revived by a few in the present century, largely among the Baptists.

The last judgment has been in Christian theology a most dreadful event, described with details sometimes grand and picturesque, often grotesque. As a means of impressing the imagination of the ignorant and superstitious, both Catholic and Protestant, and compelling them into the churches, it has stood supreme. The heavens rolled aside as curtains; Christ upon a high throne, no longer meek and persuading, but awful and relentless, surrounded by the angels and clothed with omnipotence; the graves opening; the sea giving up its dead; the terrible dividing of saint and sinner; the bliss of the one fate, the horror of the other, — these were the elements of the "Great Assize." Whatever may have been the thought of the more intelligent and spiritual, to the common mind and in the common preaching this judgment turned practically upon submission to the Church, or belief in the power of Christ to save those who trusted in him. Calvinism draws the line between the elect and the non-elect, Arminianism between those who accept and those who reject Christ according to the trinitarian conception of him; by all, "good works" not springing from faith in Christ are counted as of no value. It is but just to add that this whole doctrine, though unchanged in the creeds, has undergone an immense softening and disintegrating in the preaching of the day. Fear is less often appealed to as a motive to faith; and the love of God and of Christ and the beauty of holiness are the common grounds for urging conversion.

Universalists commonly believe in a final judgment, at first having held that it assigned all men to happiness. Later they have maintained a difference in verdict, but a final restoration. The New Church holds the beautiful doctrine that the judgment proceeds upon natural principles, each soul going, as it were, by its own specific gravity to the place, circumstances, and society for which it is fit by its actual moral condition. The Unitarian coincides in this view, holding that judgment is not entirely deferred, but is largely immediate, the soul being visited at once with that new vision or blindness, new strength or weakness, new sensitiveness or dulness in moral and spiritual things, which are the natural and just consequences of righteousness or of sin. But since the conventionalities and wrong judgments of this world hide, even from the soul itself, its real moral condition, it may well be that its emergence into a life which is purely spiritual will be a revelation to itself, as well as to others, of its actual worth. The old picture of the judgment is, of course, now rendered absurd by the changed idea of the universe, resulting in the disappearance of the old conception of heaven as a place over a stationary earth, or hell as a place within it.

The condition of the two classes of saints and sinners after the judgment has commonly been described in the terms of the Book of Revelation. Heaven is a place of rest and worship, resulting in happiness unspeakable, but apparently monotonous and tedious; hell is a place of torment, commonly described as inflicted by fire. Though the Catholic Church denies that the flame is material, it has always presented the torment under that figure, and made the most of it. The same is true of the Evangelical Protestant. As to the eternity of both conditions, all but Liberals are strongly agreed.

But against nothing in the popular theology have Liberals protested more indignantly than against infinite punishment for anything that can be done by finite man in so short a life as that which he spends on the earth. The Universalists led in this protest, and Unitarians have followed. An increasing number of Evangelicals more or less boldly renounce the belief. In the Church of England men like Stanley, Robertson, Maurice, Farrar, and Kingsley, have done so, claiming that the omission of the Article on eternal punishment from the original Forty-Two in compiling the present Thirty-Nine justifies them. In great numbers of pulpits the doctrine is scarcely heard, though it remains in the creeds and covenants. The Catholics soften it by assigning to infants not baptized only loss of spiritual happiness, leaving them natural enjoyment in their own place. The Liberals also deny the resurrection of the body, which is the belief of the rest of Christendom. The New Church maintains that a "spiritual body" is within our material body in this life, and is disengaged at death to become the tenement and organ of the soul hereafter. The Apostles' Creed, however, most widely held of all formularies, asserts "the resurrection of the body," — a phrase which, however it may be explained away, has a very clear meaning. The Liberal, however, shrinks from attempting to define the future life with much detail. A purely spiritual life is too foreign to our imagination, which is used only to material surroundings, to admit of much dogmatism. It should be enough to know that wherever or amid whatever circumstances the soul may be placed, it is still under the care of a just, loving, and almighty God.

QUESTIONS.

On what are all Christians agreed as to the future life? How did the early Christians look upon death? What changed this view? How do the Catholic and the two kinds of Protestants each meet death? Why? What difference as to the significance of death is there between the Evangelical and the Liberal views? With which do the Catholic and Greek Churches agree? What is the doctrine of purgatory? of probation after death? What is the common Christian view of the future fate of the heathen? What did the first Christians believe as to the second coming of Christ? What texts can you remember which support this belief? What revivals of it have occurred? What is the common belief now? Do you ever hear it spoken of? What becomes of the soul between death and the judgment, according to common belief?

What was the early Christian belief as to the millennium? What does this word mean? Does any one hold this belief now? What are the elements of the popular idea of the last judgment? What great pictures or sculptures of it have you seen, or do you know of? On what does the judgment practically turn among Catholics? among Evangelical Protestants? How does Calvinism draw the line? Arminianism? What is thought of good works? How has the common preaching on this point changed? What is the Universalist belief? that of the New Church? of the Unitarians?

What has furnished the common vocabulary for describing the future life? How are the two conditions thought of? How large a part of Christendom believes in eternal punishment? What is the main Liberal argument against it? Who led the protest against it? What great men besides avowed Liberals have followed them? How do the Catholics soften this doctrine for infants? How far is this reasonable? What is the common Christian belief as to the resurrection of the body? the belief of the New Church? of the Apostles' Creed? What is the general attitude of Unitarians toward the details of the hereafter?

REFERENCES.

Alger's *A Critical History of the Doctrine of a Future Life*, with bibliography. For Jewish ideas as preparatory to Christian, see C. H. Toy's *Judaism and Christianity*, chap. vii. For the Catholic view, see Addis and Arnold. For a recent Calvinistic view, see *The Doctrine of Eternal Punishment*, by W. G. T. Shedd. For a Methodist view, *Lost Forever*, by Prof. L. T. Townsend. A collection of opinions by thinkers of all schools on the question, "Is Salvation Possible after Death?" has been published by T. Whittaker, of New York, under the title, *Probation: A Symposium*. The Andover view is given in the sermons of Newman Smyth, and in *Dorner on the Future State*, with Introduction by Newman Smyth; and the liberal Anglican, in Farrar's *Eternal Hope*. Swedenborg's views are given in his *Heaven and Hell*. For the Unitarian side, see Martineau's *Seat of Authority in Religion*, pp. 546-573; American Unitarian Association Tracts, Fourth Series, Nos. 26, 27, 42, 78, and 81; Channing's sermons, "The Moral Argument against Calvinism," "Immortality," and "The Future Life;" Hedge's *Reason in Religion*, book ii. chaps. 6, 9, and 10; S. J. Barrows's *The Doom of the Majority of Mankind;* E. H Sears's *Foregleams and Foreshadows of Immortality*.

8. THE CHURCH AND THE SACRAMENTS.

> One holy Church of God appears
> Through every age and race,
> Unwasted by the lapse of years,
> Unchanged by changing place.
>
> Her priests are all God's faithful sons,
> To serve the world raised up;
> The pure in heart, her baptized ones;
> Love, her communion-cup.
>
> The truth is her prophetic gift,
> The soul, her sacred page;
> And feet on mercy's errands swift
> Do make her pilgrimage. — *Samuel Longfellow.*

The Church. — There is no satisfactory evidence that Jesus founded or prepared for an organization to perpetuate his work. The few passages of the Gospels in which the word "church" occurs are explainable on other grounds, and some are under suspicion of being later interpolations. After the death of Jesus there is no reference to any such instructions, and the whole matter is left in too great doubt to admit of positive assertions on so important a matter, though they are still made by many. The first Christian bodies grew up naturally around the Apostles or other preachers, and apparently were congregational in government; but the need and the habit of drawing more closely together led to organization on the Roman political pattern, and soon the present Roman Catholic system can be seen in process of formation. The Roman Catholic idea of the Church is that of a visible institution, founded by Jesus, placed in care of his Apostles after his death, and by them handed down to successors authorized by them to rule. It is the representative of God upon earth, the repository of His power to save, which He gives through the sacraments when duly administered. It alone has the right to interpret the revelations made in the Bible, and it alone receives, through its infallible head, such new truth as becomes necessary for human guidance.

The Reformers set aside the idea of a visible Church, the High Church Anglicans and Episcopalians alone retaining a more or less clear shadow of it. Evangelical Protestants believe that the true Church is *invisible*, being composed of the elect alone, the signs of election being clear and satisfying faith and the good life which flows from faith. "The Church is the society of believers in which the word is preached and the sacraments duly administered." The visible Church may contain some who are not true believers; but inasmuch as all who are true believers are sure to enter the Church which Christ has established, the Evangelical Protestant commonly holds, with the Westminster Confession, that "outside of the visible Church there is no ordinary possibility of salvation."

The Unitarian maintains that the visible Church is a voluntary association of those who seek religious and moral quickening, and who unite upon certain views by which this quickening seems best secured. Membership in it does not imply any superiority to those out of it, in any sense whatever. It is simply the school or college of the moral and spiritual life. But Unitarians believe still more in an invisible Church. In the words of Dr. Channing, "There is one grand, all-comprehending Church. . . . All Christians and myself form one body, one Church, just as far as a common love and piety possess our hearts. . . . No man can be excommunicated from it but by himself, — by the death of goodness in his own breast."

The *form* of the Church differs among Protestants. Some join their congregations into larger bodies, which they call "The Church," the general body having control over the single church. This control is sometimes exercised by individuals called bishops, as in the Episcopal (hence this name) and Methodist Episcopal churches, or by representative bodies, as among the Presbyterians and Universalists. Others maintain the independence of the single congregations, all associations of these being purely voluntary and advisory, as the Congregationalists (Trinitarian and Unitarian) and Baptists.

There is also a difference as to the terms of admission into the Protestant churches. Often Unitarians require only signature to a constitution, sometimes to a covenant or statement of faith and purpose, though baptism is frequent. Most other Protestants require baptism, the condition on which this is granted being generally the relation of a definite religious change or experience involving the profession of a satisfactory faith (Congregationalists, Baptists, many Presbyterians, and others), or upon assent to a creed or catechism (Episcopalians, many Presbyterians, Universalists).

The Clergy. — The idea of the clergy in Protestant churches is widely different from that in the Roman and Greek churches. In the latter the priests are chosen by their superiors, — the bishops, etc., — and are by them enabled to dispense supernatural grace through the sacraments. In a certain measure this view as to power through the sacraments is held by the High Church Episcopalians and by the Lutherans. But all Calvinistic Protestants and their descendants hold that all believers are priests alike, and receive grace directly from God, not through sacerdotal agency. Their ministers are chosen by the congregations, though under certain restrictions where a power is recognized above the congregation, as by the Presbyterians, and differ from their brethren only officially and by natural gifts or special education. This distinction is vital, and must be clearly understood.

The Sacraments. — The Roman Catholic Church has seven sacraments, or channels of divine grace — baptism, Eucharist, confirmation, penance, holy orders, matrimony, and extreme unction. Protestants have kept only the first two. The other five are considered in the chapter on "The Catholics." There is this further and vital distinction between the two parties, — that the Catholic considers his sacraments to be in themselves the vehicles of grace, whatever the character of the priest may be, so long as he is in regular standing in the Church, and whatever may be the belief of the recipient; the Protestant considers baptism or the communion as simply *occasions* when Christ comes with special power, the effect upon the recipient depending entirely upon his own faith, or spiritual condition. The High Church Episcopalians and the Lutherans approach the Catholics in giving a mystical or magical efficacy to these rites.

Baptism. This rite originated in the warm Oriental countries, where cleanliness was especially necessary, and where a new ablution was made the symbol of the purity of heart required of those who were admitted to religious sects. Whether it was a Jewish rite before the time of Christ or not, is uncertain. Its first appearance in the Bible is in the account of John the Baptist. Although there are texts which seem to represent Jesus as enjoining baptism, it is remarkable how little he says about it; and though he himself submitted to baptism by John, he never baptized any of his disciples, and there is no proof that all even of the Apostles underwent that ceremony. It is impossible for any one who understands the true distinction between Christianity and Judaism to believe that Jesus meant to make any ceremony indispensable to salvation.

Yet baptism became universal among his successors under the form of immersion, was believed to have a supernatural efficacy, and by 200 had come to be considered essential to salvation. Even infants dying without it were shut out of the kingdom of heaven, though this involved no torment, as in the case of adults, but only loss of supernatural blessedness. Natural happiness in some separate region could still be theirs. At the Reformation, the form having changed during the Middle Ages to sprinkling or pouring, the Lutherans continued this belief, holding out some hope for the children of parents in the Church, but showing little mercy to others, though allowing that God's purposes here are inscrutable. The Church of England held substantially this position. The Calvinists, however, denied all supernatural efficacy to baptism, and held that only the election of God saves. The rite became thus the seal or sign of a salvation already effected, being given only to those who could show the faith which election involves. The children of the elect who died in infancy, whether baptized or not, were considered saved, for "the promise is to you and to your children." The Baptists, however, denied that infant baptism had any meaning whatever, since an infant could not be said to have the faith implied in it; while for adults they restored the primitive form of immersion. The Friends abolished the rite entirely, as they did all other religious ceremonies. The sects which require infant baptism expect that when the children come to the age of reason they will become members of the Church by profession of their own faith or conversion, — an occasion called among Catholics and Episcopalians "confirmation." Liberals (Unitarians and Universalists) look upon baptism as an act of public consecration of one's life to God, and upon infant baptism as an act of dedication of the children by their parents to the service of God, and of consecration of the parents themselves to the religious training of their children. Some make it also the occasion of "christening," or giving the "Christian" name. No efficacy, of course, is attributed to the ceremony except its power over the hearts of those concerned in it.

Communion.— This ceremony is called by the Catholics the "Mass" (from the words *missa est*, with which the congregation was once dismissed), or the "Eucharist" (from a Greek word, which means "giving thanks"), because of the prayer of thanksgiving in it; and by Protestants the "Communion" (with each other and with Jesus), the "Lord's Supper," and the "Last Supper."

The accounts of the last supper which Jesus ate with his Apostles do not seem to imply that he meant to institute a religious ceremony, still less a mystical or supernatural rite. It was the Passover meal. He knew it was his last; and with a yearning for remembrance among those whom he left behind he asked them to recall him whenever they came to the point in that yearly meal where the loaf is formally broken and the cup passed. This wish was gratified by his disciples after the daily meal which they were accustomed to take together — the *agape*, or "love feast" — during the first days of the new religion in Jerusalem. The *agape* was given up early in the second century (for the excesses sometimes connected with it, see 1 Cor. xi. 20-22, 27-34); and the commemorative part, which had already begun to take on a mystical meaning, changed in this direction still more rapidly. At the end of the second century non-communicants were sent out of the church before the ceremony. Soon it was commonly believed that the glorified Christ dwelt in the elements as the Logos had once dwelt in the human body. In 831 Paschasius Radbert, a

French abbot, maintained that the bread and wine were actually changed into the body and blood of Christ. This change was called *transubstantiation*, or exchange of substance. The view gained ground, and was formally adopted in 1215.

Protestantism has almost exactly retraced the path of this development. The Lutherans went back as far as "consubstantiation," or the *union* of Christ's body and blood with the bread and wine, the former being received by all who take the latter. Calvin maintained only a spiritual presence of Christ, who is received by the believer alone. Liberals adopt the purely commemorative use, as Zwingli taught, restoring the primitive custom.

The Catholic gives only the bread to the laity, reserving the cup for the priest alone. The Baptists of America refuse to admit to communion those who have not received baptism by immersion. This is called "close communion." The Orthodox Protestants commonly invite to remain only those who are in good and regular standing in Evangelical churches. The Unitarians invite all to remain who are so minded. The Catholic holds Mass several times on Sunday, besides frequent celebrations during the week, and masses for the dead by special arrangement. Many Episcopal churches have communion every Sunday, sometimes twice, and some of them every morning in the week. Most other Protestant churches have it on the first Sunday of every month, after the morning service.

QUESTIONS.

Did Jesus found a church? Did the Apostles? How did the first churches grow up? What is the Catholic view of the Church? What is its relation to the Bible? What view did the Reformers take? What was their distinction between the visible and the invisible Church? What does the Unitarian hold as to the visible Church? as to the invisible? What differences in the organization of churches are there among Protestants? What differences in terms of admission?

What is the conception of the clergy in the Roman and Greek Churches? among the Protestants? What is the Catholic view of the sacraments? the Protestant view? How did baptism originate? When do we first find it mentioned in the Bible? What was the relation of Jesus to it? Is it likely that he considered it essential to salvation? Why? What change came over it after New Testament times? What view of infant baptism arose? What is the Lutheran view of baptism? the Calvinistic? the Baptist? that of the Friends? What is confirmation? What is the Liberal view of baptism? of infant baptism?

What various names are given to the communion service? What was probably the meaning of Jesus' words at the Last Supper about "remembering" him? How was his wish at first gratified? What was the difference between the *agape* and the Lord's Supper? What changes did the communion service undergo in Catholic history? What is transubstantiation? consubstantiation? What was Calvin's view? Zwingli's? How does the Catholic administer the elements? What is "close communion"? How is the invitation commonly given in Orthodox churches? in Unitarian churches? How often is the Mass celebrated in Catholic churches? the communion in Episcopal churches? in other churches? Do you attend communion? Why?

REFERENCES.

The various views of Christians may be found in the works on general theology named at the beginning of the chapter. See also Dean Stanley's *Christian Institutions;* Channing's sermon on "The Church;" Theodore Parker, *Discourse of Matters pertaining to Religion,* chap. v. Albert Barnes (Presbyterian) opposes Episcopacy in *The Apostolic Church;* F. D. Maurice gives a moderate view of it in *The Kingdom of Christ.* Hooker's *Ecclesiastical Polity* is a standard on the Anglican side. Newman in his *Apologia pro mea Vita* tells the story of his change from the Anglican to the Roman Church. See also *Congregationalism,* by H. M. Dexter; Cardinal Wiseman's *Lectures on the Real Presence in the Holy Eucharist* (Catholic); A. W. Little's *Reasons for being a Churchman* (High Church Episcopal); J. W. Nevin's *The Mystical Presence* (Calvinistic); A. N. Arnold's *Prerequisites to Communion* (Baptist); S. G. Bulfinch's *Communion Thoughts* (Unitarian); Martineau's *The Seat of Authority in Religion,* pp 127-169, 513-546.

William Wall's *The History of Infant Baptism* is a standard work. J. B. Mozley's *The Primitive Doctrine of Baptismal Regeneration* gives the Anglican view. Francis Wayland, *Principles and Practice of Baptist Churches;* Leonard Woods (Congregationalist), *Lectures on Infant Baptism.* See also Smith's Dictionary of Christian Antiquities, article "Baptism."

CHAPTER II.

THE ROMAN CATHOLICS.

There is one body, and one Spirit, . . . one Lord, one faith, one baptism, one God and Father of all. — Eph. iv. 4–6.

Name. — The official name of the organization is "The Roman Catholic Church," — *Roman*, because its centre is at Rome, Italy; *Catholic* (or universal), because it claims jurisdiction over all mankind.

History. — The Roman Catholic Church is in form the Roman Empire extended over the world with ecclesiastical instead of secular functions. The graded system of officers, the skilfully codified law, and the assumption of supreme authority are closely imitated from the ancient Roman dominion. The process was natural. Whether Peter was ever in Rome, as Catholics claim, or not, and whether his primacy among the Apostles was granted or not, whoever was the head of the churches in Rome would become the head of all the churches of the Empire. The first bishops about whom we are certain were men of great force of character and executive ability; and as the emperors grew feebler and less respected, the ecclesiastical authorities came to the front. The earnestness of Christian zeal and confidence stepped into the place of the decaying public spirit and private manhood. The transfer of the seat of government to Constantinople, in 330, left the Bishop of Rome in still greater prominence. At last, in Leo the Great (440–446), the Church came to a full consciousness of its opportunity, and shaped its course accordingly. Under Gregory the Great (590–604) the Church was roused to a missionary spirit; and by 750 all Europe, even to Norway and Iceland, was under its teaching. Meantime, by the Seven Great Councils (325–787), the doctrines of the Church had been defined. The gift of a large territory to the Pope by Pepin, king of the Franks (755), laid the foundation of the "temporal power." The "Isidorean Decretals," a collection of documents purporting to be very ancient, but largely forged, — especially the "Donation of Constantine," by which sovereignty over the West was given to the Pope, — strengthened the papal authority over the provincial bishops. Corruptions crept in, which were stoutly opposed by Gregory VII. (Hildebrand), who closely organized the Church throughout. Under Boniface VIII. (1294–1303) the papal power was at its height; but from this time its decline was speedy. The resistance of kings, the rising national consciousness, the quickening of intellectual life, the revolt of the popular moral sense against the corruptions of priest and pope, and the rivalries of competing popes, — all combined to check and retard the progress of the Church. Councils for internal reform having failed, the Reformation began outside. Its progress was stopped and much ground won back by the counter-reformation within the Church, led by the Jesuits, and formulated by the Council of Trent (1545–1563).

The chief events in the history of the Church since the Council of Trent have been the proclamation of the doctrine of the "Immaculate Conception of the Virgin Mary" (1854); of the "Syllabus of Errors" (1864), in which the Church set itself squarely against modern intellectual tendencies; and of the "Infallibility of the Pope" (1870); the abolition of the "Temporal Power" in the same year; and the "Old Catholic" movement under Hyacinthe, Döllinger, and Reinkens, — an attempt to bring back the Church to the position of the earlier centuries, when councils, not Popes, were the source of authority. The attitude of the Church is now very different from that which it took in the Middle Ages, even in lands where it contains the majority of Christians. Its reliance is, to a larger extent, upon moral and spiritual means of influence, its internal condition is purer, and its spirit more earnest; but its pretensions to universal authority and its ambition to realize these remain, of course, unchanged.

In the United States settlements were made by Catholics in Maryland under Lord Baltimore (1634), and in other parts, — as Florida, Louisiana, New Mexico, and California, — which were settled by Catholic nations. The first bishop was appointed in 1789 at Baltimore. The growth of the Church has been mainly from immigration, — as from Ireland, Southern Germany, Italy, and the French part of Canada. Its later career in the United States has been marked by its opposition to the public-school system and its establishment of parochial schools of its own.

Doctrines. — The distinctive doctrine of the Roman Catholic Church, and one which must be thoroughly understood before its history and claims can be comprehended, is that it is the divinely established and sustained Church of God upon the earth, and His *only* Church. It was instituted by Jesus Christ in the solemn words which made the Apostle Peter its foundation rock. Its legitimacy is secured by an unbroken succession of Popes. By their infallibility under the guidance of the Holy Spirit it is kept from error in the interpretation or unfolding of doctrine. It is thus a supernatural institution, and therefore cannot submit its teachings to natural reason, or allow its spiritual authority to be controlled by any earthly power. It must obey God rather than man.

The Catholic doctrine of the infallibility of the Pope needs to be distinctly understood. He is not personally, but *officially* infallible; that is, he is not beyond error in his opinion upon ordinary matters, but only when pronouncing judgment upon matters of doctrine or morals formally laid before him by the Church. The judgment which he then pronounces is final, irrevocable, and infallible. This has nothing to do with the Pope's personal character, any more than with his personal knowledge or mental power. The Church claims that no such decision of Pope or General Council has ever been revoked.

As a source of truth, the decisions of the Church must take precedence of any private interpretation of Scripture. As the Supreme Court is to the Constitution of the United States, so is the Church to the Bible. The consequence, the *reductio ad absurdum*, of the Protestant principle of private judgment is the number of contradictory sects and the variety of individual opinions in the different commentaries. An infallible Book is of no value without an infallible Church to guarantee the correctness of its text, the faithfulness of translation, and the truthfulness of interpretation. The Church does not encourage the indiscriminate reading of the Bible by the uneducated; but it regards the Bible as the inspired Word of God, of which it, not the uneducated reader, is the divinely appointed interpreter.

The central part of its *worship* is the Mass. High Mass is sung; low Mass is read. There are two essential parts of this service, — the change (transubstantiation) of the bread and wine into the body and blood of Christ, and the offering or sacrifice of them for the sins of the people. The Catholic puts the most literal construction upon the words of Jesus, "This is my body; this is my blood" (Matt. xxvi. 26, 28). He believes that though to the senses the elements remain the same, in substance they are changed into the veritable body and blood of the Lord. These are then sacrificed at the altar in perpetual memorial of the original sacrifice upon the cross. The bread, which is baked in the form of little round cakes, or wafers, is after consecration distributed to the communicants. The wine, however, is drunk only by the priest. The reasons for this are, first, that the Church teaches that "Christ is contained whole and entire under each species" (see 1 Cor. xi. 27, — the word "or" in Revised Version); secondly, practical considerations, — as the quantity of wine that would be needed, the undesirability of many drinking from one cup, and the danger of dropping or spilling.

Admission into the Catholic Church is by baptism in the name of the Father, the Son, and the Holy Ghost. Inasmuch as all men inherit the taint of sin from Adam, and are born enemies of God, a new birth, or regeneration, is necessary. Even infants who are unbaptized, though they do not go to torments, fall short of the perfect happiness of the saved. If any man be "heartily sorry for his sins, and loves God with his whole heart, and desires to comply with all the divine ordinances," the pouring of water upon him becomes the vehicle of supernatural grace, washing away original sin, and begetting a new and spiritual life. This life is constantly fed by reception of the Lord's body in the Holy Communion, and thus is prepared for the heavenly mansions.

The Holy Communion and Baptism are called "sacraments." A sacrament is the visible sign of invisible grace. There are seven in all in this church, the remaining five being Confirmation, by which baptized persons of ripe years are *confirmed*, or strengthened in soul by the reception of fresh supplies of divine grace; Penance, or absolution for sins by the priest; Extreme Unction, the anointing of the sick with holy oil, usually when they are expected to die; Orders, for priests and other ecclesiastics; and Matrimony, by which special grace is given that the wedded couple may live together in love and harmony.

Some other peculiarities of worship should be noticed. The *Latin language* only is used by the priests in the Mass and in the administration of the sacraments, because this was the common language when the Church was established; because a common language is still needed by a church which extends over the world; because she wishes her liturgy to be always and everywhere the same, safe from the changes which come to all living languages; and because the worship, being addressed to God, not to men, may as well be in Latin as in any other language. The congregation follows the worship by means of a translation. The *lighted candles* upon the altar commemorate the time when the Christians worshipped in the dark catacombs, and are symbols of him who is the light of the world, of our light which should shine before men, and of spiritual joy. *Incense* is an emblem of prayer, ascending like smoke from hearts burning with love. The *flowers* are meant to adorn the place where God comes to dwell. The *vestments* of the priest are signs of his sacred and peculiar office, and are intended to be beyond the influence of changing fashion.

Besides conducting public worship, the priest deals with his people individually by the confessional. The Catholic Church claims that power was given to it to forgive sins (Matt. xvi. 18, 19 : John xx. 21-23). To receive this forgiveness, the sinner must not only repent, but if possible confess his sins to the priest, promise amendment and restitution, and submit to whatever penance may be imposed upon him. It is claimed that in this way control or influence over people is secured better than in any other way, and for better results. It is in the power of the Church also to give *indulgence*. This word is used by the Church in its original sense of gentleness or mercy, not in its present sense of condoning weakness. It is not permission, but remission. The consequences of any sinful act are three, — the stain of guilt upon the soul, eternal punishment (if the sin be mortal), and the temporal consequences which may follow either in this life or in purgatory. The first two are washed away by baptism or absolution. It is the temporal punishment only that is remitted in an "indulgence." The merits of the innocent Christ, and those of the saints and martyrs whose sufferings were greater than their sins required, constitute a "treasury" upon which the Church can draw in behalf of sinners who are truly repentant. On condition of good deeds to be done by them, — as almsgiving, pilgrimages, etc., — a remission of temporal suffering is assured. If time is named, as a "forty-days indulgence," it means so much remission as would have been secured by forty days of penance under the old laws of the Church. The system is evidently easy to abuse, as to misunderstand; but the doctrine of the Church that an indulgence is useless without sincere repentance and amendment must be carefully separated from the misinterpretations and misuse of its officers.

Besides the worship of God, the Catholic Church teaches the invocation of saints, including the Virgin Mary, as intercessors with God. As the Protestant asks his friends or his minister to pray for him, so the Catholic asks his more powerful friends in heaven to pray for him. The Church encourages also the use of images, especially of the crucifix, as aids to the imagination in devotion, since they make the object of worship more real, as a photograph makes our distant friends. But it does not allow worship of the image itself.

It holds also to an intermediate state between hell and heaven, called purgatory, or the place where lesser sins can be expiated, or sins not fully punished here may receive the remainder of the penalty due them (1 Cor. iii. 13-15). Those who die in grave unpardoned sins go into eternal and irremediable torment; but those who are in purgatory may be prayed for, and so helped. For the Church holds that prayers for friends in purgatory are as efficacious as prayers for friends in distant lands, or in peril or sin on the earth.

The Catholic Church admits no divorce from marriage (Matt. xix. 3-9). It allows separation, but no re-marriage. It praises celibacy as superior to the wedded life (Matt xix. 12; 1 Cor. vii. 32, 33), and as following the example of Jesus and all the Apostles except Peter, who, it claims, gave up his wife when he was called (Matt. xix. 27). It demands celibacy of its clergy, because of the sacredness of their office and their greater ability to concentrate themselves upon their work. It regards the married state as a holy sacrament instituted by Christ for those who have not been called to a higher state.

On many points the Catholic Church holds the same belief as the "Evangelical" Protestant churches; namely, the inspiration of the Bible, the Trinity, the deity of Christ, the sin of all men in Adam and their merited eternal punishment, their redemption by the suffering and death of Christ, the resurrection of the dead, and the everlasting happiness of the saved. An important difference, however, arises between the two bodies as to justification, — the Protestant making faith alone the ground of acceptance with God, the Catholic requiring both faith and the reception of the sacraments. Infants are justified by baptism, which conveys to them sanctifying grace, and restores to them the righteousness lost at the Fall. On coming to the use of reason, those who have been baptized in infancy must have faith in God and love to God.

Government. — The head of the Church is the Pope, — "vicar of Christ, head of the bishops, and supreme governor of the whole Catholic Church, of whom the whole world is the territory, or diocese." He is also patriarch of the West and bishop of Rome and its district, and was temporal ruler over the "Pontifical States" till these were absorbed in the Kingdom of Italy. He is absolute in power and infallible as above defined. He is elected for life by the *cardinals*, of whom there are seventy-four, who were originally occupants of parishes in Rome, but have now larger powers and often distant residences. The government of the Church is carried on by a number of councils, or ministries, called "congregations," each presided over by a cardinal, composed of distinguished ecclesiastics, and caring for some department, — as Inquisition, Propagation of the Faith (*Propaganda*),

Bishops, etc. Out in the world the work is presided over by archbishops and bishops, who receive power from the Pope over special districts, or dioceses, and have under them priests, who come into direct contact with the people in administering sacraments and doing parochial work. There are various other offices, not necessary to describe.

Statistics. — The number of Catholics in the world is difficult to determine, since the Church publishes no official list. Tolerably trustworthy authorities give over 210,000,000, of whom 154,000,000 are in Europe. There are 74 cardinals, 920 bishops and archbishops, 165 vicars, etc.

In the United States there are (1890) one cardinal, 14 archbishops, 74 bishops, 8,463 priests, and adherents estimated between eight and thirteen millions, probably about ten millions. There are 102 colleges, 635 academies, and 35 theological seminaries.

The Roman Catholic stands at the opposite extreme of the line of Christian bodies from the Unitarian, representing the most complete submission to authority as opposed to reliance upon the inner voice and light of reason and conscience, and close and complete organization as opposed to individualism and voluntary association. It is a fair question whether there is any halting-ground between the two. The Catholic seems to be right in claiming that an infallible Book without an infallible Interpreter cannot be a ground of certitude in religion, and that the number of Protestant sects proves this. The Evangelical Protestant position is a mixture of authority and reason in varying and uncertain proportions, and without the strength of either. The same is true of its varying forms of church government.

Yet, though at the opposite extreme as to the *grounds* of belief, the Catholic often approaches the Unitarian in single points of belief, and seems really broader than the Evangelical Protestant. He is freer than the latter in his handling of Scripture, feeling secure from serious error under the control of the Church; gives more credit to the every-day virtues of mankind, — as honesty, purity, and charity, — sneering less at "mere morality;" and is more generous and kindly in his view of the future life so far as purgatory is concerned. Even his doctrine of the infallibility of the Pope hints of the ever-present Spirit, whose revelations did not cease eighteen centuries ago. The Catholic Church deserves also great credit for its principle of the equality of all men before God, building its costly churches among the poor as well as among the rich, and making the two classes equal in the house of worship. Its confessional, though open to terrible abuse, has done immense good in controlling the lives of many, especially of the young women in large cities, who often have no other guidance.

In a wider, historical way the civilized world owes a great debt to the Roman Church. During the chaos which followed the overthrow of the Roman Empire by the Northern barbarians, the Church was the only power which was respected. It conquered the conquerors, and mollified to some degree their rough manners. It still has a hold upon classes among us which no other religious body seems able to reach. It became the refuge of men of letters, and the guardian of manuscripts. It encouraged art and music. Within itself rank counted for little or nothing, and the highest offices were open to men of humblest birth who had the ability to reach and fill them.

Yet it must be admitted that the fundamental principle of the Catholic Church, that it claims an authority in religious matters which nothing else on earth can have, directly antagonizes the fundamental principle of modern life, that truth comes through the individual reason, not through institutions. Such power as the Catholic Church claims *might* be confined only to spiritual matters, and be used only persuasively; but history has shown that supposed infallibility, whether in Catholic or Protestant, whether in sacred or secular affairs, is too great a temptation for human nature to bear. Both the political power which is free from responsibility to the people and the intellectual power that is free from open discussion have proved insufferable tyrannies and bars to progress. The divine right of kings is gone; the divine right of churches must go. The latter already denies the free use of reason, and given power to enforce its claims, may easily menace civil and religious liberty in the future as it has in the past. That the Catholic Church is thoroughly sincere and earnest in its own belief makes it all the more formidable.

QUESTIONS.

What is the official name of those who are commonly called the Catholics, and what does it mean? What is the relation of the Roman Church to the Roman Empire? Describe the process of replacement. When and by whom was its opportunity made clear? Who was the great missionary Pope? How were the doctrines first defined? What is meant by the "temporal power," and how did it begin? What were the "Forged Decretals"? Who was the greatest reforming and organizing Pope? When was the power of the Church at its height? What causes led to its downfall? What was the Reformation? the counter-reformation? What great council fixed the modern policy of the Church? What are the chief events since then? What gives strength to the Catholics here?

Name the distinctive doctrine of the Roman Catholic Church. What is meant by the "infallibility" of the Pope? What is the relation of Church authority to the Scriptures? What is the Mass? What does "transubstantiation" mean? What constitutes admission into the Church? What does baptism imply? What is a sacrament, and how many are there? Why is Latin used? What do the candles, incense, vestments mean? What is the doctrine of the confessional? Do you think it would be useful to you? What is an "indulgence"? What wrong ideas of this are among Protestants? How do you think it could be abused? What is the "invocation of saints," and what can be said for it? What against it? What is "purgatory"? Compare this view with that of many Protestant sects. What is the Catholic doctrine of divorce? of celibacy?

Who is the head of the Roman Catholic Church? What other offices does he hold? Who are the cardinals? What are the "congregations"? Name some of their departments. What other officers are there? How many Catholics are there in the world? in this country?

What are the main points of difference between Catholics and Unitarians? In what points do they approach each other? Wherein are they more liberal than "Evangelical" Protestants? For what do they deserve credit? Why should they be opposed? Do you think a Catholic can be a patriot? a scientist? What is his position toward our public schools? How does this follow from his doctrine? Would he persecute to-day, if he had power, as he did in the Middle Ages? What has America to fear from him? What do you think of the Catholics you know? What is your chief objection to them? What good can you see that they do here? Do you think they are sincere? How ought we to act toward them?

REFERENCES.

The best popular work on the Catholic side, for both doctrine and history, is Addis and Arnold's *Catholic Dictionary*, which is semi-official. La Harbe's *Catechism* contains a short summary. Longer histories are Alzog's, in three volumes, and Döllinger's, in four. By Protestant authors, an admirable epitome is J. H. Allen's *Outline of Christian History;* good is J. H. Blunt's *Key to Church History*, 2 small volumes. On the whole, the best history for common reading is Fisher's. Besides the general histories of Neander, Gieseler, Hagenbach, see Milman's *Latin Christianity*, 8 vols.

(to about 1450); Ranke's *History of the Popes in the Sixteenth and Seventeenth Centuries*; and Macaulay's famous review of it in his *Essays*; Bryce's *Holy Roman Empire*; Lea's *Sacerdotal Celibacy* and *Inquisition*; Lecky's *History of European Morals*; Encyclopædia Britannica, articles "Popedom," "Roman Catholic Church" (the latter valuable as to government), and "Jesuits." As to the Church in America, see histories by J. G. Shea, Prescott's *Mexico*, Parkman's *Jesuits in North America*, and many references on special periods and phases at the close of Fisher.

For the best popular compend of Catholic doctrine, see Cardinal Gibbons's *The Faith of Our Fathers*. Newman's *Apologia* is in every way important, but especially as showing the relation, in his mind, between the Churches of England and Rome. See, also, Martineau's *Authority in Religion*, book ii. chap. 1. *Per contra*, see R. F. Littledale's *Plain Reasons against joining the Church of Rome*. The great creeds are given in Schaff, vol. i.

CHAPTER III.

THE OLD CATHOLICS.

WHEN Peter was come to Antioch, I withstood him to the face, for he was to be blamed. — GAL. ii. 11.

THE Vatican Council of 1869–70 was a triumph of the "Ultramontane," or extreme papal, party in the Roman Catholic Church. By the decree of papal infallibility it placed the Pope beyond the power of councils, and thus of bishops or national churches. Most of the powerful minority of eighty-eight dissentients and ninety-one non-voters, out of the whole number of seven hundred and forty-four, after a long and often bitter struggle, accepted the decree. But Dr. Döllinger, of Bonn, Germany, the foremost of German Catholic scholars, refused, and with his colleague, Professor Friedrich, was excommunicated in 1871. In September of that year a conference of five hundred delegates was held in Munich, and an attempt was made at union with the Greek and Russian churches and an "understanding" with the Protestant and Episcopal communions. The consecration of Dr. Reinkens as bishop by a Dutch bishop gave the advantage of "apostolic succession;" the Prussian government legalized the body, and for a while it gained rapidly among the cultivated people of Germany and Switzerland. In Paris, Père Hyacinthe (Loyson), the famous preacher at Nôtre Dame, a devout believer in the rights of the Gallican Church as against absolute papal power, became an ally. The design of the Old Catholics was to return to the ancient faith and practice of the Church as laid down by the Seven Great Councils, before 787, untainted by papal usurpations and later doctrines. This would include the supremacy of councils, the equality of laity with the clergy in them, the marriage of priests, the use of the vernacular in public worship, and the abolition of compulsory fasting and confession. More emphasis was also laid upon the authority of the Scriptures.

But the movement made no impression upon the masses; was, like Protestantism, essentially Teutonic in its range; and was bitterly fought by the Catholic Church, whose influence at length brought also political pressure to bear upon it. Of late years it has made no gains, and is probably declining.

QUESTIONS.

What was the occasion of the Old Catholic movement? What does "Ultramontane" mean? Was the council a unit on the doctrine of infallibility? What did the beaten party (for example, Dr. Newman) do after the decision? Was this right? Who were the leaders in the new movement? Who was its first bishop? What was its first condition? What is its condition now, and why? What are its main doctrines? Where does it stop short of Protestantism? Ought Unitarians to sympathize with it, and how far?

REFERENCES.

See Encyclopædia Britannica, "Old Catholics;" Schaff, vol. i. pp. 191-202; *Catholic Reform*, by Father Hyacinthe; *The New Reformation*, by Theodorus.

On the Vatican Council, see Schaff's *The Vatican Decrees; The Pope and the Council*, by James (ascribed to Döllinger and Friedrich); *Letters from Rome on the Council*, by Friedrich and others (from the Old Catholic point of view); and a recent work by Thomas Mozley.

CHAPTER IV.
THE EASTERN CHURCH.

THE disciples were called Christians first in Antioch. — ACTS xi. 26.

Name. — The full name is "The Holy Oriental Orthodox Catholic Apostolic Church," the emphasis being upon the word "Orthodox," as in the name of the "Roman Catholic Church," the emphasis is upon "Catholic."

History. — The Eastern Church holds the birthplace of Christianity, Jerusalem, and the place where it was christened, Antioch. Its language is largely that which Jesus and the Apostles spoke, and the great Councils which first defined the faith of Christendom were summoned and controlled by Greek emperors and bishops. But after those Councils it became stagnant, and except in Russia, has made no advance and no conquest, while it contains the lowest types of Christianity to be found, — as the Christians of Abyssinia, and even some of the Russian sects. With the increasing prominence of Russia, Greece, and the Balkan realms, however, the Eastern Church may yet revive and spread.

The Council of Nicæa (325) recognized three Patriarchs, or heads of main divisions of the Christian Church, — those of Rome, Alexandria, and Antioch. Two more, at Jerusalem and Constantinople, were afterward added. Differences of language and customs, added to distance, naturally separated the eastern part of the Roman Empire from the western. Rome addressed itself more and more to conquering spiritually the barbarian hordes who had conquered her materially, and perpetuated in the Papacy the practical and legal ability which had created and regulated the Empire. In the East, not Roman law but Greek philosophy was the heritage of the Church, and even the common people speculated on those questions of the divine nature which were settled in the first great Œcumenical Councils. While the Latin Church became more united, the Greek became more divided. At the

A STUDY OF THE SECTS.

Third Council (Ephesus, 431) Nestorius, bishop of Constantinople, was condemned for having assigned two natures to Christ in such separation that Mary could not be called the "Mother of God." The large secession of the *Nestorians* ensued. At the Fourth Council (Chalcedon, 451) the doctrine of two natures in Christ, united without change or confusion, gave rise to the *Monophysite* or one-nature schism, which includes to-day the Jacobites of Syria, the Copts of Egypt, and the Abyssinians. At the Sixth Council (Constantinople, 680–681) the doctrine of two wills, divine and human, in Christ, was proclaimed, and the *Maronites* seceded, but in 1182 returned to Roman rule, retaining some peculiarities in their ritual.

More important was the separation from the Latin Church. In 589, at a Council in Toledo, Spain, not œcumenical and therefore not authoritative, there was added to the clause in the Nicene Creed, "I believe in the Holy Ghost, who proceedeth from the Father," the words "and the Son." Against this the Eastern churches protested as a heresy, contrary to the true doctrine of the Trinity. To theological dissension abundant political jealousy was added, and at last, in 1054, Leo IX. excommunicated the Eastern Church. The treatment of Eastern Christians by the crusaders from the West, culminating in the sack of Constantinople by them, 1204, intensified the quarrel, which, in spite of many attempts, has never been closed.

Meantime the Mohammedans swept over the East, but were not converted to Christianity, as the northern barbarians were by the Roman Church. In the period including the capture of Jerusalem in 637 and that of Constanstinople in 1453 all the old domain of the Eastern Church fell into their hands. Its organization was kept up, but its life largely departed. But new domains had been added by missionary zeal, especially in Russia, which, accepting Christianity in 992, now contains two thirds of all Eastern Christians.

Doctrine. — The Eastern Church, not being a formal unit, has no authoritative creed. It holds, however, to the creeds laid down by the first seven Œcumenical Councils, especially the one commonly known to us as the Nicene. In 1643 and 1672 creeds were made by the Synod of Jerusalem which are now virtually agreed upon. Their substance is given by the Encyclopaedia Britannica, article "Greek Church," as follows, the small capitals marking differences from the Roman Catholics, the italics those from the Protestants:—

"Christianity is a divine revelation communicated to mankind through Christ; its saving truths are to be learned from the Bible *and tradition*, the former having been written, *and the latter maintained uncorrupted*, through the influence of the Holy Spirit; *the interpretation of the Bible belongs to the Church, which is taught by the Holy Spirit*, but every believer may read the Scriptures.

"According to the Christian revelation, God is a Trinity; that is, the Divine essence exists in Three Persons, perfectly equal in nature and dignity, the Father, the Son, and the Holy Ghost; THE HOLY GHOST PROCEEDS FROM THE FATHER ONLY. Besides the Triune God there is no other object of divine worship, *but homage may be paid to the Virgin Mary, and reverence to the saints and to their pictures and relics*.

"Man is born with a corrupt bias, which was not his at creation; the first man, when created, possessed IMMORTALITY, PERFECT WISDOM, AND A WILL REGULATED BY REASON. Through the first sin Adam and his posterity lost IMMORTALITY, AND HIS WILL RECEIVED A BIAS TOWARD EVIL. In this natural state man, who even before he actually sins is a sinner before God by original or inherited sin, commits manifold actual transgressions; *but he is not absolutely without power of will toward good, and is not always doing evil*.

"Christ . . . by his vicarious death has made satisfaction to God for the world's sins, and this satisfaction was PERFECTLY COMMENSURATE WITH THE SINS OF THE WORLD. . . . This divine help is offered *to all men without distinction, and may be rejected*. In order to attain to salvation, man is justified, and when so justified CAN DO NO MORE THAN THE COMMANDS OF GOD. He may fall from a state of grace through mortal sin.

"Regeneration is offered by the word of God and in the sacraments, *which under visible signs communicate God's invisible grace to Christians when administered cum intentione*. There are *seven* mysteries, or sacraments. Baptism *entirely destroys* original sin. In the Eucharist the true body and blood of Christ are *substantially present; and the elements are changed into the substance of Christ, whose body and blood are corporeally partaken of by communicants.* ALL Christians should receive the bread and THE WINE. *The Eucharist is also an expiatory sacrifice.* The new birth when lost may be restored through repentance, which is not merely (1) sincere sorrow, but (2) *confession of each individual sin to the priest, and* (3) *the discharge of penances imposed by the priest for the removal of the temporal punishment which may have been imposed by God and the Church. Penance accompanied by the judicial absolution of the priest makes a true sacrament.*

" The Church of Christ is the fellowship of ALL THOSE WHO ACCEPT AND PROFESS ALL THE ARTICLES OF FAITH TRANSMITTED BY THE APOSTLES AND APPROVED BY GENERAL SYNODS. *Without this visible Church there is no salvation.* It is under the abiding influence of the Holy Ghost, and *therefore cannot err in matters of faith.* Specially appointed persons are necessary in the service of the Church, *and they form a threefold order, distinct jure divino from other Christians, of Bishops, Priests, and Deacons.* THE FOUR PATRIARCHS, OF EQUAL DIGNITY, HAVE THE HIGHEST RANK AMONG THE BISHOPS; AND THE BISHOPS, *united in a General Council, represent the Church, and infallibly decide,* under the guidance of the Holy Ghost, all matters of faith and ecclesiastical life. . . . *Bishops must be unmarried,* and PRIESTS AND DEACONS MUST NOT CONTRACT A SECOND MARRIAGE."

They must, however, be married at ordination.

A priest of the Eastern Church is called a " pope," which means " papa," and corresponds to the Catholic " father." This church has prayers for the dead and a somewhat indefinite belief in a purgatory, but rejects the use of unleavened bread in the Eucharist; gives the Eucharist to babes as well as adults; makes the priest and people stand during prayer; baptizes by immersion; anoints the sick with oil, but has no " extreme unction," — that is, at death; abhors the use of images in churches, but permits fervent homage to pictures; allows divorce, and follows the

Mosaic Law in abstaining from things strangled and "unclean" meats.

The liturgies of the Eastern Church are naturally very ancient, the most common being that of Saint James. Unlike the Catholic ritual, the Eastern is commonly in the vernacular, with the advantage that where Greek is spoken the New Testament is read and understood in the language in which it was written. The services of the Russian Church, especially, are very elaborate, and the vestments of its priests gorgeous.

Government. — The Eastern Church has now four Patriarchs, — of Constantinople, Antioch, Jerusalem, and Alexandria. They are supreme in their districts, having metropolitan. or chief, and suffragan, or deputy, bishops under them. But their power has been much curtailed by the formation of various national churches, — as those of Russia, under a Holy Governing Synod appointed by the Czar, which has authority over sixty-three divisions called *Eparchies*, each under a bishop; of Roumania, under a metropolitan and bishops; of Greece, under the king as head, with a synod like the Russian; of Servia; of Montenegro, etc. There is no single authority over the whole Church. except a possible Œcumenical Council, which has never been summoned since the separation from Rome.

Statistics. — There were in 1890 about 92.000,000 Eastern Christians, of whom 76,000,000 are regular adherents of the Greek Church, mainly in Russia; 11,000,000 are in Russian sects; while there are 2,300,000 in the Armenian (Monophysite) Church, 1,500,000 Jacobites, and 400,000 Nestorians, in virtual agreement with the rest, but separate ecclesiastically as they are politically.

QUESTIONS.

What is the name of the Eastern Church ? Why is it called also the Greek Church ? What advantage has it over the Roman Church in locality ? in language of the people ? Has it been progressive ? What different work have the two churches taken up ? Who are the Nestorians ? the Maronites ? When and why did the two churches separate ? What different relations had they to the barbarians ? Which have been the more civilized, the Greek Christians or the Mohammedans ?

A STUDY OF THE SECTS.

What are the foundations of the belief of the Eastern Church? What does "Œcumenical" mean? What do you know of the Nicene Creed? What is the Eastern doctrine of the Bible? How does this differ from the Protestant? What is its doctrine of the Trinity? of total depravity? of the atonement? of regeneration? of baptism? of the Eucharist? of the Church? What is the difference between the Roman Pope and an Eastern pope? What other beliefs of the Eastern Church can you mention? Compare the doctrines in general with the Roman and Protestant. What can you say of the liturgies? What is the government? Who are the patriarchs? Does the Eastern Church seem attractive to you? Why? More or less so than the Roman? Which stands nearer to Unitarians? Which has the better future before it?

REFERENCES.

An admirably clear and concise article in the Encyclopædia Britannica, "Greek Church." Dean Stanley's picturesque *Lectures on the History of the Eastern Church* is especially full on the Russian Church, and has a good map. Gibbon, chaps. xlvii. lv., as well as all chapters relating to the Eastern Empire. Fisher, see Index, "Church, Eastern," and "Greek Church." Schaff, vol. i. pp. 43-82, gives an account of the various creeds, and vol. ii. pp. 275-445, the creeds themselves. Prof. A. V. G. Allen, in *The Continuity of Christian Thought*, gives a fascinating account of the Greek theology and its influence upon modern Christian thought. J. M. Neale, *The Holy Eastern Church*, 5 vols.

CHAPTER V.

THE PROTESTANTS.

THAT no man is justified by the law in the sight of God, it is evident: for, The just shall live by faith. — GAL. iii. 11.

Origin of the Name. — At the second Diet, or congress, of the German princes, called by the Emperor Charles V. at Speier (Spires), in 1529, a former edict of toleration to the Lutherans was rescinded; and the edict of Worms, by which Luther was declared an outlaw and his writings were condemned, was pronounced still in force. Against this act the Lutheran princes at the Diet made a formal protest: "In matters which relate to the glory of God and to the salvation of our souls, we must all stand before God and give account of ourselves to him." Hence the name "Protestant," or "protester." It was afterward widened, and is so used to-day, to cover all Christians who protest against the doctrines and practices of the Catholic Church.

History. — The Reformation had been long growing, and sprang from several roots. First, there was a *political* restlessness under the yoke of what was felt more and more keenly, as the nations began to form and to become self-conscious, to be a foreign tyranny. The Church held one third of the land of Europe, immense endowments of cathedrals, monasteries, etc.; and received enormous incomes from various tithes, fees, etc. These were burdens and drains upon the national strength; and the kings, nobles, and people became on this account hostile to Rome. This explains the protection of the Reformers by many princes. Secondly, there was a growing *intellectual* pressure against the narrowness of the Church. The Crusades, which were foreign tours of vast multitudes whose minds were broadened and aroused, the revival of learning and study of the ancient classics, the invention of printing, the discovery of America and of the way around the Cape of Good Hope, and the general awakening of the human mind — a stretching, as it were, in the broader spaces and opportunities of study and commerce — made old ideas and ways no longer possible. Thirdly, the *moral* sense revolted against the corruption of the priesthood, which is now acknowledged by both sides to have been very great, and which extended often to the Popes themselves. Fourthly, the *religious* instinct rebelled against the choking of the way between the soul and God by the "dead works," the ritual, and discipline of the Church. A long series of protests which had not availed, because "the fulness of time" had not come, gave their momentum to the movement under Luther.

Few however, wished or expected to break away from the Church. Its right to rule was universally conceded. Reform, not revolution, was the aim; and had the Church been as shrewd before the Reformation as it became after, it might for a long time have kept its integrity. But reform within having been defeated, the Church swept on to rupture and loss. When the movement was over, it was found that the division was essentially one of race, — between Teutonic and Latin, between Northern and Southern Europe; and so it still remains.

The detailed history of this crisis must be studied elsewhere. But we must follow Protestantism into its own lamentable, though perhaps inevitable, divisions. The first was between Luther and Zwingli on the subject of the Eucharist, which broadened into the more disastrous one between Lutheran and Calvinist, or, as it was called, between " Evangelical " and " Reformed." The Lutheran party became stationary and practically national, and so remains. It was Calvinism which led Protestantism to its widest and bravest conquests in Switzerland, France, Holland, England, and New England. The Huguenots, the Puritans, the Covenanters, the defenders of Holland against Philip, were all Calvinists. So were their descendants, the Presbyterians, Congregationalists, Baptists, and some minor sects. The Church of England, though influenced by Calvinism, claims now not to be Protestant, or to have been "reformed" in the same sense as "the sects," but to be the branch in England of the one Catholic, or universal, Church, cleansed of the errors which the other branches, the Roman and Greek Churches, still hold. The sway of Calvinism was first broken by the Friends, with their doctrine of "the inner light," but later and more seriously by the Methodists, with their denial of predestination. The swiftly moving " Liberal " or rationalistic tendency has taken shape in the Unitarians, and less clearly in the Universalists. As against these " Liberal Protestants," or " Liberal Christians," the other sects have taken the name of " Evangelical," from the Greek word for Gospel (Latin *evangelium*), implying that they alone hold " Gospel truth." The "Evangelical Alliance," formed in 1846, excludes Unitarians, Universalists, Friends, and the New Church.

A truer classification of Protestants would be according to the *source* of their beliefs : namely, first, the *Church* party, which looks to the decisions of the visible, organized Church for its authority, including High Church Episcopalians, who thus properly belong with the Roman and Greek Churches; secondly, the *Scriptural* party, which bases its belief directly upon the teachings of Scripture, including the sects commonly called Evangelical; and the *Rational* party, which looks to the individual reason, enlightened from all sides, as sole source of belief, represented by the more advanced Unitarians and many Universalists. A large part of both these bodies is, however, professedly Scriptural. Those of the Friends who have remained true to their primitive doctrine of the "inner light" are virtually rationalistic; so is the New Church, though nominally Scriptural. The Scriptural party shades off by imperceptible degrees into rationalism, and indeed is colored throughout by it. The coming division of Christianity is undoubtedly to be into the party of the Church and that of the Reason, in which division we see the old one of ritual and spiritual religion virtually emerging again.

Doctrine. — Protestantism, as has been said, is a revival of the Christianity of Paul as against the Christianity of Peter, — of spiritual religion as against ritualism. As Paul swept aside the Jewish rites as unnecessary, and made Christianity begin with a spiritual act, faith, so Protestantism at length swept aside all the complicated ritual of the Roman Church, and taught the same immediate relationship between the soul and its God.

More particularly, the position of Protestantism is as follows:

1. Man is justified — that is, accepted as righteous by God — on condition of faith alone in Christ, which faith is a personal trust in him and living union with him. Without this faith no deeds are acceptable. Good works are the result of, not the preparation for, faith. The Romanist maintains that man is justified by faith *and works*, faith being assent and submission to God as revealed through the Church, and good works — that is, the deeds commanded by the Church — being conditions of justification, not merely its results.

2. The Spirit of God is given *directly* in response to faith. The Romanist maintains that it comes through the *sacraments*, — as baptism and the Eucharist, — administered by duly authorized officials of the Church.

3. Hence the Protestant holds to both an *invisible* Church, made up of all believers, Christ being the head, and a *visible* Church, made up of the various denominations who hold the true faith, — the former being the essential thing. The Catholic admits no such distinction, holding that the Church of Rome is the one and only Church of Christ, outside of which there is no ordinary possibility of salvation.

4. Hence the great difference between the two as to the source of authority. The Protestant maintains that the Bible alone, as read by the believer in the light of the Holy Spirit given to him in consequence of his faith, is the source of belief. The Romanist claims that while the Bible is inspired and infallible, the Church, which superintended its formation and preservation, is alone qualified to interpret it, and that the decisions of the Councils and Popes are of equal authority with it. Hence the Roman Church discourages the irresponsible reading of it by the laity. This Church has also accepted the Apocrypha as part of the Bible, and the Latin Vulgate, an ancient translation, as of equal authority with the original. English-speaking Catholics use the Douay Version instead of the so-called Version of King James.

5. From the distinction between the invisible and the visible Church comes an important distinction between the two conceptions of the ministry. The Protestant considers all believers to be priests in the sense of being able to approach God directly and to give significance and value to their own spiritual acts. For example, the efficacy of the sacraments depends, not upon who administers them, but upon the spirit in which they are received. The minister, though "called" to his office by the Holy Spirit, is yet essentially one of the members of the church, differing from the others only in personal fitness and education. The Roman ecclesiastic, priest or bishop, however, is invested with supernatural powers, as in a special sense the representative of God. Through him alone do the sacraments have efficacy. This power comes by the "apostolical succession," — that is, by the transmission of authority from Christ through the Apostles and their successors, the Roman bishops, in an unbroken line. This neces-

sity the Protestant, except the Anglican, denies, holding that the clergy are immediately commissioned by the Holy Spirit.

6. The Protestant reduces the seven sacraments to two, — baptism and the Lord's Supper; and with the exception of the Lutheran and the Anglican, denies to these any necessary conveyance of divine grace to the partaker. The Romanist maintains that the sacraments are supernatural channels for the communication of spiritual life to the recipient, independently of his or the priest's character, — baptism removing the stain of original sin, and the Eucharist repeating the sacrifice of Christ on the cross for the partaker's sake. The Protestant assigns all the benefit of these rites to the faith of the partaker in them. He denies transubstantiation, or the change of the elements into Christ's body and blood; refuses, therefore, to *adore* them; and grants the cup as well as the bread to the laity. Many Protestants also reject infant baptism. As to the other sacraments, *confirmation* is often replaced by admission to the church on confession of faith; *penance* is entirely swept away, together with auricular confession and priestly absolution; the doctrine of indulgences, which started the Reformation, is wholly set aside; *ordination* is often made an act of the congregation in the exercise of their own priestly functions, and the celibacy of the clergy is not required; *matrimony* is divested of many restrictions laid upon it by Romanists, — as refusal to unite with those outside the Church unless by dispensation, and then only with those properly baptized, — divorce being more liberally allowed; and *extreme unction* is abandoned.

7. Some minor differences may be considered together. The Protestants do not believe in purgatory, holding to heaven and hell only. They refuse any worship to the Virgin Mary or the saints or to images and relics, which the Romanist gives, though in different senses of the word "worship."

The Romanist and the Evangelical Protestant agree, however, on many points, — the inspiration and authority of the Bible; the Trinity; the deity of Christ; the fall of man and his consequent helplessness and need of redemption from without, the redemption coming through the sacrifice of Christ; heaven and hell.

A STUDY OF THE SECTS. 75

Statistics. — Of the 150,000,000 Protestants in the world, 47,000,000 are said to be Lutherans, 25,000,000 Methodists, 24,000,000 Episcopalians, 20,000,000 Presbyterians and Reformed, and 13,000,000 Baptists, though where any of these faiths are "established," it is the whole population which is often included in these figures. In the United States there are said to be over 50,000,000 Protestants, including most of the 140 "religious bodies" reported in the census of 1890. The official reports of the various sects show the number of *communicants* to be about 14,000,000, of whom 4,980,000 are Methodists, 4,292,000 Baptists, 1,229,000 Presbyterians, 1,086,000 Lutherans, 620,000 Disciples of Christ (1889), 491,000 Congregationalists, and 480,000 Episcopalians. The usual estimate of *adherents* is three and one half times the number of communicants. Of 18,000,000 scholars in the Sunday-schools of the world, one half are in this country. There are 143,761 churches and 95,000 ministers.

Unitarians consider, not only that they are Protestants, but that they alone are true to the fundamental Protestant principle of the direct communication of the soul with God. They charge the Evangelicals with having displaced the barrier of the Church and its rites to replace it, not only with a literal Bible upon which they cannot agree, and which they have made an unwilling obstacle to the progress of truth, but with creeds defining the meaning of the Bible, which they have made often of equal and even superior authority to the Scriptures. Unitarians consider the Bible as a *record* of a revelation in its earlier stages, but not as the finished revelation itself; and reject creeds as unjustifiable limits to the freedom, and so to the reality and sincerity, of thought. They hold that God speaks still to the minds and souls of men, revealing fresh truth, as Jesus foretold (John xvi. 12, 13). The divergence of Unitarians on other points of doctrine will appear as those points come up for special consideration.

QUESTIONS.

What does the word "Protestant" mean? When and how did it arise? Who are included under it now? What were the causes of the Reformation? What was the aim of the Reformers? Do you think that the Roman Church could have been kept whole forever? How are Protestants and Catholics now divided? Who was the first Protestant leader? What was the first division among the Protestants? What was the greatest division? What was the course of the two parties? Which has done the world the more good? What is the position of the Church of England toward the Reformation? What was the first break in Calvinism? What was the point of difference? What was the more serious break? On what doctrine? What is meant by Liberal Protestantism? Why should it be called "Liberal"? What is the meaning of Evangelical? Is its use justified? What sects does it include? What other classification could be made? Where would you place the Baptists? Methodists? New Church? Episcopalians? Universalists? Friends? Name some signs of rationalism among these. How do you think Christians will be divided in future?

What ancient tendency is represented in Protestantism? Can you trace both kinds of religion in single sects? Among the Baptists? Episcopalians? Unitarians? What is the difference between Romanist and Protestant as to faith and works? salvation? the Church? the source of authority? How does the Protestant Bible differ from the Romanist? How do Romanist and Protestant differ as to the priesthood? What is meant by the "apostolical succession"? What is the Protestant doctrine of the sacraments? How do the two parties differ as to the Eucharist? divorce? indulgences? adoration of saints? future state? On what points do the two agree?

Is the Unitarian a Protestant? Why? In what fundamental point does he differ from the "Evangelicals"? What is the difference between the Bible as *being* the word of God and *containing* the word of God?

REFERENCES.

Perhaps the best handbook is *The Era of the Protestant Reformation*, by F. Seebohm. Longer and more reflective is *The History of the Reformation*, by Prof. George P. Fisher. Still longer and more standard, Ranke's *History of the Popes*, and D'Aubigné's *History of the Reformation*; J. H. Allen's *Christian History in its Three Great Periods*, vol. iii, and *Outline*, chaps. vii.-ix.; Encyclopædia Britannica, "Reformation," "Luther," etc.; *The Reformation* (Handbooks for Bible-Classes), T. M. Lindsay, Edinburgh, T. & T. Clark; Schaff's *Creeds of Christendom*, vol. i., especially pp. 924-928, where the agreements with and differences from Romanism are clearly given; Charles Beard, *Hibbert Lectures for* 1883, *The Reformation of the Sixteenth Century in its Relation to Modern Thought and Knowledge;* W. E. H. Lecky, *Rationalism in Europe;* Dorner's *History of Protestant Theology*, 2 vols. Bibliography at end of Fisher's *History of the Christian Church*, and of his *History of the Reformation*.

Section I.
THE EVANGELICAL PROTESTANT SECTS.
1. THE LUTHERANS.

WHILE one saith, I am of Paul; and another, I am of Apollos; are ye not carnal? Who then is Paul and who is Apollos, but ministers by whom ye believed, even as the Lord gave to every man? I have planted, Apollos watered; but God gave the increase. — 1 Cor. iii. 4-6.

Name. — The name Lutheran was, like the name Christian, first given in contempt by enemies. In time its application was widened by Catholics to all opponents of Rome. Among Protestants the name is applied to those whose creed is the Augsburg Confession. In Poland and Austria their official name is "The Church of the Augsburg Confession," but they are generally known as "The Evangelical Lutheran Church."

History. — The history of the Lutherans after the death of their leader is very painful. Instead of standing united and firm against their still powerful enemy, the Roman Church, they broke into the most bitter controversies among themselves and with the Calvinists, under cover of which the Romanists regained much of the ground they had lost, and the banner of aggressive Protestantism was taken up by the Calvinists. Melanchthon, the friend of Luther, found himself diverging from him on the doctrines of the sacrament and of predestination. The lamentable disputes between the two parties should be read in Schaff (vol i. pp. 268-307). They were terminated in 1577 by the "Form of Concord," which most signed, but many rejected and reject still. The excessive emphasis on dogma led to two reactions, — one of the heart, called "Pietism," under Spener (1635-1705), much like Methodism; and one of the head, called "Rationalism," which resulted in the severe criticism of the Bible that has marked much of later German scholarship, reaching its climax in Strauss, Baur, and the Dutch Kuenen and Wellhausen. In Prussia, in 1817, and in a few smaller States, a forced union was made by the secular authorities between the Calvinists and the Lutherans under the name of "The United Evangelical Church." The stricter Lutherans resisted this, and made the sect of "Old Lutherans," who were finally given legal footing; but many emigrated to America. To-day Lutheranism is the *established* religion in Denmark, Sweden, and Norway, and the *prevailing* religion in Saxony, Hanover, and northern Germany generally, in Baden and Würtemberg in the south, and in some districts of Russia,—as St. Petersburg, Livonia, and Finland. The German element in Hungary and Transylvania is Lutheran, the Magyars being Calvinist.

In the United States, the first Lutherans came from Holland, in 1621, and settled in New Amsterdam, or New York; but the first organized church and minister were Swedish, at Christiana (now Wilmington), in Delaware, 1638. This minister translated Luther's Smaller Catechism into the Indian tongue, and was the first missionary to the Indians of North America. The first *German* Lutheran church was organized in New York, 1644. There was not much growth until the first half of the next century, when large numbers of German immigrants came over. Aid was asked of the home churches; and in 1742 came Dr. Henry Melchior Muhlenberg, who was the virtual founder of the Lutheran denomination in this country. The first synod was organized in Philadelphia, 1748. The Lutherans were intensely patriotic during the Revolution, and induced many Hessians to desert, thousands of whom, after the war, settled with them permanently.

But divisions rent the churches here as at home. The German language was at first used exclusively in the churches. English was introduced into one church in 1819, and it remained the only one for years. Much disputation ensued on this point. The "General Synod of the Evangelical Lutheran Church of the United States" had been established in 1820. It adopts only the Augsburg Confession as its doctrinal basis, and allows a liberal construction of even this.

In 1847 the "Synod of Missouri, Ohio, and other States" was formed,—generally called "Missourians,"—very active and strict in doctrine and discipline, powerful chiefly among the Germans of the West. They were incorporated in 1872 into the "Synodical Conference of North America." It requires its ministers to subscribe to the whole Book of Concord, "as the pure, unadulterated explanation and exposition of the divine word and will." During the late war, in 1863, the "General Synod of the Southern States" was formed, in doctrinal agreement with the "General Synod." In 1867 the "General Council" was formed, accepting the "unaltered Augsburg Confession in its original sense," — of doctrine intermediate between the other two bodies. Besides these are several other bodies and independent churches.

Doctrine.— The Evangelical Lutheran churches agree upon the Apostles' Creed, the Nicene Creed, the Athanasian Creed, and the Augsburg Confession. The stricter churches add to these the "Apology of the Confession" (prepared by Melanchthon as an answer to the "Confutation" of the Catholics, promulgated by the Diet of Augsburg in 1630 as a reply to the "Confession"); the "Articles of Smalcald" (a creed prepared by Luther to express his belief at a council called by the Pope at Mantua, in 1537, and signed by a convention of Protestant theologians at Smalcald, in Thuringia); the two Catechisms, Large and Small, written by Luther to replace the Catholic catechisms for the young; and the "Form of Concord," prepared by six divines in 1577. Together these nine creeds form the "Book of Concord."

The characteristic doctrines of Lutheran, as distinguished from Calvinist churches are these: —

1. They teach *consubstantiation*, or the real presence of Christ's body and blood *in*, *with*, and *under* the elements, literally eaten by unworthy as well as by worthy communicants. This doctrine must be distinguished from the Roman Catholic doctrine of *transubstantiation*, which teaches that bread and wine are changed *into*, do not merely coexist with, the body and blood of Christ. Calvin taught a *spiritual* presence of Christ at the Eucharist, enjoyed by believers only.

2. Behind this doctrine lies that of the ubiquity of Christ's glorified body. "The human nature, while retaining its inherent properties, may and does receive the attributes of divine glory, — majesty, power, omniscience, and omnipresence." Hence it

is present, as God is, in all places and things, the Eucharistic elements included, at the same time.

3. With the supernatural Eucharist goes a supernatural baptism, by which the child is regenerated, and without which there is ordinarily no salvation. In and with the water, as in and with the Eucharistic elements, goes a divine saving power.

4. The Lutherans hold that atonement was made for and salvation freely offered to *all* men, and that no one is lost save by his own refusal to repent and believe. They therefore deny the Calvinist doctrine of election and an atonement limited to the elect. As one is free to take divine grace, so one may afterward fall from it. The doctrine of the perseverance, or necessary continuance in grace, of the believer is therefore also rejected.

Lutherans are also more conservative in the retention of many church festivals and usages of the Catholic Church, though their tendency is now toward agreement with other Protestants in such non-essential matters.

In other doctrines the Lutherans are mainly at one with the rest of Evangelical Christendom.

Government.— The organization of the Lutheran churches varies in different nations. In Germany, which was divided at the Reformation into small States, each obliged to follow the religion of its prince, the ruler naturally took the place of the bishop, and became the head of his churches. Under him, and largely appointed by him, was the *consistory*, or council, — the executive body. The congregations have little power. The rules of the churches differ greatly; in 1846 more than one hundred and eighty different constitutions could be counted.

In Norway and Denmark the Roman Catholic bishops were replaced by Lutheran bishops, who are, however, appointed by the king, as head of the Church. In Sweden the Roman bishops were converted; so that the apostolic succession is preserved, though no doctrinal use is made of the fact. There is also an archbishop (of Upsala).

In the United States the congregation has more power. It appoints its own pastor, who is then, however, responsible to the Synod in doctrine and discipline. The District Synod is made up of delegates, lay and clerical, from the churches, and sends delegates to the General Synod.

Lutheranism deserves honor as having been the "old guard" of Protestantism, — the first form in which the movement took shape. But it proved reactionary within and an impediment to the success of the movement without. It turned its energy against heresies in its own ranks rather than against the common enemy, whose disastrous recovery of ground must be largely attributed to Lutheran narrowness and disputatiousness. The sword of conquest passed into the hands of the Calvinists. Even in this country the Lutherans have proved reactionary, joining hands in the West with the Romanists against the public schools, and stoutly maintaining, not only their original doctrine, but the language of the land they have left in the land that has received and sheltered them.

To the Unitarian the Lutheran history is valuable as showing the disastrous effects of limiting truth by the words rather than by the spirit of a single man, though he be as great as Luther, and by creeds which not only circumscribe truth, but dictate even what shall be read in the Bible. Such a course leads, not only to divisions and controversies, but to reactions as violent as the action, and resulting in the overthrow of the creeds so vehemently urged. That the "rationalism" and "destructive criticism" which characterize German thought to-day should have sprung up in the bosom of a church so sternly resolved to keep thought in bonds is very suggestive to all those who consider creeds conservative; while the spirit in which the controversies were carried on shows afresh how far dogmatic clearness may be from the spirit of Christ.

Statistics. — There are in the world about 47,000,000 Lutherans. In the United States there were in 1890, it was estimated, about 4,000,000. The churches report 1,086,000 *communicants*, 7,948 congregations, 4,692 clergymen. There are 57 synods; 23 theological seminaries, or departments; 28 academies; 10 female seminaries; 48 benevolent institutions; and over 100 periodicals in English, German, Norwegian, Danish, Icelandish, and Finnish.

QUESTIONS.

What was the origin of the name? What are the official names now? What can you say of the German Lutherans in their early history? Did this follow naturally from Luther's doctrine of private judgment? What were the points of controversy? Do they seem to you worth while? What were the consequences to Protestantism? How was it ended? What reactions followed? Were these natural? Why? Where are Lutherans most numerous in Europe? Who were the first Lutherans in this country? On what were they divided? Who was their great organizer? Name some of their divisions to-day.

What are their standards of belief? What is their doctrine of the Eucharist? of Christ's body? of baptism? of the atonement? Are they conservative or progressive generally? How are they organized? What is the tendency in this country? Why? How many are there in the world? How many here? What is your impression concerning them in general? What honor is due them? What may be charged against them? What lessons do they teach the Unitarian?

REFERENCES.

The best account of both history and doctrine is in Schaff, vol. i pp. 220-349, vol. iii. pp. 1-193; Fisher's *Reformation*, chap. v., and other works on this period; McClintock and Strong; and the Lives of Luther, especially Köstlin's. For later history, see J. H. Allen's *Christian History in its Three Great Periods*, vol. iii. chap. ix.; Hagenbach's *History of the Church in the Eighteenth and Nineteenth Centuries;* Hurst's *History of Rationalism;* Krauth's *Conservative Reformation*, and Wolf's *The Lutherans in America*.

---

2. THE REFORMED CHURCH IN AMERICA.

Knowing that a man is not justified by the works of the law, but by the faith of Jesus Christ, even we have believed in Jesus Christ, that we might be justified by the faith of Christ, and not by the works of the law.— GAL. ii. 16.

Name. — The first title was " The Reformed Protestant Dutch Church in North America," — " Reformed," as Calvinistic, not Lutheran; "Protestant," as against Rome; "Dutch," as distinguished from the "English," or Episcopal Church, which competed with it, and after the English conquest of new Netherlands, in 1664, oppressed it. The word "Dutch" was added in 1694; but in 1867 the present name, "The Reformed Church in America," was taken.

History. — The Reformed churches in the United States are slips from the Calvinistic churches of Europe. They are divided into the Dutch and the German, chiefly for national reasons. The Dutch was the first to be transplanted. The principle of justification by faith, on which the Reformation of Luther was based, was preached in Holland half a century before his day, but made little impression. When the Reformation was under way it was from Calvin, not Luther, that Dutch Protestantism took shape. Its struggles against the Spanish power of Charles V. and Philip II. are famous in history. The church took shape in a synod at Antwerp in 1563, when the Belgic Confession was adopted. Its influence in Europe was very great; and through the English Protestants who took refuge in Holland — among them our "Pilgrims" — it affected England also. It was in this church that the famous Arminian controversy took place, ended at the Synod of Dort, in 1619, by the triumph of Calvinism and the banishment of the Arminians.

The first Reformed church in New Amsterdam (later New York) was established by the Dutch settlers of the province in 1619. There were but five churches when the English, in 1664, took the province. Life became a somewhat hard struggle to them. The attempt to become independent of the church in Holland, in 1755, resulted in a fierce struggle and division; but in 1792 this came to an end, and the present organization was formed.

Its growth was much hindered by the sole use of the Dutch language in service and sermon till 1764, and by its dependence and divisions. Though one of the oldest bodies in the country, it is not large, though it is wealthy and influential. It cares greatly for an educated ministry, and was the first body to institute systematic theological instruction in this country.

Doctrine. — The Reformed Church is essentially Calvinistic in doctrine. Its standards are the "Belgic Confession," the

"Heidelberg Catechism," and the "Canons of the Synod of Dort," which are coincident with the Westminster Confession. It used the liturgy adopted in 1568 at Wesel, based on Calvin's, translated into English in 1667, when singing in English was also introduced. The ministers often wear the Genevan gown.

Organization. — The Reformed Church is essentially Presbyterian in government, though the bodies have different names. The "Consistory" corresponds to the "Session"; the "Classes" to the "Presbytery," the "Particular Synod," and the "General Synod."

There are also a "Board of Foreign Missions," with work in China, India, and Japan; with a "Woman's Board," a "Board of Domestic Missions," a "Board of Education" to aid theological students, a "Board of Publication," etc.

Statistics. — The report of 1889 gives 36 classes, 546 churches, 566 ministers, 88,812 communicants, 103,101 in Sunday-schools and catechumen classes. For religious and benevolent purposes $282,000 were raised, and for congregational uses $971,000. The receipts for home missions were $60,000, for foreign $132,000. There are two theological schools, — at New Brunswick, N. J., and at Holland, Mich.

QUESTIONS.

What is meant by the "Reformed" Church? Why was it called Dutch? What is its origin? How is it divided, and why? Which came here first? What was its history in Holland? What had our Pilgrims to do with it? What was its attitude toward Arminianism? Where was the first church here built? What was its fate? What was the dissension between it and the home church? What hindered its growth? What is its character now? What is its doctrine? What are its standards? How is it governed?

REFERENCES.

For the Church in Holland, see Schaff, vol. i. pp. 502-523, the "Confessions" in vol. iii.; also Motley's *Rise of the Dutch Republic* and *United Netherlands;* and Prescott's *Charles V.* For the Church in America, see a good article in McClintock; and *A Manual of the Reformed Church in America*, by Edward T. Corwin.

3. THE EPISCOPALIANS.

Let all things be done decently and in order. — 1 Cor. xiv. 40.

Name. — The legal name in England is "The Church of England." By this is implied, not only that it is the national church, — that is, the nation organized for religious purposes, — but that it is the branch in England of the Catholic or Universal Church of which the Roman and Greek Churches are also branches, though they have added false doctrines to those handed down from the Apostles.

The name in this country is "The Protestant Episcopal Church in the United States of America." The word "episcopal" comes from the Greek *episcopos*, or overseer, of which Greek word our word "bishop" is a contraction.

History. — The Church of England claims to have been founded by Oriental Christians, and not by missionaries of the Church of Rome, of which it kept for a long while its independence. The first historic evidence of Christianity in Britain dates back to about 300, and the Church soon had bishops of its own. Saint Patricius, or Patrick, was sent as missionary to Ireland, where the Church became strong, and noted for its learning. From Ireland went missionaries to the north of Scotland.

The invasions of the Danes during the fifth and sixth centuries practically exterminated the British Church, the remains being driven into Scotland and Wales; but in 597 Christianity was reestablished by Austin, the missionary of Pope Gregory the Great, and he became the first Archbishop of Canterbury. About the same time representatives of the old British Church came down from Scotland; and disputes arose on points of ritual between them and the Roman priests, which were settled in favor of the latter at the Council of Whitby, in 664. The Church of Rome therefore claims not only to have founded the Church of England as a branch of itself, but to have received formal recognition at Whitby, — both of which points the Church of England denies, claiming distinct origin from and equality with the Church of

Rome as also a branch of the One Holy Catholic and Apostolic Church. It is certain that no part of Europe was more independent of Rome than England, or more sturdy in its resistance to her exactions. The reforming spirit was active; and while Luther was beginning the German Reformation, a gentler band of scholars, led by Sir Thomas More, John Colet, and the German Erasmus, were pleading and working for purer morals, a broader spirit, and a more learned clergy in the Church. With Luther, however, they had no sympathy or co-operation; and Henry VIII. wrote an abusive book against him. The refusal of the Pope to annul the marriage of Henry to his first wife precipitated a crisis; and Henry forced the Houses of Convocation to make the king, instead of the Pope, the head of the Church of England. The doctrines of the Church, including transubstantiation, remained otherwise unchanged. Under Edward VI. (1547–53) the first Prayer Book and Forty-Two Articles were published. Under Elizabeth the Prayer Book was revised into virtually its present shape, and the Forty-Two Articles abridged to the present Thirty-Nine.

The act of Uniformity attempted to stop further reform, and establish one Church again throughout the kingdom. But then arose the "Puritans," or those who wished worship to be still further purified from things suggestive of Papistry, and to retain nothing that was not expressly commanded or sanctioned by Scripture, dividing into Presbyterians, and later Independents, or Congregationalists. Baptists and "Quakers" also became numerous.

The cessation of the long religious disputes in 1688 was followed by great weariness and laxity during the last century, and the condition of the Church and clergy was disgraceful. The first reaction came in Methodism, which was continued in the Church by the Evangelical or "Low Church" movement. But the sternness of its dogmatic emphasis led to the liberal, or "Broad Church," movement, under Thomas Arnold, Maurice, Whately, Kingsley, Stanley, Jowett, Temple, and others. This, in turn, roused the "Tractarian" or "High Church" movement, under Newman, Keble, Pusey, and their friends, who invoked

A STUDY OF THE SECTS.

against the disrupting influences of German rationalism, which threatened to undermine faith in the Church standards and doctrines, the aid of ritual to preserve due reverence for the unrevealed mysteries of God.

The influence of the Tractarian movement has been very deep and lasting, and by its emphasis upon the divine origin and office of the Church has stimulated very powerfully the zeal of its members to make it effective. Within thirty years as many millions of pounds have been spent in restoring its cathedrals and churches. Great attention has been paid to the enrichment of the services, to work among the poor and sick, and to the wider problems of modern civilization. What the Council of Trent was to the Roman Church, — emphasizing its peculiar doctrines, but setting it upon a more earnest and effective basis, — that the High Church movement has been to the English Church, which, though ministering to a decreasing proportion of the population, was probably never more in earnest than to-day.

In the United States. — The first settlers of Virginia, in 1607, were members of the Church of England, and churches were founded also in New York and other cities. In New England the Church obtained foothold with great difficulty, the people being Puritan, and remembering their contests with the Church in old England. The royal governors, however, maintained it; and the Church, in return, when hostility to and finally war with the mother country arose, was loyal to the crown, its ministers and people being for a long time extremely unpopular for having taken the "Tory" side. When the United States became independent of England, the Church deemed it necessary to make a separate organization. Never having had bishops of its own, it sought the ordination of some by the English Church. The clergy of Connecticut, having elected Dr. Samuel Seabury, sent him to the Archbishop of Canterbury for consecration. He, however, found himself unable to ordain him without requiring the oath of allegiance which all candidates had to take. Dr. Seabury therefore was consecrated by three Scotch bishops at Aberdeen, in 1784. In 1787 Dr. White, of Pennsylvania, and Dr. Provoost, of New York, were consecrated at Lambeth, England, by the

Archbishops of Canterbury and York and two bishops, the disability having been removed. Having now three prelates of its own, the Church here was henceforth competent to its own management. A provisional liturgy, called the "Proposed Book," was issued in 1786, which differed in many respects from the English Prayer Book; but a more conservative spirit prevailed, and in 1789 the present book was adopted. Subscription to the Thirty-Nine Articles is not required of the clergy here as it is in England. The legal name was fixed as "The Protestant Episcopal Church in the United States of America." This name is, however, very distasteful to the growing High Church party, who dislike to be classed among Protestants. They propose to change it to "The American Catholic Church," with a fair prospect of final success.

Doctrines.— The doctrines of the Church of England are to be found in its "Book of Common Prayer," "Thirty-Nine Articles," and "Homilies." These were adopted by the Protestant Episcopal Church of the United States, with a few changes, the chief of which was the omission of the Athanasian Creed.

These formularies are the result of two streams of influence, — one from the long-established use of the Catholic Church, the other from the German Reformers. The former predominates in the Prayer Book, the latter in the Articles and Catechism. The Morning and Evening Prayer and the Litany are substantially translations from the Catholic Breviary. The Communion Service is also a translation from the Latin service of the Mass, but with a larger admixture by the Reformers.

All the forms of worship of this Church are prescribed and regulated by the Prayer Book. No extempore prayer is allowed, and the lessons from Scripture are assigned by unvarying rule. The hymns also must first be approved by the proper authorities.

It is very difficult to expound the doctrines of the Church of England. In its three parties it contains the three forms under which Christianity exists in the world, elsewhere in separate sects. The High Church, which is now predominant, represents the Church idea, and is essentially to be ranked with the Roman and Greek Churches. The Low Church, which has shrunk very much in numbers and influence, represents the Scriptural idea, and is essentially Protestant. The Broad Church is really rationalistic, and ranks with the Liberal sects. The difference between these parties within the Church is really greater than between them and the sects which stand for their fundamental tendencies; but they all find support in the formularies of the Church, owing largely to that difference in the origin of the latter which has been explained.

The Church of England, which will be understood to include the Episcopal Church of our own country, agrees with the Roman Catholic Church in believing in "One Catholic and Apostolic Church," — that is, in an external and visible institution, having authority over all the world given it by Jesus Christ and transmitted through the Apostles and the bishops ordained by them in direct and demonstrable succession to the present day. Of this Church it claims to be a legitimate branch, ministering to the English nation, or *the* Church *in* England. It differs from the Roman Church in denying supremacy to the Bishop of Rome, and in rejecting such doctrines as it claims were not of apostolic origin, but have been added in later days, — as the papal infallibility, transubstantiation, communion in one kind, purgatory, etc. It concedes to the Roman and Greek Churches, however, apostolic authority in all other things in their own territory, they being with itself branches of the Catholic or universal Church. Though not pronouncing officially upon the validity of ministers not episcopally ordained, this Church virtually denies it, not allowing them to minister in its pulpits or at its altars, and generally forbidding its own clergy to officiate in churches of other faiths.

The apostolic descent of the Church of England gives, it is claimed, validity to its sacraments, of which it maintains two, baptism and the Supper of the Lord, instead of the Roman seven. The sacraments are "outward and visible signs of an inward and spiritual grace," given in or with them to the partakers. By baptism divine strength descends into the soul, contending with original sin, disposing to righteousness, and remitting previous actual sin. As stated in the order for infant baptism, the child is "regenerate." In the communion the body and blood of Christ are present in the bread and wine, conveying new strength to the soul of the partakers.

But it is upon these doctrines of the Church and the sacraments that the divergence of opinion already mentioned chiefly occurs. The above is the High Church view. The Low Church, — which on this point may be said to include both the Evangelical and the Broad Church parties, — while admitting the apostolic authority of its clergy, ascribes to it little practical value. The Evangelical churchman, like the Protestant, lays emphasis upon justification by faith, — that is, direct faith in Christ, — to which an apostolic clergy and sacraments may be helps, but are not indispensable. His tendency is to disregard the Church as an external institution, going immediately to the Bible, and trusting in the immediate action of the Holy Spirit upon the reader's heart. Baptism and the Eucharist are to him rather symbols than divine instrumentalities. The Evangelical churchman is virtually a Protestant, separated from other Protestants mainly by his use of the Prayer Book. The Broad Churchman, like all so-called liberals, lays stress upon character, values the Church and its sacraments as means of influencing the soul, and has less to say of faith in its theological sense. On the other hand, many High Churchmen are hardly to be distinguished from Romanists in their views of the necessity of baptism and of the Real Presence in the Eucharist, some even maintaining transubstantiation. They also grant higher power to their clergy, — in receiving confession, imposing penance, and granting absolution.

Besides these most characteristic doctrines, the Church of England holds to the Trinity, as defined especially in the Nicene Creed, including the deity of Christ and of the Holy Spirit; the inspiration of the Bible, though the Broad Churchmen are very lax herein; the taint of original sin, predisposing to evil; predestination and election, in which the Evangelicals are decidedly Calvinistic, though High Churchmen and Broad Churchmen are as clearly Arminian; the resurrection of the body, though with much divergence as to what this means; and eternal punishment of the wicked, though Broad Churchmen like Maurice, Kingsley, and Archdeacon Farrar have openly denied this, it having been omitted from the Articles, though it is plainly implied in the Litany.

Organization. — The highest officers in the Church of England are the archbishops, or metropolitans (Canterbury and York). The legislative power lies in the two Convocations, presided over by the two archbishops, and consisting each of two houses, the upper containing the bishops, deans, archdeacons, and abbots of the archdiocese, the lower the representatives of the clergy. Their decisions, however, must be ratified by Parliament before becoming law, and they cannot even be assembled without writ of the crown.

The bishops have jurisdiction over the churches in their respective territorial dioceses. They alone can administer confirmation, ordain priests and deacons, or dedicate new churches. The twenty-four senior sees send their bishops to the House of Lords. They are nominated by the crown, and elected by the chapter of their cathedral. The cathedral is the chief church of the diocese, and is so called from the bishop's seat (*cathedra*), which it contains. Hence, also, the cathedral church or city is called his " see " (*sedes, siège*). This church is administered by the chapter, which consists of the dean, or presiding officer, and (usually) four canons, who take turns in conducting the services. Each diocese has also from two to four archdeacons, who are in many ways the executive officers and aids of the bishop. Next come the priests, and finally the deacons, in which office every priest must serve at least a year before ordination to the priesthood. A curate is an assistant to the incumbent of a parish, and may be either a priest or a deacon.

The Church of England is the Established Church of England and Wales. In Scotland the Established Church is Presbyterian, while in Ireland there has been none since the disestablishment of the Anglican Episcopal Church in 1869. By the " Established Church " is meant the official or national Church. The sovereign must be a member of it. Its prelates are peers of the realm. Its liturgy is used upon all official occasions and in all government institutions where any devotional exercises are held ; and it retains the churches, churchyards, and other ecclesiastical property held by the Church before the changes made by Henry VIII. and his successors. This property constitutes its endowment. Formerly it levied compulsory rates upon all taxable property; but these are now abolished along with most other peculiar privileges,— as the power to perform the marriage ceremony or the sole right of its members to be elected to Parliament.

In the United States the Episcopal Church is upon a level with all other religious bodies before the law. It has no archbishops. The bishops are elected by the conventions of their dioceses, the election being ratified by the General Convention or its representatives, in which both lay and clerical delegates vote. They are consecrated by other bishops, at least three being necessary. There is but one cathedral, that at Albany, but more are planned. The legislative body is the General Convention, which meets once in three years. It consists of the "House of Bishops" and the "House of Deputies," to the latter each diocese sending four clergymen and four laymen, and each Missionary District one. There is also an informal but very interesting body called the "Church Congress," here as well as in England, for discussion of important questions. Beside the bishops there are priests and deacons, with archdeacons and other officers, as need requires.

Statistics. — There are in the Church of England 2 archbishops, 28 bishops, 30 deans, 74 archdeacons, and about 13,000 parochial clergy. The number of people nominally connected with the Church is about 13,000,000, though there are accommodations for less than half that number. The number of active members is probably less than that of the "dissenters." It contains, however, most of the nobility, as well as the royal family. It is very wealthy, its annual income being estimated at over £7,000,000, or $35,000,000. The salary of the Archbishop of Canterbury is $75,000 a year, the lowest salary of any bishop being $12,000, though a large part of these sums is usually spent in charities and upon the needs of the diocese. The "livings," or endowments, of the parochial clergy are also often large, though a thousand of them receive less than $250.

In the Protestant Episcopal Church of the United States there were, in 1890, 50 bishops, besides 17 missionary bishops, nearly

4,000 clergy, 3,500 parishes, and over 480,000 communicants. Their total contributions for church and missionary purposes, $11,277,000. There were also in the Sunday-schools over 360,000 scholars and 29,000 teachers.

The Episcopalians have been the best representatives in this country of good taste and good manners in worship. The dignity and verbal simplicity of its liturgy and the æsthetic excellence of its music, architecture, and appointments have done much to correct on the one hand the coldness and stiffness of Puritan services, and on the other hand the "revival" extravagances of a new country. Its chief emphasis is not upon the sermon, as in most Protestant churches, but upon the service. It has paid great attention to the organization of parishes for charitable work, and has had great success in the "free-seat" system, as opposed to the sale or rental of pews. In many philanthropic directions, as temperance and social purity, it has done good service, while some of its bishops have been very outspoken on the great social problems of the day.

All this has increased with the growing claim to be *the* Church in America, — the sole legitimate representative of Christ, — at least, as compared with the other Protestant sects. This also gives it a strong hold upon the reverence and loyalty of its members, and a growing attraction for the conservative classes, — those of wealth and social rank. But another and less agreeable consequence is an increasing exclusiveness and withdrawal of fellowship from other bodies. As *the* Church, it declines to consider itself on a level with "the sects," works less and less with them, and holds its clergy at a distance from theirs. It stands thus in contrast with the rapidly growing sense of fellowship among the different branches of the Christian Church, and the tendency to a working, if not to a corporate, unity. To Liberals this assumption and the exclusiveness which follows from it cannot but be repulsive, and the beauty and dignity of its worship cannot hide the fact that the Episcopal Church stands in the way of one of the most beautiful manifestations of the Christian spirit. Nor can they fail to see that though the Apostles' Creed is made the standard of belief, yet the Book of Common Prayer virtually implies when it does not plainly assert many doctrines which Liberals have put aside as untrue. The baptismal service, especially, in declaring the child "regenerate by baptism," strikes at the root of Protestantism; while the Litany contains petitions which no Unitarian can offer. While, therefore, he may admire the beauty and dignity of the liturgy, sincerity forbids him to use it.

QUESTIONS.

What is implied in the title, "The Church of England"? What does "Episcopal" mean? Are any other bodies Episcopal? Why? What does the English Church claim as to its origin? What does the Roman Church say to this? What can be said on either side? What was the Church's attitude toward the German Reformation? Who led the English movement? What else do you know of any of them? What led to the break with Rome? When was the first Prayer Book compiled? When the present one? Who were the Puritans? Would it not have been better to concede something to keep the "dissenters" in the Church? What bodies can you think of who have come out of this Church? What condition succeeded that of dispute? What reactions came from it? Who led them? What can you recall about any of these men? How do your sympathies turn? What has been the influence of the High Church movement? Who brought the Church to this country? How did it stand in New England? What was its attitude during the Revolution? How was the Church organized in this country? What is its name here? What change is proposed? What does this imply? What do you think of it?

What are the standards of doctrine? What influences formed them? What restrictions are placed upon worship? What difficulty is there in expounding the doctrines? What are the three parties? What tendencies do they embody? How are they really affiliated? What is the High Church view of the Church? How does it look upon the Roman and Greek Churches? How do they look upon it? What view of the clergy does this involve? what of the sacraments? What is the view of baptism? of the communion? How do the Low Church views differ from these? How do those of the Broad Church? How do the parties differ on the inspiration of the Bible? on predestination? on eternal punishment?

What grades of officers are there in the Church of England? What is a cathedral? a deacon? a curate? What is meant by the "Established Church"? How is it governed in England? What officers has the Church here? What is the governing body? What other body is there?

What do the Episcopalians best represent? In what ways? What have they done for parish work? for free churches? for philanthropic causes? What has given importance to these? What other effects has it had? What criticism can you make on its attitude to other bodies? What do you think of its doctrines? How far can you use its liturgy? What do you think of liturgical service in general? What are its advantages? its disadvantages?

REFERENCES.

For the sources of the history and the standard books, see the bibliography at the close of Fisher; Schaff, vol. i. pp. 592-665; Fisher, Index, "England" and "England, Church of;" C. Arthur Lane, *Illustrated Notes on Church History*, 2 small volumes; Green's *Short History of the English People*, chaps. vii. and viii.; Herford's *Story of Religion in England*. For the Roman Catholic side, see Lingard's *History of England;* and for the Puritan, Neal's *History of the Puritans*. For later history, see W. N. Molesworth's *History of the Church of England from 1660;* Lecky's *History of England in the Eighteenth Century;* Tulloch's *Movements of Religious Thought in Britain during the Nineteenth Century;* Newman's *Apologia*,[1] and his *Letters;* Thomas Mozley's *Reminiscences of the Oriel Movement;* and G. G. Perry's *History of the Church of England in the Nineteenth Century*, 3 vols.; also lives of Keble, Pusey, Whately, Wilberforce, etc. The history in this country has lately been told anew by S. D. McConnell in his *History of the American Episcopal Church*. See also Bishop W. S. Perry's *History of the American Episcopal*

---

[1] Cardinal Newman was the leader of the Oxford or Tractarian movement in the Church of England, which, starting with the assumption that there *is* a visible and authoritative Church on the earth, strove to believe that the Anglican is that Church. Newman became a Roman Catholic in 1845, and his mature views upon this point are of great weight.

"I cannot tell how soon there came on me, but very soon, an extreme astonishment that I had ever imagined it [the Church of England] a portion of the Catholic Church. . . . I saw it as it was, — . . . a mere national institution. . . . And when I looked back upon the poor Anglican Church, for which I labored so hard, and thought of our various attempts to dress it doctrinally and æsthetically, it seemed to me to be the veriest of nonentities. . . . And as to its possession of an episcopal succession from the time of the Apostles, . . . I must have Saint Philip's gift, who saw the sacerdotal character on the face of a gayly-attired youngster, before I can by my own wit acquiesce in it; for antiquarian arguments are quite unequal to the urgency of visible facts" (*Apologia*).

"Why should I wish to see it [the Anglican Church] overthrown? While Catholics are so weak . . . it is doing our work; and though it does harm in a measure, . . . the balance is in our favor" (*Apologia*).

"As to your question about the growth of Church principles in the Anglican Church, I rejoice in the fact; but as to the *why*, . . . it may be to prepare for a large addition of members to the Roman Catholic Church" (Letter to Canon Maccoll).

Church, 2 vols.; Palfrey's *History of New England*; and Foote's *Annals of King's Chapel*.

For doctrine, consult the *Book of Common Prayer*, which contains the Creeds and Thirty-Nine Articles; Schaff, vol. iii. p. 486, has the Articles and the American revision of them; J. H. Blunt's *Annotated Book of Common Prayer*; J. R. Lumby, *The Creeds*; Bishop Pearson's *Exposition of the Creed*; A. W. Little (High Church), *Reasons for being a Churchman*; R. F. Littledale's *Plain Reasons against joining the Church of Rome*; E. Hatch's *Organization of the Early Christian Churches*; and Hooker's *Ecclesiastical Polity*.

---

4. THE REFORMED EPISCOPALIANS.

O FOOLISH Galatians, who hath bewitched you, that ye should not obey the truth? . . . Received ye the Spirit by the works of the law, or by the hearing of faith? — GAL. iii. 1, 2.

THE Reformed Episcopal Church, as its name indicates, is a secession from the Protestant Episcopal Church of the United States of America.

In October, 1873, the General Conference of the Evangelical Alliance met in New York. In the general communion service which was held, Assistant Bishop Cummins, of Kentucky, and the Dean of Canterbury, England, participated. This drew out a public protest from the bishop of New York, in which a large part of the Episcopal Church warmly sympathized. This seemed to Bishop Cummins the climax of the tendency to High Church ritualism and exclusiveness; and he resigned his position, and left the Church. He was formally deposed, but proceeded to form a new organization, at a council held in New York, Dec. 2, 1873. Since then it has grown steadily, though not rapidly.

Doctrine. — The standard of belief is the "Thirty-Five Articles," a revision of the English Thirty-Nine, in which the Apostles' (except "He descended into hell") and Nicene Creeds are accepted. The Liturgy was also revised, in general agreement with the first revision of the American Church in 1786, omitting from the baptismal service the thanksgiving for the "regeneration" of the child, and changing throughout the words "priest" and "altar" to "minister" and "Lord's table." The general position of the new body may best be seen in the

DECLARATION OF PRINCIPLES.

"I. The Reformed Episcopal Church, holding 'the faith once delivered to the saints,' declares its belief in the Holy Scriptures of the Old and New Testaments as the Word of God and the sole Rule of Faith and Practice; in the Creed 'commonly called the Apostles' Creed;' in the divine institution of the Sacraments of Baptism and the Lord's Supper; and in the doctrines of grace substantially as they are set forth in the Thirty-Nine Articles of Religion.

"II. This Church recognizes and adheres to Episcopacy, not as of divine right, but as a very ancient and desirable form of church polity.

"III. This Church, retaining a Liturgy which shall not be imperative or repressive of freedom," etc.

"IV. This Church condemns and rejects the following erroneous and strange doctrines as contrary to God's Word:—

"*First*, That the Church of Christ exists only in one order or form of ecclesiastical polity.

"*Second*, That Christian ministers are 'priests' in another sense than that in which all believers are 'a royal priesthood.'

"*Third*, That the Lord's Table is an altar, on which the oblation of the Body and Blood of Christ is offered anew to the Father.

"*Fourth*, That the Presence of Christ in the Lord's Supper is a presence in the elements of Bread and Wine.

"*Fifth*, That Regeneration is inseparably connected with Baptism."

The Reformed Episcopalians are thus simply *belated Puritans*. They are those of the Protestant or Pauline wing who can no longer endure the Churchly or Petrine tendencies of the Episcopal Church. In their emphasis upon the Bible as the rule of faith and upon justification by faith as their leading doctrine, in their assertion that the Liturgy is not obligatory but expedient and voluntary, and that the Episcopal form of government is not essential, that the minister and people are equal, and in their protest against belief in the supernatural effect of the communion and of baptism, they are thorough-going Evangelical Protestants.

Organization. — The Reformed Episcopal Church retains the threefold order of bishops, priests, and deacons, though holding them as not essential, and recognizing the validity of the ministry of other churches. It may claim for its bishops an apostolic succession through Bishop Cummins, though the Mother Church demands ordination by *three* bishops; but it does not regard this as necessary, and even considers the doctrine "unscriptural and productive of great mischief."

Statistics. — There were in 1890 106 churches and missions, with 9,500 communicants and 12,000 members of the Sunday-schools. The church property amounts to $1,250,000, and the annual contributions for all purposes to $175,000. There are two periodicals and a theological school.

So far as the Reformed Episcopal Church is a protest against the theory of an authoritative and exclusive Church and of supernatural sacraments, it has our sympathy. It has long been a mystery to us how so many men of trusted integrity and frankness could remain in the English and Episcopal Churches with their known disbelief in so many points of its doctrine and usage. So far, however, as it not only embraces but emphasizes the Evangelical doctrines, it holds us off. Apparently it lays greater stress on these doctrines to make up for its falling away from the "Church" position. As it differs from conservative Congregationalists or Presbyterians only in government and liturgy, we may look for an ultimate union between it and some such body, especially as there seems a strong tendency among them toward liturgical service and episcopal government.

QUESTIONS.

Analyze the name and explain its parts. What was its origin? In your judgment was it right for officers of the Episcopal Church to receive communion from officers of "the sects"? On what theory of that church would it be right? on what theory wrong? Do you think Bishop Cummins was right in leaving his church? Was it right in deposing him? What are the standards of doctrine of the Reformed Episcopal Church? What change was made in the Apostles' Creed? what in the baptismal service? What did the words omitted imply? What reason have you for thinking them wrong? What is the difference between a priest and a minister? an altar and a communion-table? What is this church's view of the Scriptures? How does this differ from the High Church view? What is its doctrine of the Church? of Episcopacy? How do these vary from the High Church doctrine? What does it condemn in the Eucharist? Why? What is the ecclesiastical position of the Reformed Episcopalians? Who were the Puritans?/ What sects came from them? 'What is their organization? How does it differ in theory from that of Episcopalians? Wherein can we sympathize with the Reformed Episcopalians? Wherein must we differ? What is the general impression they make on you? What is likely to be their future?

REFERENCES.

Schaff, vol. i. pp. 665–668; the Articles are in vol. iii. pp. 814–827. *What do Reformed Episcopalians believe?* by Bishop Cheney. See also their journals of the Councils, and published sermons and tracts; *Why I became a Reformed Episcopalian*, by Bishop Nicholson. *The Memoirs and Letters of George David Cummins* gives an inside view of the origin of the church.

---

5. THE PRESBYTERIANS.

SPEAK thou the things which become sound doctrine. — TITUS ii. 1.

Name. — The name Presbyterian is derived from the Greek word *Presbuteros*, which means *elder;* and is applied in the New Testament (as in Acts xiv. 23) to those who presided over the churches. The word *episcopos*, or overseer, is also used (as in Acts xx. 28). The Episcopalian maintains that the latter designates a higher officer, whom he calls a bishop. The Presbyterian maintains that it is but another name for the same officer (Titus i. 5, 7), and therefore declines to recognize a third order of clergy above elders and deacons. A Presbyterian therefore is one who believes, first, that the highest officer in the church is the presbyter or elder; and secondly, that the government of the church should rest, not in the bishop, as in Episcopacy, nor in the separate congregation, as in Congregational churches, but in representative bodies of presbyters.

History. — Presbyterianism as a form of church government existed somewhat indefinitely in the earlier years of the Continental Reformation, but it took clear shape in the *Institutes* of John Calvin. His purpose was to oppose to the closely organized Roman Catholic Church, which rested on tradition, an equally strong organization based on Scripture. It proved of immense service. It became the polity of the Huguenots, and largely of the Dutch, Poles, and the provinces of the Rhine, rivalling and often combating Lutheranism. It was the form of government under which the best stand was made by Protestantism against Romanism, — as in Switzerland, Holland, and Scotland.

As a sect, its most remarkable history and influence was in Scotland, where its champion was John Knox. It became to that country what Episcopalianism was in England, — the rallying point of the nation against the ecclesiastical and political tyranny of Rome. In 1560 it became the Church of the kingdom; equally hostile to Catholicism, which it made punishable by death, and to Protestant dissenters. In 1578, in its Second Book of Discipline, it established the graded series of church courts now generally held. The organization of these proved of great service in concentrating and training the middle class in their contest with the nobility. A long struggle with the crown led to the overthrow of Presbyterianism and the virtual establishment of Episcopacy in Scotland by Charles I. The resistance rose to a climax in **1638,** when the "Covenant," or solemn agreement of the Scotch people to oppose Prelacy to the death, was signed amid great and univerversal excitement, first in the churchyard of the Grey Friars at Edinburgh, then everywhere else in the kingdom. Presbyterianism was restored, and Scotland faced Charles with a powerful army. In 1643, the aid of the Scotch Presbyterians having been sought by the English Parliamentary party in revolt against Charles, the "Solemn League and Covenant" was signed between the two, who bound themselves to strive to "bring the churches of God in the three kingdoms to the nearest conjunction and uniformity of religion." The execution of this design was entrusted in England to the "Assembly of Divines at Westminster," which met in the Abbey, July 1, 1643. This body the Presbyterians controlled; and the creed drawn up by it, the famous "Westminster Confession," became the standard of Presbyterianism in general, and so remains to-day. In June, 1647, Presbyterianism was made the national religion of England, as it was of Scotland, though the sudden rise of the Independents, or Congregationalists, to power under Cromwell overthrew its supremacy. At the Restoration, under Charles II., Presbyterianism was suppressed both in Scotland and in England, Episcopacy becoming the national church. The struggle of the "Covenanters" against the persecution that followed is one of the noblest chapters in history. In England the Presbyterians form to-day one of the smaller "dissenting" bodies. After the Revolution of 1688 Presbyterianism was quietly restored in Scotland, where it remains to-day as the Established Church. But the old spirit of jealousy of the civil power survived and led to many divisions. In 1733 Ebenezer Erskine led a secession on behalf of the right of the congregations to reject an unacceptable minister sent by the Presbytery, and formed the "Associate Synod." This divided in 1747 into "Burgher" and "Anti-burgher" synods on the question of an oath required by certain cities. From the latter split off the "Constitutional Associate Presbytery," and from the former the "Original Burgher Synod." Meantime the "Presbytery of Relief" had in 1752 divided from the main body on the same general principle, but united in 1847 with the Burghers and Anti-burghers into the "United Presbyterian Church." But in 1843 a most enthusiastic rebellion against the main church was led by Drs. Chalmers, Guthrie, and Candlish, by which nearly one third of the ministers gave up their manses and livings, and formed the "Free Church of Scotland" on the right of the congregation to choose its own minister without control of the State or patron. It speedily provided for its own support by raising large sustentation and building funds, and is a prosperous body. But in 1874 the Established Church gave up patronage and control of pastorates, and has grown rapidly. A Book of Common Order, or liturgy, has been compiled, and organs and hymns admitted. There is much liberality of doctrine, shown especially by the "Scotch Sermons" published in 1880.

In the United States. — The first Presbyterian churches were founded by the Huguenots, but of these only one, in Charleston, S. C., remains. Large immigrations from England, Scotland, Ireland, Holland, and Germany followed. The first Presbytery, however, was not organized till 1706, in Philadelphia, and the first Synod till 1729. A division rose early between the "Old Side" and the "New Side," nominally on the question of revivals, but really upon larger questions of progressive doctrine; and this division, like that upon State interference in Scotland, has run through Presbyterian history in this country. During the Revolution the Presbyterians were, as ever, strongly on the side of freedom. In the early part of this century, they grew rapidly, but the old controversies assumed a more definite shape in the dispute as to whether the atonement was for all men or only for the elect; and in 1837 the denomination split into Old and New School, and was not united again till 1869. A still older secession was that of the Cumberland Presbyterians, who, having been cut off for introducing into their churches during a revival a number of ministers not well educated nor willing to subscribe to the extreme doctrines of the Confession, formed a body which still continues separate, and has become very large. They revised the Westminster Confession, holding milder views on predestination, and denying unconditional election and infant damnation. The Scotch divisions have also been perpetuated in this country, though they have no application here. In 1858 the southern churches of the New School seceded on the question of slavery, forming the "United Synod;" and in 1861 the southern section of the Old School followed, joining the "United Synod" in 1865, and forming "the Presbyterian Church in the United States."

Doctrines. — The Presbyterians hold, on the whole, the doctrines as well as the church government which were formulated by John Calvin, and by him made the standing-ground against Romanism.

These doctrines were restated in the Westminster Confession, which is the standard of all the main bodies of Presbyterians, and in the "Larger" and "Shorter Westminster Catechisms." The American churches, however, omit those passages which relate to the union of Church and State, limiting the duty of the latter to protection of all denominations alike.

The first point to be noticed in Presbyterianism is its frank and full declaration of the supremacy of Scripture as authority for all belief: " All things in Scripture are not alike plain in themselves, nor alike clear unto all; yet those things which are necessary to be known, believed, and observed for salvation, are so clearly propounded and opened in some place of Scripture or other that not only the learned, but the unlearned, in a due use of the ordinary means, may attain unto a sufficient understanding of them" (Westm. Conf., chap. i. sect. vii.). Herein the Presbyterians lift the standard of Protestantism as against the Catholic doctrine of tradition and the right of the Church to be the sole interpreter, more firmly than the Lutherans and the Episcopalians. Yet the emphasis laid upon the value of the Westminster Confession, and the obligation upon all the clergy to sign it, seem practically to bring back the old principle, and to betray an unwillingness to leave the Bible to "the use of the ordinary means." Yet the Bible remains as court of final appeal.

Presbyterians hold to the Protestant distinction between the visible and the invisible Church, all parts of the former being "subject to mixture and error." Yet out of the visible Church " there is no ordinary possibility of salvation." Calvin strove to make the Presbyterian Church the established Church at Geneva, and this was the ideal of the Church in Scotland. The different position of the Presbyterians in America seems to mark a great change in this doctrine.

As in Presbyterianism we leave entirely behind the idea of supreme Church authority, so we leave the idea of the sacraments as material channels of supernatural grace. Both consubstantiation and transubstantiation in the Eucharist are denied. Christ is present only spiritually, "the body and blood of Christ being not corporally or carnally in, with, or under the bread and wine, yet as really, but spiritually, present to the faith of believers in that ordinance as the elements themselves are to the outward senses." Unworthy persons do not receive, therefore, the essential element in the ordinance (Westm. Conf., chap. xxix. sect. vii.). Baptism is "a sign and seal of the covenant of grace," but in itself conveys no grace.

Another new, and though minor yet practically important, doctrine which the Presbyterians brought in is that of the Sabbath. The Catholics, Lutherans, and Anglicans, while insisting on Sunday as a day of rest, did not insist upon the cessation of all pleasure. Nor did Calvin himself. It is to the Presbyterians that we owe what is called "the Puritan Sabbath."

The essential doctrine of Presbyterianism is the absolute and unquestionable sovereignty of God, which, though just and loving, is above the comprehension of the human intellect, as it is beyond the influence of human character. The Confession must be read to show how thoroughly this doctrine is worked out. It is best known under the form of "the five points of Calvinism."

1. *Total Depravity.* "From this original corruption [that of our first parents after the Fall], whereby we are utterly indisposed, disabled, and made opposite to all good, and wholly inclined to all evil, do proceed all actual transgressions" (Westm. Conf., chap. vi.).

2. *Unconditional Election.* Out of the universal wreck, though all souls deserve to perish, God determines to save some, but irrespective of their own acts or merits. "By the decree of God, for the manifestation of His glory, some men and angels are predestinated unto everlasting life and others foreordained unto everlasting death. These angels and men, thus predestinated and foreordained, are particularly and unchangeably designed; and their number is so certain and definite that it cannot be increased or diminished. Those of mankind that are predestinated unto life, God, before the foundation of the world was laid, according to His eternal and immutable purpose, and the secret counsel and good pleasure of His will, hath chosen in Christ, unto everlasting glory, out of His mere free grace and love, without any foresight of faith or good works, or perseverance in either of them, or any other thing in the creature, as conditions, or causes moving him thereunto; and all to the praise

of His glorious grace. The rest of mankind God was pleased, according to the unsearchable counsel of His own will, whereby He extendeth or withholdeth mercy as He pleaseth, to pass by, and to ordain them to dishonor and wrath for their sin, to the praise of His glorious justice." (Westm. Conf., chap. iii. sect. iii. v. and vii.). The latter part of this passage Presbyterians call the doctrine of "preterition," or passing by; and distinguish between it and "reprobation," or fixing the non-elect in their sin. The Confession also asserts the freedom of the human will, leaving the apparent contradiction between it and divine sovereignty unsolved, as beyond the reach of the human intellect.

3. *Particular Atonement.* The sacrifice of Christ is not for all men, but only for those who are chosen, and who therefore have received as a gift the very *faith* by which the merits of Christ can be appropriated.

4. *Effectual Grace.* Those who are chosen are saved, not by anything they may do for themselves, but by the power of God working in them "to will and to do of His own good pleasure." "Yet so as they come most freely, being made willing by His grace" (Westm. Conf., chap. x.).

5. *The Perseverance of the Saints,* — that is, the preservation of the elect to the end. "They whom God hath accepted in His Beloved, effectually called and sanctified by His Spirit, can neither totally nor finally fall away from the state of grace; but shall certainly persevere therein to the end, and be eternally saved" (Westm. Conf., chap. xvii.).

Whether the Confession teaches the damnation of non-elect infants and heathen is debated by many Presbyterians, but the prevalent belief in earlier days would seem to confirm the charge that it does so teach. "Elect infants, dying in infancy, are regenerated and saved by Christ through the Spirit. . . . So are all other elect persons, who are incapable of being called outwardly by the ministry of the Word. Others, not elected, . . . cannot be saved; . . . and to assert that they may is very pernicious and to be detested" (Westm. Conf., chap. x.).

In other points, as the Trinity, the deity of Christ, eternal punishment and reward, etc., the Presbyterians substantially hold the faith common to Evangelical Christians.

Government. — A complete church has three classes of officers, — the teaching elder, or pastor; the ruling elders, who with the pastor constitute the "church session," to govern the congregation; and the deacons, who manage the financial affairs. The churches in a certain district unite in forming a "presbytery," which is made up of the pastor and one ruling elder from each church session. A number of adjacent presbyteries unite to form a "synod," to which are sent all the ministers and one ruling elder from each session within the region covered by the presbyteries. The highest court is the "General Assembly," to which the presbyteries elect an equal number of ministers and ruling elders as delegates. These bodies form a series of courts for the adjustment of all difficulties and the enactment of all needed regulations, appeal being made from lower to higher as in the secular courts. The result is a very compact and effective organization.

Statistics. — There are said to be over 20,000,000 Presbyterians (3,500,000 communicants) in the world, including, however, the "Reformed" churches. The largest number in any European country is in Scotland, — 3,600,000. In the United States there are (1890) 1,229,000 communicants and (estimated) 3,500,000 adherents. Of these 775,903 communicants (30 synods, 213 presbyteries, 6,894 churches) are in the Northern body, 168,971 in the Southern, 163,216 in the Cumberland, and 103,921 in the United.

Many Unitarian churches in England are related to the Presbyterians as most of those of New England are to the Congregationalists. It was from them that our churches were developed, sometimes gradually, sometimes suddenly and with controversy. Yet no branch of Protestantism seems further away from us than the Presbyterians. They are compactly organized, and their churches are ruled by higher bodies; while ours are very loosely attached to one another, and would resent any interference with their congregational independence. We are descended from the side of Cromwell in the great division of the seventeenth century. Again, the Presbyterians have the most systematic and authoritative form of faith among Protestants, while we steadfastly refuse to formulate our belief at all. Doubtless many of us have envied them their "body of divinity," and their unity upon it; but the revision movement of 1889 has brought to light a long-hidden and extensive rebellion against the most extreme doctrines of the Confession, and the fact that they have been lying unused in many a church It is precisely this temptation to insincerity, this hindrance to freedom of expression if not of thought, which Unitarians dread when tempted to adopt a creed. It is needless to add that in the doctrines themselves we stand far away from the Presbyterians, they emphasizing the sovereignty of God, we the dignity of man.

Yet they deserve well of Protestants for their frank proclamation of the Scriptures as the sole standard of belief. Neither the Lutherans nor the Church of England did this unreservedly. The Presbyterians are thus the "color-guard" of Protestantism. And they deserve the respect of thoughtful people for their equally frank and sturdy facing of the facts of human life. The truth in the doctrine of predestination has already been pointed out (p. 35). Calvin and modern science are at one here so far as this world is concerned. And, finally, the Presbyterians deserve the gratitude of all lovers of freedom for the courage and persistence with which they faced both the Roman Church and the Church of England, in the interests not only of religion, but of political liberty. They represented the people in their struggle with nobles and kings. It was from them that the Puritans of Massachusetts Bay came, and though they soon became congregational in polity. the doctrines of Presbyterianism remained long in power, and should be remembered as the doctrines of those who determined the destiny of the New World.

QUESTIONS.

What does the word "Presbyterian" mean ? How does a Presbyterian differ in polity from an Episcopalian? from a Congregationalist? From whom did Presbyterianism take shape ? Tell what you know of him. What was his purpose ? How far did he succeed? Where was Presbyterianism most successful? How did it stand politically? What was the "League and Covenant"? Why were the Presbyterians hostile to Cromwell ? What do you know of the Covenanters? What secessions have happened? What is the "Free Church of Scotland"? How does it differ from the Established Church ? Who brought Presbyterianism to this country? What division runs through its history here ? What were "Old School" and "New School" ? Who are the Cumberland Presbyterians ?

By whom were the Presbyterian doctrines formulated? In what documents are they contained ? Why is the Confession called the "Westminster"? What do the American churches omit? What is the Presbyterian ground as to Scripture? Why is it important to notice this? How do Presbyterians regard their Confession? Is there any inconsistency here? What difference does it make whether the Westminster Assembly or the Vatican Council be made the authority as to what Scripture teaches? What do Presbyterians hold as to the Church? Are they anywhere the Established Church? What do they believe as to the sacraments? How does this differ from Romanism? from Anglicanism? What is their idea of the Sabbath? How does this differ from the Roman Catholic idea? from the Jewish? Ought we to say Sabbath or Sunday? What is the essential doctrine of Presbyterianism? Name "the five points of Calvinism." Do you think that anybody is utterly unable to do any good? Is there a distinction between a sinful disposition and sinful acts? How deep does sin go? What is the difference between predestination and preterition? Does the latter word really relieve God from blame for eternal damnation? How far is your faith the result of your own effort? Is it not to some extent the gift of God? Is particular atonement just? Would a universal atonement be just? What is "effectual grace"? What does the word "grace" mean? How does it differ from partiality? Is not God, then, a "respecter of persons"? What does "the perseverance of the saints" mean? As far as you can see, do all saints persevere to the end? Do you think that the Confession teaches the damnation of infants? Would it be any more unjust to damn infants than adults who cannot help themselves? Does not the doctrine of predestination *necessarily* involve both?

How are Unitarians related to Presbyterians? How do we differ from them in government? in the matter of a creed? What objection to a creed appears in their recent history? On what points is revision demanded? What have they done for Protestantism? for the philosophy of life? for political freedom? for Massachusetts and America?

REFERENCES.

For history, Schaff, vol. i. pp. 669-813; Green, *Short History of the English People*, chap. viii.; Encyclopædia Britannica, article "Presbyterianism;" McClintock and Strong; Lives of Calvin and Knox. On Calvin, see Schaff, vol. i. pp. 421-467; Merle d'Aubigné's *History of the Reformation in the Time of Calvin*, vol. vi. chaps. 1-15.; A. P. Stanley's *Lectures on the History of the Church of Scotland*. For a graphic account of the Disruption of 1843, see *Life of Dr. Guthrie* and that of Dr. Chalmers. On the history in various countries, see Drysdale's *History of the Presbyterians in England*; A. F. Mitchell's *The Westminster Assembly: Its History and Standards*; Neal's *History of the Puritans*; Carlyle's *Cromwell*; C. A. Briggs's *American Presbyterianism*; E. H. Gillett's *History of* the *Presbyterian Church;* L. W. Bacon's *Genesis of the New England Churches;* and the histories of Palfrey and Bancroft. For doctrine, Schaff as above; also vol. iii. pp. 600-676, where the Westminster Confession and Catechism are given in full. Dr. C. A. Briggs, in *Whither,* maintains that the later Presbyterians have departed from the Confession, and throws much light upon its original meaning. H. B. Smith's *Christian Theology;* C. Hodge's *Systematic Theology,* 3 vols., and his *Discussions in Church Polity;* Thomas Witherow's *Which is the Apostolic Church;* Froude's "Calvinism," in *Short Studies,* vol. i.; S. J. Barrows's *The Doom of the Majority;* Michael Wigglesworth's *The Day of Doom;* and the writings of Jonathan Edwards show what New England Calvinism was.

---

6. THE CONGREGATIONALISTS.

The churches of Christ salute you. — Rom. xvi. 16.

Name. — A Congregationalist is one who believes that every congregation should govern itself, instead of being governed by bishops, as the Episcopalians are, or by a series of courts, as the Presbyterians are. In this wider sense the name belongs also to Baptists, Unitarians, and other Sects; but it is usually assigned to and claimed by the denomination which first made the congregational principle its characteristic. As the first Unitarian churches in New England were mainly of this denomination, many of them retain the name "Congregational," to which, as being still self-governed, they are strictly entitled. The Trinitarian Congregationalists in Massachusetts are popularly called "the Orthodox," as holding to the old creeds. The Congregationalists of England, where the denomination began, called themselves "Independents" until this century, but now belong to the "Congregational Union of England and Wales."

History. — The Independent principle marked the third step in the revolt from Roman Catholicism in the English Reformation, the Anglican being the first, and the Presbyterian the second. Of the Puritan party, who wished to preserve the national Church, but to *purify* it still further from the errors of Rome, rejecting all rites, vestures, festivals, etc., not expressly authorized by Scripture, some gave up their demands in face of the Church's stern resistance, but others began to ask themselves what authority the Church, or anybody but Christ, had to control the worship of any one. This led to withdrawal, not only from the Church of England, but from its first offshoot, the Presbyterian Church, which also claimed authority over the single congregation. The first Independent church was founded at Norwich, in 1580, by Robert Browne. It was at once assailed by State persecution and popular ridicule, and called "Separatist," or "Brownist." It soon found itself obliged to leave the country, and went to Middleburg, in Zealand, but there was broken by poverty and internal dissensions; and its people returned to England, Browne joining the Church of England again.

More successful and creditable was the work of Henry Barrowe and John Greenwood, who founded a church in London, in 1592. They were both put to death the following year, but the church removed to Amsterdam. This church differed from Browne's in not being governed directly by congregational vote, but by the board, or "Session," of elders, including pastor and teacher, which it first chose, and then obeyed. So far it followed the Presbyterians, but there stopped, acknowledging no higher authority. This form of government, sometimes called "Barrowism," became the model of the Congregational churches for a long time, both in England and in New England.

More celebrated and permanent was the church gathered at Scrooby, England, and emigrating first to Amsterdam, then to Leyden. From the Leyden church, under John Robinson, came the permanent Congregationalism both of England and of New England. In 1616 Henry Jacob returned to London and founded there the first Independent church that remained alive in England. There adherents multiplied fast, and under Cromwell the Independents became masters of England. In 1658 the Savoy Council was held in London, which virtually adopted the Westminster Confession, except as to church government. At the Restoration the Independents were roughly handled by Charles II., and by the "Act of Uniformity" in 1662. Two thousand ministers were deprived of their livings, and further oppressed. Upon the site of the old Fleet Prison, where some were confined, their descendants have built a Memorial Hall and Library. After the Revolution of 1688 the denomination obtained toleration, and is now one of the most influential in the kingdom.

From Leyden went also those "Pilgrim Fathers," under Elder Brewster and Deacon Carver, who founded the church in Plymouth in the New World. They were Barrowists, but of a mild type.

But American Congregationalism in the main is descended from churches which at first hated Independency, — those of Massachusetts Bay and Connecticut. From 1620 to 1640 it is estimated that twenty-two thousand Puritans came to New England on account of persecution. They did not mean to leave the "Mother Church," but only to change some of her usages. But in the new land and under Plymouth influence they speedily became self-governing, and in time most sturdy opponents of the Church of England. At the first Synod, in Cambridge, Mass., 1648, the Barrowe principle was adopted. Gradually, however, the authority of the elders decreased, and the congregation acquired full power, which it still holds.

Congregationalism was virtually the "established church" of New England. In the beginning church and town were but the same community in different capacities. All voters were church members, and all adult male church members were voters. Money was raised by taxation for church expenses, as for other town needs. As the population grew diverse in religious belief, it was at first arranged that all should be taxed to support the Congregational Church who could not prove that they supported any other; and finally, but not till 1833 in Massachusetts, all church taxes were remitted, and the Congregationalists became before the law but one sect among many. The suffrage question was more troublesome. For many reasons the proportion of church members to the male population decreased, till it was only one fifth. To meet this difficulty, the "Half-way Covenant" was arranged in 1662, by which persons of discreet lives were admitted to all the privileges of the church except that of coming to the Lord's Supper, on simply giving public assent to the covenant of the church, instead of, as before, being required to give proofs of "regeneration." In time unconverted persons were received at communion also. Against the latter, and indeed against what he deemed the general decline of religious interest, Jonathan Edwards protested; and about 1740, under his lead and that of Whitefield, the English preacher, a revival called "The Great Awakening" swept over New England, followed by reaction, and by theological divisions which have never been healed. Arminianism, or the assertion of the freedom of the will as against predestination, largely replaced Calvinism; and a liberal movement began, culminating in the early part of this century in the Unitarian defection, which took away most of the older churches in Massachusetts, including the one in Plymouth and the "First" churches in Boston, Salem, Dorchester, Roxbury, and other large places, and obtained control of Harvard College. In consequence of the latter fact, Andover Theological Seminary was established, in 1808, which has of late years led in the heresy of "future probation."

The growth of Congregationalism in this country was much hindered by the "Plan of Union" with the Presbyterians in evangelizing the newly opened West. The adherents of the two bodies in any town were to unite in one church, choosing which body they were to affiliate with, and when becoming Congregationalist, were allowed a certain relation with the Presbyterian Synods. But this was found more useful to the latter than to the former; and in 1852 the "plan" was abandoned, the Congregationalists having, it was estimated, lost some two thousand churches. Since then the denomination has been increasingly active in home missionary work, and has grown in numbers, though not in proportion to the population. The American Board of Commissioners for Foreign Missions was established in 1810.

Government.—The Congregationalists are not *a* church, as the Episcopalians and Presbyterians are, but are gathered into *churches*, each sufficient unto itself, and denying the right of any other earthly authority to control it. They believe that this was the polity of the churches mentioned in the New Testament, and that only two classes of church officers are there mentioned, — the pastors, or elders, and the deacons.

The "church" is the assembly of believers around a "covenant," or "declaration of faith," to which they agree. There is usually, but not always, associated with the church another body, called the "society," commonly made up from the attendants upon public worship, whether they are members of the church or not. The society ordinarily owns the ecclesiastical property, and pays the expenses of public worship. Neither baptism nor attendance upon communion is requisite to membership, nor any profession of belief. It represents to-day the citizens of the old town system, who were not church members, but were taxed to support the church, and thus had a right to its public services. The pastor of the church is the minister of the society, and the two bodies unite in settling him. The deacons are officers of the church, assist at the communion service, and take charge of the poor-funds. Members are admitted to the church by vote, — having previously appeared before an examining committee, who require evidence of their conversion, — and by publicly entering into covenant with the church, having received baptism, and commonly also by a public profession of belief.

Though the churches are thus independent of one another's control, they have a fellowship of sympathy, which they often use to ask advice, — as in settling or dismissing a pastor. Then a "council" is called of ministers and delegates, either chosen at will or from a definite circle of churches, by whose decision the church commonly abides. It may, however, act in every case alone; and other churches, if disapproving, can only withdraw their fellowship and countenance. It is customary, when members remove, to give them letters to any other church in the fellowship. No letters, however, are given to unevangelical churches.

The churches of a district are usually united into a Conference, and the Conferences of each State into State Conferences. The National Council, meeting tri-ennially, is representative of all the churches in the country, each Conference sending a delegate for every ten churches, and each State Conference one for each ten thousand communicants, the delegates being half lay, half clerical. These bodies, however, are all merely deliberative and advisory, all approach to control being jealously watched and resisted.

Doctrine. — By the fundamental principle of Congregationalism there can be no creed binding upon all churches. There is no body with power to make one. Each church makes its own. There is therefore more or less diversity of belief within certain limits, which makes a general statement somewhat difficult.

At first, Congregationalists were as strictly Calvinistic as the Presbyterians. The Cambridge Synod, in 1648, and the Savoy Conference, in 1658, substantially adopted the Westminster Confession. The "Shorter Catechism" and Wigglesworth's "Day of Doom" were text-books in New England schools. But on both sides of the Atlantic the original doctrines have been somewhat modified.

The "Statement of Doctrine" ecommended in 1883 by a commission appointed by the National Council is the most prominent recent utterance. It has been said to give "the low-water mark of Congregational belief;" that is, no fuller statement could receive the assent of all its compilers, who represented the different wings of the denomination. The Bible is received as authority for teaching and conduct, as being "the record of God's revelation of Himself in the work of redemption," and "written by men under the special guidance of the Holy Spirit." The Trinity is affirmed substantially in terms of the Nicene Creed. "III. We believe . . . that our first parents by disobedience fell under the righteous condemnation of God; and that all men are so alienated from God that there is no salvation from the guilt and power of sin except by God's redeeming grace. . . . VI. We believe that the love of God to sinful men has found its highest expression in the redemptive work of His Son; who became man, uniting his divine nature with our human nature in one person; . . . whose sacrifice of himself for the sins of the world declares the righteousness of God, and is the sole and sufficient ground of forgiveness and of reconciliation with Him. VII. We believe that Jesus Christ . . . sends the Holy Spirit to convict [men] of sin, and to lead them to repentance and faith; and that those who through renewing grace turn to righteousness, and trust in Jesus Christ as their Redeemer, receive for his sake the forgiveness of their sins, and are made the children of God. VIII. We believe that those who are thus regenerated and justified grow in sanctified character through fellowship with Christ, the indwelling of the Holy Spirit, and obedience to the truth; that a holy life is the fruit and evidence of saving faith; and that the believer's hope of continuance in such a life is in the preserving grace of God. IX. That to Jesus Christ . . . Christians are directly responsible in faith and conduct; and that to him all have immediate access without mediatorial or priestly intervention. . . . We believe . . . in Baptism, to be administered to believers and their children as the sign of cleansing from sin, of union to Christ, and of the impartation of the Holy Spirit; and the Lord's Supper as a symbol of his atoning death, a seal of its efficacy, and a means whereby he confirms and strengthens the spiritual union and communion of believers with himself. XII. In a final judgment, the issues of which are everlasting punishment and everlasting life." To this Statement a "Confession of Faith" is added, in which the person to be admitted into the church states his belief in the words of the Apostles' Creed.

Statistics ("Year Book," 1890). — The Congregationalists have in the United States 4,689 churches, the largest numbers being in Massachusetts (557), Michigan, Connecticut, New York, and Iowa, — very few in the South; 4,408 ministers; and 491,985 members. There are also 580,672 pupils in Sunday-schools. The benevolent contributions were $2,398,037. The home expenses were about $5,000,000.

The American Board of Commissioners for Foreign Missions spent about $670,000, and have 472 missionaries and assistants. There are also a College and Education Society, expending $110,000; the American Congregational Union, about the same amount for building churches and parsonages; the American Home Missionary Society, about $512,000. The American Missionary Association spends $323,000, mainly upon colored people in the South; a Sunday-School and Publishing Society, about $17,000,— the New West Education Commission spending on the children and youth of Utah and adjacent States and Territories $78,000. There are also Women's Boards for foreign and home missionary work.

The Congregationalists have 7 Theological Schools (notably Andover, Oberlin, and Yale), with 490 students; and a large number of colleges and universities were founded either wholly or mainly by them.

The Congregationalists are especially interesting to Unitarians as being the mother sect from which their own was born, or considered in another and truer way, — since many Unitarian churches are older than any Congregational churches in this country, — as brothers of the same family, though we are not allowed by them to sit around the same table or live under the same roof. Yet the two bodies still have some institutions in common, — as the funds for supporting aged clergymen or their widows; and as experience and advancing thought mellow the former doctrines of the Trinitarians, the distance between the more liberal among them and the more conservative among the Unitarians has lessened. It is to the Congregationalists that we owe our democratic form of church government; our free order of worship; our love of an educated ministry, on which the Puritans so nobly insisted; and indeed, through the doctrinal discussions which they loved and stimulated, that loyalty to truth and that liberal and progressive tendency which are so prominent among us.

In a larger sense, we are as Americans indebted to them for the impetus which they gave to education at the beginning of their settlement in New England, and which has always marked that section and all other sections of the country which it has influenced. And the republican form of government is due in no small degree to the free and representative character of their churches and councils. The prayer meeting, with its freedom of speech to all, was the father of the town meeting. The Revolution was largely due to the influence of the Congregational ministers, in marked contrast to the Toryism of the Episcopalians.

Our divergence from their doctrines, though greater in appearance than in reality, and differing very much according to the church or to the writer with which we compare ourselves, is still very great, and until they change much faster than they have, is irreconcilable. The step which our fathers took, like that of the Reformers three centuries before, was greater than they knew. Our name emphasizes one of the least of our differences. The doctrine of the Trinity is one of the most harmless of the older tenets. Dr. Channing's sermon on "The Moral Influence of Calvinism" opens the real gulf between the two parties. So long as the Congregationalists hold to a helpless human nature, a vicarious atonement, and eternal punishment for temporal sins, our position and our mission must be separate from theirs. The Andover view of a possible extension of probation into the next life, so that heathen and others who have not had a fair chance to receive the Gospel here shall have it hereafter, though held by a large section of the denomination, is not yet dominant; and if it were, though it might bring other changes in doctrine in its train, it would leave much divergence unchanged. Not until they give fuller and franker recognition to the rights of reason and conscience as authority for truth, as against a mere textual use of the Bible, can the two bodies come together again. Nevertheless, the growing respect and love of each for the other must be emphasized, with the consciousness of a common ancestry and of common traditions, which compel to a common love of truth and duty.

QUESTIONS.

What does "Congregationalist" mean? Who else are entitled to the name? Are Unitarians? Why? What relation do the Congregationalists hold to the Presbyterians? to the Episcopalians? to the Puritans? What were they first called? Why? What is the difference between a Brownist and a Barrowist? Trace the fortunes of the Scrooby congregation. When were the Independents masters of England? Recall what you know of Cromwell. What was the Savoy Confession? the Act of Uniformity? When did the Independents get toleration in England? What was the difference between the "Pilgrims" and the Puritans of Massachusetts Bay in intention? in church government? When did the latter change, and how? What was the relation of Church and State in Massachusets? When did this cease? By what steps? What was the "Half-way Covenant"? What did Jonathan Edwards do? What was the consequence? What is Arminianism? What success had Unitarianism? What was the "Plan of Union"? its result?

How do Congregationalists differ from Episcopalians in church government? from Presbyterians? What is their distinction between "church" and "society"? What was the origin of it? What are deacons? How are members admitted? What is the relation of churches to each other?

How much authority has a council? Can a letter to a Unitarian church be obtained from a Congregational church? What is the National Council? What authority has it?

Have Congregationalists a common creed? Why? What was their original doctrine? What is the best statement of their present belief? Is there any difference between a revelation and the record of a revelation? What is their doctrine of God? What do you think of their doctrine of the fall of man? of his condition? What is their belief about Jesus? What is implied in the word "sole"? Is not the question of predestination evaded in Article VII.? What truth or fallacy can you find in Article VIII.? What relation of faith and works is stated there? Can a believer fall from grace, according to this? What is the bearing of Article IX. on the Catholic Church? on Presbyterianism? What is the doctrine of the sacraments? Compare it with the Catholic and Lutheran. What is the view of the Last Judgment? Do you think this statement of faith is very definite? Why?

What is the relation of the Congregationalists to the Unitarians? What do we owe to them? What does America owe to them? Wherein do we still differ from them? Have you read Channing's sermon? How do you like Congregationalists generally? What great preachers of theirs can you think of?

REFERENCES.

The most convenient authority is *A Hand-Book of Congregationalism*, by H. M. Dexter, a condensation of his larger work, *Congregationalism: What it is*, etc. George Punchard's *Congregationalism in America from 1629 to 1879*. In Schaff, see vol. i. pp. 820-840; vol. iii. p. 707 (the Savoy Declaration), p. 910 (the American Creed of 1883). McClintock and Strong; Encyclopædia Britannica, articles "Independents" and "Congregationalism;" Green, *Short History*, chaps. 7 and 8; Fisher, pp. 611-615; R. W. Dale's *A Manual of Congregational Principles* (in England). The racy biographies of John Todd and Lyman Beecher, and Mrs. Stowe's *Minister's Wooing, Poganuc People*, and *Oldtown Folks*, give pictures of New England ministers and church life in the early part of this century. Palfrey's *History of New England*; Sprague's *Annals of the American Pulpit*, vols. i. ii. iii.; George E. Ellis, *The Puritan Age in Massachusetts*; Brooks Adams, *The Emancipation of Massachusetts* (not good-tempered or just, but containing interesting facts); J. K. Hosmer, *Young Sir Harry Vane*. Leonard Bacon, *Genesis of the New England Churches*, emphasizes the distinction between "Pilgrim" and "Puritan," giving most of his book to the former. John Fiske's *The Beginnings of New England* is valuable, especially for its admirable first chapter.

A STUDY OF THE SECTS. 119

7. THE BAPTISTS.

BURIED with him in baptism, wherein also ye are risen with him.
COL. ii. 12.

Name. — The word "Baptist" is derived from the Greek Βαπτίζω (*baptizo*), meaning (Thayer's Greek-English Lexicon of the New Testament) "to dip," "to immerge." The name first given, though never accepted, was "Anabaptists" (or Again-baptists), because they denied the validity of infant baptism, and obliged people baptized in infancy to receive the rite again.

History. — The denial of the validity of infant baptism and the insistence upon immersion as a form have probably been held by individuals, though not by churches, from the beginning of Christian history. They are found in various sects or parties of the Church during the Middle Ages, notably the Waldenses; but it came into prominence, very soon after Luther had stirred up the latent heresies and dissatisfactions of Europe, in the sect called the Anabaptists. Unfortunately, the main doctrine became mixed with various fanatical and even immoral doctrines, which had no real bearing upon it, and for which it was in no way responsible. The doctrine found more worthy support in Zurich and among the Mennonites of Holland, who were devout, peaceable, and pure people, abstaining from participation in civil government, and maintaining the right of religious liberty. In fact, the first one who ever proclaimed this right was Balthazar Hubmaier, one of the original Anabaptists of Germany, who was burned at the stake in 1528.

It was in Holland that the English Independents, or Brownists, first came into contact with Anabaptist doctrines; and one of their ministers in Amsterdam, the Rev. John Smyth, became a convert to them, and formed a new church, part of which came to London in 1612. The early history of the sect there is uncertain; but it is known that a church existed in 1633, and from that time adherents multiplied fast. They were opposed by all the sects then in existence, and were persecuted through all the changes of religious control. The Revolution of 1688 gave toleration to them, as to all dissenters; but they soon divided into "General Baptists," who believed that the atonement was for all men to accept or reject, and "Particular Baptists," who believed that it was for the elect alone. The latter is the Baptist sect of to-day. The former divided again into "Old Connection," who became generally Unitarian, and "New Connection," who correspond to what we call Free (Will) Baptists.

The founder of the denomination in this country was Roger Williams, a clergyman of education and prominence in the Church of England, who became an Independent, fled to this country in 1631, and was pastor of the church in Salem. Denying the validity of the royal charter to the colony, and the right of the magistrates in matters of religion, he was banished by them, went southward through the woods, and founded a settlement, which in gratitude he named "Providence." There, having become a convert to the Baptist doctrines, he had himself immersed by a layman, whom he in turn baptized in the same way, with ten others, and then founded in Providence the first Baptist church in America, 1638. The sect spread rapidly. In Massachusetts it was bitterly persecuted, — partly on mere theological grounds, partly because of the persistence of the Baptists in annoying ways, partly from fear of the effect on the attitude of the crown toward the colony. They were at length allowed freedom of worship, and in 1833 participated in the equality of all sects before the law. In Virginia also they were persecuted by the Episcopalians, any man who refused to bring his child to "a lawful minister" to be baptized being fined two thousand pounds of tobacco. Equality was granted there in 1785.

The Baptists originated in the laboring classes of Germany, and still have their strength in the middle classes of English and American society. Over three fourths of those in this country are in the former slave States, and they divide the negroes with the Methodists. The largest numbers in any State are in Virginia and Georgia, though they are very strong in Massachusetts and Rhode Island. They have not in the past been as insistent upon the education of their ministers as the Congregationalists, especially in the South.

Government. — The Baptists are congregational in their polity; that is, every church governs itself, and formulates its own creed and covenant, owning no control from any human authority, Christ being the head of the Church, and the Bible the only source of doctrine. There are associations of churches for mutual sympathy and for co-operation in common causes; but congregational independence is jealously guarded.

Doctrines. — Being congregational in polity, the Baptists can have no creed binding upon all churches. Each congregation is supposed to draw up its own statement of belief from its own study of the Scriptures. Yet few denominations have greater unity in doctrine. The Northern Baptists accept what is called the "New Hampshire Confession" (1833); while those of the South and of England are more attached to the "Philadelphia Confession," which appeared first in London in 1677, and was adopted early in the last century by the "Philadelphia Association." They are, however, not authoritative statements, and they differ little from each other.

The Baptist doctrine is Calvinistic, and is therefore essentially the same as that of the Congregationalists, baptism and its implications excepted. The Baptists have, however, kept Calvinism far more intact than the Congregationalists. Their peculiar doctrines are: (1) Denial of the validity of infant baptism. The ordinance, they affirm, is to be given only on profession of faith in Christ, and is therefore meaningless when applied to infants. They can find no case of infant baptism in the New Testament. (2) Insistence upon immersion as the only valid form of baptism. They claim that this was the original form as it was adopted and urged by Jesus, and is implied in the language used by Scripture, — as in descriptions of baptism (Matt. iii. 16; John iii. 23; Acts viii. 38, 39), and in Paul's frequent figure of baptism being a burial and resurrection. They baptize either in natural bodies of water or in tanks prepared beneath the pulpits of their churches. (3) "Close Communion," — that is, exclusion from the celebration of the Lord's Supper of all such as have not been immersed. This doctrine, however, has during this century been given up by many English Baptists. (4) Freedom of worship to all. This has, of course, ceased to be a distinctive mark of the Baptists, but was so once, and deserves to be still mentioned.

There are several sects who are Baptists as to baptism, but vary on other points. Some of them are mentioned here only for convenience, as they have no real connection with the Baptists. Most numerous are the Freewill Baptists (115,000), who began in New Hampshire, in 1780, and now call themselves Free Baptists. They are Arminian, — that is, they deny predestination and limited atonement, and assert the "free will" of all men to accept or reject the terms of salvation, — and hold "open communion." The Mennonites (93,000) are of Dutch origin, rejecting infant baptism, but using pouring as a form. The "Church of God," or "Winebrennarians" (about 30,000), — so called from their founder, Rev. John Winebrenner, — left the Lutherans, in 1820, on the question of revivals. They baptize by immersion, but are Presbyterian in polity. The "Tunkers" 100,000) are of German origin, immerse forward instead of backward and do it thrice, observe the rite of foot-washing, and object to "hireling" ministers and to organs. The "Seventh-Day Baptists (9,000) observe Saturday as the Sabbath. The "Six-Principle Baptists" (1,450) have for their creed the six points in Hebrews vi. 1. They live mostly in Rhode Island. The "Anti-Mission" or "Anti-Effort Baptists" (45,000) oppose all missionary, Sunday-school, or other efforts for conversion, as interfering with God's work. The "Christian Baptists" deny the Trinity.

Statistics. — There were in 1890 ("Year Book") 32,588 "regular" Baptist churches in the United States, with 21,175 ministers and 3,070,000 members, of whom 2,267,206 were in the domain of the Southern Convention, and about equally divided between the whites and the negroes. There were 17,696 Sunday-schools, with 1,211,696 pupils. The church property is valued at over $58,000,000; while nearly $7,000,000 were paid for current expenses, over $1,000,000 for missions, $228,000 for education, and nearly $2,000,000 for building, poor, etc. They have 7 theological schools; 31 colleges; 32 seminaries for females, 46 for males and coeducation, 17 for negroes, and Indians. There are 106 periodicals, including those for Sunday-schools. The foreign mission work of the Northern Baptists (279 missionaries, 134,113 converts) is carried on through the American Baptist Missionary Union, with two societies of women; and the home mission work by the American Baptist Home Missionary Society, with also two women's societies. The Southern Convention has corresponding apparatus.

In Great Britain there are nearly 330,000 Baptist communicants; in all Europe, 400,000; in the world, 3,701,882.

We owe a debt of gratitude to the Baptists for their unflinching defence and consistent allowance of strict religious freedom. That it is so common now is due in no small degree to their early and constant advocacy of it. Their Congregationalism has also played its part in the development of free institutions. Their stout attack upon infant baptism in the days when it was universally a superstitious rite, partaking of the character of magic, must also be praised, even by those who now practise that beautiful rite on rational, symbolic grounds. Their early enthusiasm in the foreign missionary movement, dating from 1792, when William Carey led in the formation of their missionary society, gives them, next to the Catholics and the German Pietists, the credit of having been its leaders.

On the other hand, must we not see in their emphasis upon an outward form, as that of baptism, a survival of the Jewish or Petrine spirit? Can we think it in accordance with the spirit of Jesus, whatever texts may be insisted upon? He certainly gave baptism no such prominence in his teachings; and his general emphasis upon the inner life, and his general tendency away from forms, even from those which he found in use and continued to permit, seem thoroughly inconsistent with the Baptist position. There should be no doubt, let it be granted, that immersion was the form in use in his day; but even the Catholic Church, usually so insistent upon primitive ceremonies, has changed it to sprinkling or pouring, according to its wise policy of conforming to the demands of changing climates and customs in non-essential matters. That the Baptists should insist upon transferring to cold and icy regions the forms natural only to warm ones is a rigor of ritualism against which real Christianity must protest. As to infant baptism, it is now among most Protestant bodies symbolical of the parent's desire that the child should be considered as adopted by the Church until he is of age to choose for himself, and of the parent's determination to care for his religious welfare, to " bring him up in the nurture and admonition of the Lord," and not at all of any change wrought in the child himself. The Baptist protest, once universally needed, and still valid as against Catholics and High Church Episcopalians, who look upon baptism as "regenerating" by virtue of the divine grace which it conveys, is not applicable to this interpretation. The logical consequence of the insistence upon immersion — namely, exclusion from the communion of all not so baptized — makes it still more to be regretted, and sets the Baptists, who cling to it, the more squarely against the progress of Christian union.

QUESTIONS.

What does the word "Baptist" mean? What was the first name given? How far back can Baptist doctrines be traced? When did they revive? Where were they found at their best? Who was the first advocate of religious liberty? How did Baptist doctrines get into England? What treatment did they receive? How was the body divided, and what became of the parts? Who founded the Baptist sect in this country? Where was the first church formed? How did the body fare in Massachusetts? When did it obtain liberty? Where is it strongest? Where at its best?

What is its church government? Has it any authoritative creed? Why? What statements of belief are popular? What is the general cast of doctrine? Are they more or less progressive than the Congregationalists? What is their doctrine as to infant baptism? Why? What as to baptism? Why? What as to the communion? Why? What as to liberty of thought? Name some other sects who are Baptist in any way. How many Baptists are there in this country? How do they compare in numbers with the other sects which we have considered?

How are we indebted to the Baptists? What was their relation to political freedom? What good can be said of their resistance to infant baptism? What have they done for foreign missions? What must we say of their insistence on a form of baptism? Was it the original form? What difference does that make? What should we do if we kept the Last Supper exactly as it was instituted? What is the form of baptism used by Catholics? Why? What ancient kind of religion is perpetuated by the insistence upon immersion? Is it really Christian? What is the prevailing Protestant idea of infant baptism? What sects practise it? What bodies hold a different idea of it? What do you think of "close communion"? What is your general impression of the Baptists?

REFERENCES.

The best manual is *Baptist Layman's Book*, by W. W. Everts, D. D. Also good are *The Distinctive Principles of the Baptists*, by A. M. Pendleton, and *The Baptist Principle*, by W. C. Wilkinson; *Baptist History*, by J. M. Cramp (popular); *A History of the Baptists*, by Thomas Armitage, D. D. (best and most comprehensive); McClintock and Strong and Encyclopædia Britannica, article "Baptists;" Schaff, vol. i. pp. 840-859. On baptism, see Smith's Bible Dictionary and Encyclopædia Britannica under this word, Thayer's Greek-English Lexicon of the New Testament under $\beta\alpha\pi\tau\iota\zeta\omega$, and the very interesting chapter i. in Dean Stanley's *Christian Institutions*. On the Baptists in this country, see Benedict's *General History of the Baptists in America*; *The Puritan Age in Massachusetts*, by George E. Ellis; Palfrey's *History of New England*; *Memorial History of Boston*; *Virginia*, by J. E. Cooke; Backus's *History of the Baptists of New England*, 2 vols.; and Cathcart's *Baptist Encyclopædia*. For the history of the minor bodies, see Goodby's *By-paths in Baptist History* and Stewart's *History of the Freewill Baptists*. For Baptist doctrines at length, see Strong's *Systematic Theology*, Hovey's *Manual of Systematic Theology and Christian Ethics*, and Butler's *Christian Theology* (Free Baptist); also Fisher, Index.

The "Philadelphia Confession" and the "New Hampshire Confession" may be found in Schaff, vol. iii.; in McClintock and Strong; and the latter in the *Baptist Layman's Book*, p. 60.

8. THE MORAVIANS.

THIS is his commandment, That we should believe on the name of his Son, Jesus Christ, and love one another, as he gave us commandment. — 1 JOHN iii. 23.

The name "Moravians" is a popular one, derived from the country of Moravia, between Austria and Bohemia, from which they originated. They call themselves *Unitas Fratrum*, or "United Brethren," but must not be confounded with the Methodist "United Brethren in the United States."

They were originally a party among the followers of John Huss (burned, 1415), and were at one time very numerous, but were almost exterminated in the Catholic reaction at the end of the sixteenth century. The present church took its rise, in 1735, from a few families of their descendants, who lived on the estates of Count Zinzendorf in Saxony, — a place which they called *Herrnhut*, or "The Lord's Protection." Thence they spread through Germany, where they are a society within the Lutheran Church, into England and the United States.

They have no formal creed; but the doctrines implied in their catechism and liturgy are Evangelical, in general agreement with the Lutherans. Their peculiarity lies rather in their very warm and sincere religious feeling, which so impressed John Wesley that he was converted and started in his great career by contact with it, and their extraordinary zeal for missionary work. Their central and vitalizing point is their personal devotion to a personal Christ. Their influence has everywhere tended to cool controversy and quicken genuine religious life.

They have bishops, presbyters, and deacons. Their bishops have no dioceses, but collectively watch over the welfare of the church, ordaining the other two orders. The legislation is in the hands of synods, the executive power in a board of bishops and elders. The church is divided into three provinces, — Continental, English, and American, — each caring for its own local affairs, but united in doctrine and missions. They have a worship partly liturgical, partly extemporaneous, with much music. Their hymns breathe a tender and sweet piety.

For their warm religious feeling and aversion to mere dogmatic controversy, we must join in the universal praise which goes out to the Moravians. They approach us doctrinally also, in that they were the spiritual ancestors of the Methodists, who broke the sway of Calvinism over Protestants. They have dropped many singular practices, — as foot-washing, and the use of the lot in choosing their ministers, and in marriage. They were the first hearty pioneers in the missionary movement, and have done more in proportion to their numbers than any other body, especially in Greenland, Labrador, among the Esquimaux, and the American Indians.

A STUDY OF THE SECTS. 127

There were in 1882 in all 10 bishops, 291 presbyters and deacons, and 18,871 communicants (in this country, 1886, 10,250); besides 26,455 communicants in home and foreign missions.

QUESTIONS.

Whence came the name "Moravians"? What do they call themselves? What was their origin? their fate at first? Whence the present church? Where do they live? Have they a creed? Where do they stand doctrinally? What is their peculiarity? their central principle? their effect on controversies? What is their polity? their worship? How are they related to us doctrinally? What have they done for missions? How numerous are they? Can you think of any Moravian hymns? Look them up in the hymn-book of your church. What founder of a great sect was influenced by them? What do you see to commend in them? what to censure?

REFERENCES.

Schaff, vol. i. pp. 874–881; Fisher, Index, Encyclopædia Britannica; McClintock and Strong, *The Moravian Manual;* Holmes's *History of the United Brethren*, 2 vols.; A. C. Thompson, *Moravian Missions.*

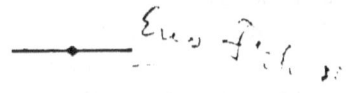

9. THE METHODISTS.

WHOSOEVER will, let him take the water of life freely. — REV. xxii. 17.

Name. — "Methodists" is a nickname given to John Wesley and his Oxford associates by another student, on account of their regular religious habits. It was originally applied to an ancient school of physicians. In England the followers of Wesley are called "Wesleyan Methodists;" in this country, "The Methodist Episcopal Church."

History. — The Methodists owe their existence as a body to a great organizer, John Wesley, and a great preacher, George Whitefield. But as Whitefield became a Calvinist, his influence practically ceased at his death; and the Methodism of to-day is mainly the work of John Wesley. He was a graduate of Christchurch, Oxford, and a fellow of Lincoln College, becoming a clergyman in 1728. His tendencies were then "High Church." From the Moravians he adopted those doctrines of conversion, assurance, and perfection which became the substance of his preaching. On May 24, 1738, he himself experienced that sudden change which it was his aim henceforth to produce in others. It was then that modern Methodism was born.

The early Methodists may be described as the revival party in the Church of England. Nothing was further from their purpose than to leave that church; but its piety was at a very low ebb.

The fervent preaching of Wesley and Whitefield was met with scorn and hostility. Almost every pulpit was closed to them, and they were often mobbed and maltreated. Whitefield then began preaching in the open air, and was soon followed by Wesley, though with great reluctance. Beginning with the colliers of Kingswood, near Bristol, Whitefield gathered thousands about him; and the new views, and still more the new earnestness, spread over the whole kingdom. Chapels were erected, lay preachers ordained; and Wesley's marvellous powers of organization consolidated the growing body, which at his death numbered nearly eighty thousand members. Charles Wesley, his brother, the hymn-writer of the movement, and also a strong preacher, composed over six thousand religious poems.

The influence of Methodism spread far beyond its own adherents. The English Church was roused to a religious life and a philanthropic zeal which have never since left her. The Evangelical movement was the Methodist wave inside the Church; and the Ritualist revival, which succeeded the Liberal reaction from this, received some of its life from the same source. Attention to the poor, both in religion and in their material condition, as in factories and mines, received a new impetus; and it is claimed that the quiet growth of England into political freedom, as contrasted with the violent revolutions and reactions upon the Continent, was partly due to the gentler spirit which the Methodist movement instilled into the lower classes.

The Methodists are by far the largest non-conformist body in England, having their strength chiefly in the middle and lower classes. Though Wesley himself never wished them to leave the Church of England, and died in its communion, his followers have been obliged to organize a separate body, and as such now exist, though with kindly feelings toward the church which they have been the last large sect to leave.

The first Methodist society in America was formed, in 1766, in New York, by Irish emigrants, under the lead of Barbara Heck. Appealed to for aid, Wesley, in 1784, ordained two "presbyters" and a "superintendent," the Rev. Thomas Coke, and sent them over. Precisely what rank Wesley meant Coke to represent in the English Church is a matter of dispute; but he was virtually a bishop. He ordained Francis Asbury, and the two were the first American Methodist bishops. Asbury's activity and success in this country were second only to Wesley's in England, and he saw his sect increase from fifteen thousand to two hundred and eleven thousand in 1816.

The career of Methodism in this country is almost as romantic as it has been successful. As a pioneer religion, pushing its way westward, and following closely the advancing settlers, it recalls the apostolic days. Already in 1799 the Methodists had adopted "camp-meetings" to draw together the scattered and churchless population of Tennessee under temporary religious influences. Their preaching was of the most glowing description, working powerfully upon crude natures, and though often producing strange nervous disturbances, making wonderful and permanent changes of character. More than any other religion Methodism adapted itself to the needs of the new country, and deserved to be called the "American religion." It has also had great influence over the negroes of the South. The colored Methodists are organized into the "African Methodist Episcopal Church" (1816) and the "African Methodist Episcopal Zion's Church;" and in 1870, by order of the Methodist Episcopal Church South, the "Colored Methodist Episcopal Church in America" was created. Slavery has divided the main church also. In 1843 the "Wesleyan Methodist Church" broke away on this question; and in 1846 the "Methodist Episcopal Church South" was formed. Other secessions have been the "Methodist Protestant Church" (1830), which like the English sect has no bishops, but is governed by conferences; "United Brethren in Christ," or German Methodists (1800); "Evangelical Association," or "Albrights" (1800); "Free Methodist Church" (1860), differing from the main body only on minor points of government or discipline.

Government.— The Methodists, like the Catholics, Episcopalians, and Presbyterians, are a visible *Church*, not merely a collection of churches, like the Baptists and Congregationalists. The separate church or congregation does not govern itself, but is governed by a central power, the General Conference.

In England the Conference is the legal successor to the almost absolute power of John Wesley, which was transferred by him in a legal instrument, the "Deed of Declaration," in 1784. The chapels had been placed in his possession, and were now given to one hundred ministers selected by him as the Conference,— a close corporation, filling its own vacancies. In their hands the power remains. There are no bishops.

In the United States power is centred in the General Conference, which meets once in four years. It is made up of delegates from the annual conferences, formerly all ministers, but since 1872 including two laymen from each conference. It elects the bishops, and is the supreme legislative body, under certain limitations as to the fundamental points of the system. The annual conferences are made up of the itinerant preachers of a certain district, and have mainly to do with their affairs. The region of the annual conference is divided into districts, each with its presiding elder and its district conference, which meets once or twice a year as directed, and is made up of the preachers, itinerant and local, in the district, and a Sunday-school superintendent and class-leader from each society, with other officers. This conference licenses the local preachers, and cares for the general temporal and spiritual affairs of the district. The quarterly conference is made up of the officers of the church, or of the several churches constituting a circuit. Besides having charge of the affairs of the church, or churches, it pronounces upon the fitness of any member who desires to preach. In each society there are also *classes*, each under its *leader*, who originally had strict oversight upon the members, visiting them once a week, advising them, and collecting their contributions, but whose duties are now much less rigorous.

The bishops are elected by the General Conference, and hold office for life. Their duty is strictly administrative. They preside at the annual conferences, without vote, and ordain the preachers and assign them to their stations. They have no dioceses, as the Episcopal and Catholic bishops, but change jurisdiction every year according to the disposition of a committee of themselves, — each having residence, however, at some one point.

The presiding elders constitute the council of the bishop who happens to have jurisdiction over their region, advising him as to the character and ability of the preachers to be assigned. They visit and preside over the quarterly conferences.

The preachers are of two kinds, local and travelling. The local preachers are not assigned nor supported, having other avocations during the week, but officiate as needed. The travelling preachers devote all their time to the work of the ministry, and are supported by the societies. They apply to the quarterly conference for recommendation to the annual conference, and if recommended, are allowed to preach on trial for two years, pursuing certain required studies. They are then ordained *deacons*, permitted to baptize and marry, but not to administer the communion. After two years more of study they are, if they pass their examinations, ordained as elders or preachers. There are also *exhorters*, who may lead prayer-meetings; *stewards*, who care for the pecuniary affairs of the society;·and a new order of *deaconesses*, women who are set apart for works of mercy and charity in the cities.

Doctrines.— The official standard is the abridgment of the Articles of the Church of England, which Wesley reduced from thirty-nine to twenty-five. Virtual standards are also Wesley's sermons and "Notes on the New Testament" and Watson's "Institutes of Theology."

The characteristic of Methodist theology is that it is *Arminian* instead of *Calvinistic*. The Methodists were the first great sect to break formally from the doctrines of Calvin. As against his doctrine of election, it proclaims free grace, — that is, the offer of salvation to all men, who are therefore lost only through their own deliberate refusal of it. This implies that the atonement of Christ was universal; that is, not intended for the elect alone, but for all men. Although Methodism admits that when properly educated a soul may pass gradually into a state of salvation, yet it looks commonly to a sudden experience, — conviction of sin, faith in Christ, and consciousness of regeneration. When this process is complete, there is an "assurance," or certainty in the mind of the convert, upon which Methodism lays great stress. It further maintains that it is possible in this life to attain to such a completeness of union with Christ that one is sinless in spirit, though errors of judgment and involuntary transgressions are still possible. This is the doctrine of "perfection." The three characteristic doctrines of Methodism are therefore "free grace," "assurance," and "perfection."

In other points it is at one with Evangelical Christendom. It holds to the universal corruption of mankind by the fall of Adam, total depravity, the Trinity, vicarious atonement, eternal bliss and torment, and the inspiration and authority of the Bible.

The worship of Methodism was at first according to the English Liturgy; but it has retained this only (abridged) in the sacraments of baptism and communion, and in the ordination service, and then only in an abridged form. Baptism is by sprinkling, though choice of other forms is allowed. Prayer is extempore, and it is but rarely that manuscripts are used in preaching.

Converts are not admitted into this church until they have spent six months of "probation" (in England three) in the class-meeting. "Love feasts" were once held in connection with the quarterly visit of the presiding elder, at which "experiences" were related, and bread and water taken in token of fellowship. Watch-meetings are often held on the last night of the year.

Statistics. — There were in 1890 in the Methodist Episcopal Church 2,236,000 members; 15,500 travelling and 13,500 local preachers, under 16 bishops, besides 2 missionary bishops; 25,000 Sunday-schools, with 2,200,000 pupils. The value of the church property is nearly $100,000,000; of parsonages, $13,000,000.

The current expenses were $11,000,000; and $1,000,000 were given for missions, besides $200,000 from the Women's Foreign Missionary Society. The Methodist Church South has 1,166,000 members; the African, 410,000; Zion, 412,000; Colored, 170,000; Evangelical, 148,700 ; the Methodist Protestant, 148,000, — making with the smaller bodies a total of over 4,980,000 members, exclusive of other attendants and children. The total Methodist constituency in the United States is claimed at 10,000,000, or one in every six of the population. The total *membership* in the world is placed at between 5,000,000 and 6,000,000, and the total number of adherents at 25,000,000.

The Methodists deserve the warmest praise for their love of the common people and their care for individuals. Beginning at a time when religion was cold and formal, and even as such confined mainly to the upper classes, they made it a warm and living reality, which laid hold of the humblest lives. No other religious body except the Catholics has so carefully searched out the individual and ministered to his wants as the early Methodists by their close organization. Much of this has changed with the loss of the first enthusiasm and with the improved circumstances of their members. In the civilization of the great West in this country they did service which cannot be forgotten.

In the evolution of Liberal Christianity they deserve mention as the first great body to break openly away from the Calvinism which prevailed at least nominally in Protestant Christendom. In denying predestination and election, they asserted the power of the individual will to control its own destiny to some extent, and so far advanced toward belief in that dignity of human nature which Channing and his followers fully maintained. The break in the chain of Calvinistic reasoning, though it has stopped here in Methodism itself, has encouraged Liberalism generally; and Unitarians have often had a more fraternal connection with Methodists than with other Evangelicals. The aid given by Unitarians to the African Methodists of the South was bestowed with all the more readiness for this reason. And while there is not much resemblance or sympathy between the emotional worship of the Methodists and our more quiet and intellectual ways, yet in the vividness of the Methodist's religious experiences, in public and private, we find something akin to our belief that the Spirit of God is active in the soul to-day as well as in the apostolic times.

But the fact that in their revolt from Calvinism the Methodists stopped with the denial of human helplessness, and cling yet to the Trinity, the deity of Christ, a vicarious atonement, a future state fixed forever at death, and a textual use of Scripture, keeps a gulf between them and us which at present it seems impossible to bridge.

QUESTIONS.

What was the origin of the name "Methodist"? Whence came its present use? What other names now honored have been given in derision? What is the English name for Methodists? Who were their founders? How did Whitefield differ from Wesley in doctrine? What was Wesley's first tendency? Whose influence changed him? What was the relation of the first Methodists to the Church of England? How did it treat them? What has been the result? Who was Charles Wesley? What was the effect of Methodism outside its own ranks? What position does it now hold in England? Who formed the first Methodist church in this country? Who were the first Methodist leaders? Compare the independence of the Methodists on reaching this country with that of the Puritans of Massachusetts Bay. Describe the career of Methodism in this country. What was the use of camp-meetings? What has Methodism done in the South?

What is the church government of the Methodists? What is the governing body called? What is the difference between the English and the American Conferences? What is the difference as to the use of bishops? What is the district conference? the quarterly? What are "classes"? What is the difference between a Methodist and an Episcopal bishop? What does the presiding elder do? What kinds of preachers are there?

What is the standard of doctrine? What is the characteristic of Methodist theology? Wherein does it differ from Calvinism? What is the difference between "free grace" and "predestination"? between "particular atonement" and "general atonement"? What kind of conversion do Methodists favor? What is "assurance"? "perfection"? How is worship conducted? What is "probation"? What position does Methodism hold among the sects in this country as to numbers?

For what two things especially do Methodists deserve praise? Compare them with the Catholics. What have they done for our West? What relation do they bear to Liberal Christianity? What do we find in their religious temperament akin to our views? On what points do we differ from them? How serious is this difference? What is your general impression of Methodism? Compare it with the other Protestant bodies which we have considered. What can you praise? What must you reject? What hymns of Charles Wesley do you know?

A STUDY OF THE SECTS. 135

REFERENCES.

The best history of Methodism is that of Dr. Abel Stevens, in seven volumes, three of general history, four of American; but a good *résumé* is James Porter's *History of Methodism*, in one volume. See also the most admirable ninth chapter in Lecky's *History of England in the Eighteenth Century*, vol. ii.; Lives of John Wesley, by Southey and by L. Tyerman, 3 vols.; *John Wesley and the Evangelical Reaction of the Eighteenth Century*, by Julia Wedgwood; Schaff, vol. I. pp. 882-904; *Life of George Whitefield*, by L. Tyerman. McClintock and Strong is very full on all points. History, doctrine, and government are summed up in James Porter's *Compend of Methodism*; Fisher, pp. 515-523, and Index.

For belief and usages, see the official *Doctrines and Discipline of the Methodist Church*. John Wesley's sermons and *Notes on the New Testament* and Richard Watson's *Theological Institutes* are virtual though not official standards. See also Bishop Foster's *Studies in Theology*. The statistics are given in the official *Minutes of the Annual Conferences*.

---

10. THE SALVATION ARMY.

A GOOD soldier of Jesus Christ. — 2 TIM. ii. 3.

THE original name was "The Christian Mission." But Mr. Booth, in correcting a proof in which the workers were described as "a volunteer army," said, "No, we are not volunteers, for we feel that we must do what we do, and we are always on duty." He substituted the word "salvation." The title spread, and was formally adopted in 1878. The title "General" was originally an abbreviation of "General Superintendent of the Christian Mission." The military idea was thus a growth.

The Salvation Army is the development of a mission undertaken in the East End of London in 1875 by Mr. and Mrs. Booth. Its aim was to reach the lowest classes of the population there religiously and morally, in this adopting the general methods of "revivalists," but with the addition of caring also for bodily needs where that was possible. Since the "army" idea was adopted, it has been carried out in great detail in organization, discipline, titles, and phraseology. Its doctrinal standard is the

"Articles of War," which each recruit signs, and which contain moderately Evangelical doctrines, probably closely resembling the "free grace" of the Methodists. It allows women to be preachers, and they are everywhere prominent among the workers. The spirit of the movement, though suffering sometimes in the hands of incompetent and ignorant people, has been admirable, thoroughly Christian in the best sense, and recalling some of the most effective periods in Christian history, — as those of the Franciscan monks or of early Methodism. Though it seems sometimes grotesque to more cultivated observers, its effect upon the lower classes has been often wonderful.

Its growth has been very rapid. It numbers to-day 2,864 "corps," in 32 different countries, 9,349 officers devoted exclusively to the work, 13,000 non-commissioned or volunteer officers, 7,000 musicians, and over 1,000,000 privates. It has a revenue of about $3,750,000 a year, and invested property of about $3,000,000. It has 32 periodicals (in 12 languages), 24 Homes of Rest, 30 Training Garrisons (for its preachers), 30 Rescue Homes for Fallen Women, etc.

Its history and hopes are given in a most interesting book by General Booth, *In Darkest England and the Way Out*, of which a digest with numerous photographs is given in the "Review of Reviews," for October, 1890; and in *Beneath Two Flags*, by Mrs. Maud B. Booth.

Section II.
CERTAIN OTHER PROTESTANT SECTS.

1. THE ANTI-SECTARIAN SECTS.

MASTER, we saw one casting out devils in thy name, and we forbade him, because he followeth not with us But Jesus said, Forbid him not, for he that is not against us is on our part. — MARK ix. 38–40.

I. **The Christians.** — The popular name is "The Christian Connection." The name "Christian" is meant to imply that the body returns to the primitive condition of Christianity before it was corrupted by creeds or by any false doctrine.

The sect exists only in the United States and Canada, and arose from the union of three distinct movements: (1) A secession from the Methodists, in 1793, in Virginia and North Carolina, led by the Rev. James O'Kelly, who had opposed in vain the power of the bishops over the assignment of ministers to churches. They were at first called "Republican Methodists." (2) A secession from the Baptists, in 1800, led by Dr. Abner Jones, of Hartland, Vermont, who was joined by many from Freewill Baptist Churches. They wished a non-sectarian Biblical basis. (3) A secession from the Presbyterians of Kentucky and Tennessee, in 1801, of people who during a great revival had fallen away from Calvinism, and embraced the doctrine of "free grace." They took the name of "Christians" in 1803, whence the name passed over to the united body.

The "Christians" believe the Bible to be divinely inspired and the supreme authority in matters of religion. Every man must read it for himself; and no creed or council can condemn him for doctrines which he honestly draws from it, nor should any church withdraw its fellowship from him for doctrinal reasons. They hold an Arian view of Christ, — that is, that he is a divine being, pre-existed, and is a mediator between God and man; but he is not God, and there is no Trinity. His atoning sufferings suffice for all men, who if they repent and have faith may be saved. They immerse in baptism, denying that rite to infants, but hold "open communion."

Their government is congregational, the various churches sending delegates to State conferences, and they to the General Conference. These are bodies of consultation, not of authority.

The increase of the Christians reached its climax in 1844, when there were nearly 325,000; but in 1888 they had declined to 142,000, with 1,755 churches and 1,344 ministers. The causes of this have been the "Millerite" or "Adventist" excitement about that time, the secession of many to the Disciples of Christ, and the growing liberality of the older bodies.

See *History of the Christians*, by N. Summerbell; Encyclopædia Britannica Supplement, vol. ii.; Dorchester's *Christianity in the United States*, pp. 315–317.

II. **Disciples of Christ.** — Popular names for this sect are "Campbellites" and "Campbellite Baptists." The members prefer to be called "Disciples of Christ" or "Christians."

The sect was founded, in 1812, by an Irish Presbyterian, Alexander Campbell, who came to this country in 1807. His purpose was to draw Christians together out of all party names, creeds, and organizations. The Disciples have no creed, but are Evangelical in belief. They steadfastly decline to explain such points as the Trinity or the atonement, holding them as revealed facts above the reach of the human intellect, and give baptism only by immersion. They are congregational in government, with the usual district, State, and national associations.

In 1888 they had 645,771 members (mostly in the West), 6,859 churches, and 3,388 ministers besides some foreign missionaries. They are increasing in number very fast. They are enthusiastic in Sunday-school work, and have paid attention to education, having 5 universities, 20 colleges, and 8 academies, and 31 periodicals of all kinds.

See Encyclopædia Britannica Supplement, vol. ii.; *The Origin of the Disciples of Christ*, by G. W. Longan; *Memoirs of Alexander Campbell*; *The Christian System*, by Alexander Campbell; Dorchester, p. 485.

III. **The Christian Union,** or **The Church of Christ in Christian Union,** was organized in Columbus, Ohio, in 1863. Its platform is " The oneness of the Church of Christ, Christ the only head, the Bible our only rule of faith and practice, ' good fruits ' the only condition of fellowship, Christian union without controversy, each local church governs itself, political preaching discountenanced." The reason for the movement was that men's " hearts were wearied with the cruel intolerance and divisions of the sects." This body is Evangelical in doctrine, congregational in government, having local councils and a quadrennial general council, and practises both kinds of baptism.

It numbered in 1889 150,000 members, with 1,500 churches and 1,200 ministers, mainly in the West, and is rapidly increasing.

See Encyclopædia Britannica Supplement, vol. ii.; Dorchester, pp. 677, 783.

Liberal Christians must sympathize with all these bodies in their protest against the narrow and trivial sectarianism which divides Christendom. It seems a pity, however, that they should have found it necessary to organize new sects. Between Unitarians and " Christians " there is practically little difference except in the mode of baptism, which ought not to be considered an essential matter; while between the " Disciples " and the " Christian Union " there seems to be no valid ground for continued separation. The three bodies together make a reinforcement to the Unitarian protest against creeds of nearly a million church members, besides those otherwise connected with these churches.

QUESTIONS.

Who are the "Christians"? What is the name commonly given to them? Where does it exist? How was the sect formed? What is its belief about the source of authority in religion? about Christ? Are they Unitarian? Are they Arminian or Calvinist as to the atonement? Are they increasing? Why?

What are the common names for the " Disciples of Christ " ? Who was their founder? What was his aim? What is the tenor of their doctrines? How do they baptize? What is their polity? Are they numerous? growing?

What is the Christian Union? What are its principles? Is it Liberal or Evangelical?

How far can Unitarians sympathize with any of these bodies?

2. THE FRIENDS.

WHEN he, the Spirit of truth, is come, he will guide you into all truth.
JOHN xvi. 13.

Name. — The full name of this sect is "The Religious Society of Friends." The name by which they are commonly known, "Quakers," is never used by themselves. It was given to them in mockery by one Justice Bennett, of Derby, England, because George Fox "bid them [the judges] *tremble* at the word of the Lord."

History. — The founder and organizer of the Friends was George Fox (1624–1690), the son of a weaver in Drayton, Leicestershire, England. He was poorly educated, and early apprenticed to a shoemaker, but was always "religious, inward, still, solid, and observing beyond his years." Brooding much in that time of religious excitement and discussion over the matters in dispute, he felt within him the stirrings and revelations of the Spirit of God, and began in 1647 to go about England as a wayside preacher of the gospel of the "inner light" as superior, though not necessarily opposed, to the authority of Church and Bible. Insisting on speaking in the churches during the services, he was repeatedly thrown into prison. But he and his fellow-preachers had wonderful success, drawing immense crowds after them, and making many converts. Hearers fell into convulsions and sometimes into insanity. The preachers themselves were often eccentric, sometimes beyond the bounds of decency. Naturally, they roused the bitter hostility of all the sects of the day, and were frequently mobbed and in danger of their lives. The language on both sides was warm, and even coarse. The Quaker was a very different being from what he has since become. He was filled with a fierce desire to convert others. He went to the United States, West Indies, Jerusalem, Malta; and Mary Fisher — for women also became preachers — visited Smyrna and Greece, and even sought audience of the Sultan. Fox did not favor the formation of a separate sect, being sure that his doctrine would conquer the Church itself; but the believers naturally drew together into organizations of their own, which in 1666 were made formal, and a discipline was established for the regulation of the lives of members.

Toleration by the English government was proclaimed in 1689; and Fox dying in 1690, the Friends changed their character very essentially. They had suffered during the age of persecution more than any other body, fourteen thousand having been imprisoned, one hundred and fifty transported, and over three hundred having died from ill-treatment or direct martyrdom. Now the body, like most of the others, lapsed into quietness and almost indolence. It became known more for its peculiarities of dress and manners than for its doctrines, ceased to convert or controvert, became a consciously "peculiar people," drew away from the rest of the Christian world, sought by strict regulations to keep its members jealously together, and grew wealthy and respectable. Its numbers rapidly declined. In 1700 there were probably one hundred thousand in the United Kingdom, in 1800 only twenty thousand, and to-day there are probably not over fifteen thousand.

To the United States they came early, two women landing in Boston in 1656. Their coming was much dreaded; and after imprisonment for five weeks they were sent away to Barbadoes. The most stringent laws were passed against Quakers coming to the colony, and against any one harboring or aiding them; but only the more were they moved to come and "bear testimony." They interrupted the Puritan services, doing strange and disturbing things "for a sign," and returned when banished. The excitement against them was great; and at last the authorities, driven beyond patience, hung four of them, Mary Dyer being one, on Boston Common. Public opinion and the order of the king condemned this, however, though the struggle against them only gradually ceased. In 1678 they settled New Jersey under Fenwick, and in 1682 Pennsylvania under William Penn; and for many years the immigration was very large. The decrease in England was nearly balanced by the increase in this country. There is a small annual growth on both sides of the Atlantic, but not in proportion to the increase of the population.

In the middle of the last century a stern attempt was made to restore strictness of discipline in the society; and it is estimated that nearly one third of its number was lost, as a result chiefly of the excommunication for marriage with the "world's people." Doctrinal discussions also rent the body. Elias Hicks, a preacher of Long Island, was accused of Unitarianism and of too free treatment of the Bible; and a division took place. He was followed, in 1827, by about one third of the American Friends, chiefly in Pennsylvania, New York, Ohio, and Maryland. Largely by the influence of the Gurney family, which included Elizabeth Fry, the majority of the Society in both countries reacted into Evangelical doctrines, and were assimilated to the popular Christianity. But John Wilbur, a Rhode Island Friend, opposed this movement, and led a return to faith in the "inner light," as well as to other doctrines of Fox and his contemporaries. The majority, however, remained "orthodox" or "Gurneyite," the Wilburites now hardly existing as an organized body.

Doctrines — The characteristic doctrine of the Friends is the reliance upon the "Spirit" as a present voice and light in every man's own soul. Reverencing the Bible as true and inspired, they maintain that the same Holy Spirit which spoke to the men of old speaks to-day, and that every man should listen for it and be guided by it. In this belief they once stood opposed both to those who hold to the Church and to those who hold to the Bible as authority. In all matters of life, as well as in doctrine, they waited for this "inner light;" and when it came, or seemed to them to come, they were fearless to the extreme.

From this main doctrine it follows —

1. That a specially educated ministry is not deemed essential. Men and women should speak from divine impulse, and not from any human ordination, and should say what God gave them to say, not what human education taught them. If any one feels constrained to devote himself to preaching, and his brethren think that he is justified in it, he may do so; but there must be no preparation, either in general or for special occasions. The only ordination is a minute of approval by the Meeting to which he belongs, which constitutes him a minister. Speech is always ex-

temporaneous. The preachers are not "settled," but often travel from place to place.

2. Though the Friends assemble at stated times for worship, no "order of service" is allowed. The Bible is not read, nor is any prayer or address necessarily made; and there is never, except as a modern innovation, singing or music of any kind. No one speaks unless "moved by the Spirit;" and when so moved, any one may speak.

3. There are no religious ceremonies. There is no baptism or communion, the Friend holding that the rites of old were but shadows of spiritual acts; and he denies that Jesus meant to institute or perpetuate them. The marriage of Friends is a simple agreement before the Meeting that the two will live as husband and wife, and the signature of a certificate by them and by the clerk of the Meeting. At a funeral the friends assemble, and after a period of silence at the house, unless some one is moved to speak, bear the body to the grave, where also sometimes "testimonies are borne" by ministers to the character of the dead. In neither marriage nor funeral has the minister necessarily any part.

In other respects the doctrines of most Friends at present are those of moderate Evangelical Christians.

Organization. — The organization of the Society was originally very close. The local society is organized as a "Preparative Meeting." It has "overseers of the Meeting," of both sexes, who watch over the lives of members; "overseers of the poor;" and "elders," who care for worship and ministry. Several Preparative Meetings unite into a "Monthly Meeting," which is the executive body, several of these into a "Quarterly Meeting," and several of these again into a "Yearly Meeting," which legislates for a certain district. There is right of appeal upward to this body. Over the Yearly Meetings there is no authority, though great deference is paid to the London Meeting, as the oldest. The children of members are themselves members by birthright. Any one who wishes to become a member makes request to the Meeting, on which a committee is appointed to investigate the case, and report.

The "discipline" of the Society was originally very severe. The private life of every member was subject to extraordinary scrutiny. All luxury or extravagance in living, amusements, even music, undue attention to dress, — especially in colors and unnecessary parts, jewelry, buttons, etc., — and too great absorption in business, were strictly repressed. Members were forbidden to go to law, but must bring their grievances before the Meeting. They were forbidden to marry outside of the Society on pain of being disowned. When two members intended to marry, they appeared before the Monthly Meeting, with the consent of their parents; a committee of men and one of women investigated the matter on either side to see that they were clear of all other engagements, and that the rights of children, if it were a second marriage, were duly cared for; and if allowed, the marriage took place as already described. All military service was forbidden. No oaths could be taken. No titles were assumed or given, not even "Mr." and "Mrs.;" no unmeaning salutations, as "good-morning," exchanged. The hat was not removed in deference to any one, even in Meeting, except in prayer, when all rose and uncovered their heads; nor was there any bowing. The primitive form of address, as "thee" and "thou," was retained; and the months and days of the week were designated by numbers, as in Scripture, not by the common names, which are of pagan origin. Tombstones above a certain small size were prohibited. Many of these characteristics, however, including the peculiar dress, are simply the remains of former customs or fashions, the ornamental being left off. They were not invented.

The Friends have always been noted for their philanthropy. They were the first to advocate the abolition of slavery. In 1761 all members were cut off who were engaged in the slave trade, and by 1784 not a Friend in America owned a slave. The modern treatment of the insane was first adopted in England by them. They have always protested against war. Their treaties with the Indians were never violated, and they have cared greatly for the remainder of the race. Elizabeth Fry was one of the first workers in prison reform. The first women preachers, and indeed the first recognition of the equality of women in religious services, were among the Friends. They have also some foreign missions. They have always taken generous care of their own poor, educating their children, and assisted each other in business.

Statistics. — There are in all about 128,000 Friends, of whom 108,000 are in the United States. Of these 78,000 are "Orthodox" (under 12 Yearly Meetings, the largest in Indiana), 24,500 are "Hicksite," and 6,000 are in smaller bodies. They have 7 colleges, besides academies, and 5 periodicals in this country. Many Meetings have also "First-Day schools."

The Friends were the first Liberal sect in the Reformation, and their rise was as remarkable as it was picturesque. They stood entirely apart from all other Christian bodies, relying on the Spirit as authority, in distinction from Church and Bible. They represent, therefore, the extreme of the Pauline or spiritual tendency. There is something magnificent in their complete trust in the inner voice and their sturdy refusal to allow anything to interfere with its being heard and obeyed.

But the almost entire abandonment of this original position, even by those who hold to the original name, who even brand it with the stigma of heresy, shows that it was premature. It was too high and ideal a faith for the mass of men to live up to. They cannot distinguish between the voice of the Spirit and mere transient or selfish impulses. The temptation to set these even above the true "inner light" is very strong, and has led to many ludicrous, as well as serious, results in practice. There is something ironical also in the way in which the ideas of the Friends, when carried out, turned back against themselves. Starting from complete individualism, each man looking within himself for guidance, they arrived at one of the most despotic and repressive codes of "discipline" which any religious or even civil society has ever adopted, and became the most persistent and even annoying proselyters of their day. In the name of pure spiritual religion they laid an emphasis on external things — as dress, speech, titles — which finally made them almost as ritualistic as their first opponents, and which became the chief peculiarity by which the world designated them. Protesting against fashion and etiquette, they fell into a fashion and etiquette of their own quite as strict as any which "the world's people" followed; and in their hostility to useless expense and luxury, they came not seldom to be known as lovers of money. That after all this the majority of the Society should turn about and renounce the pure doctrine of the "inner light," and assimilate themselves to the dogmatic and Scriptural position which Fox and Penn denounced, is surely a most striking phenomenon in religious history.

The criticism upon the Friends is that they overlooked on the one hand the "solidarity" of mankind, and on the other the revelations that come from the outer world. Other men beside themselves had "inner light," and it is by comparison and mutual clarifying that truth becomes known; and the world of Nature, as well as the world of the soul, has light to give. Nevertheless, the main point of the Friend, that the final court of appeal for every man in his questions of faith and duty must lie in his own conscience, heart, and reason, remains unassailable. It is the ground to which Liberal Christianity is rapidly transferring itself; and the Friends must be considered the pioneers and protomartyrs of modern spiritual religion.

QUESTIONS.

What is the origin of the name "Quakers"? What is the name they give themselves? Who was their founder? Relate what you recall of his life. What kind of men and women were his first disciples? How were they treated? What reaction took place? What can you say of their growth? How did they begin in this country? How were they treated? What other States did they enter? What do you know of the beginning of Pennsylvania? What reformation was attempted among the Friends? What divisions arose? What parties now exist among them?

What is their characteristic doctrine? How does it differ from that of other sects we have noticed? How does it compare with our own? What is their practice with regard to the ministry? to worship? to religious ceremonies? to marriage and burial? How are they organized? What is a "Preparative Meeting"? a "Monthly Meeting"? a "Quarterly Meeting"? Does this series of bodies resemble that of any other sect we have considered? How does it consist with the theory of the "inner light"? How did they treat private life? dress? disputes? marriage? titles? language? How far were any of these inconsistent with the main doctrine? What can you say of their philanthropy? What did they do for slavery? for the insane? for peace? for the Indians? for woman?

Where do the Friends stand in the classification of the sects? What strange transformations have they undergone? What is the danger of the doctrine of the inner light? Is it any more dangerous than following authority? Has reliance upon an infallible Church or Bible secured freedom from error? What criticism can you make upon the main point? What relation has it to ours? What impression have the Friends made upon you? Do you think their main doctrine likely to gain or lose power?

A STUDY OF THE SECTS. 147

REFERENCES.

The best (and official) manual is *A Concise Account of the Religious Society of Friends*, Thomas Evans, Philadelphia; admirable summaries in McClintock and the Encyclopædia Britannica. An excellent history and criticism by a friendly outsider is Frederick Storrs Turner's *The Quakers*. The standard history of the early movement is William Sewell's *History of the Rise, Increase, and Progress of the Christian People called Quakers*. The standards of doctrine are Robert Barclay's *An Apology for the True Christian Divinity*, etc.; the writings of William Penn — for example, *No Cross, no Crown* — and of Isaac Pennington. The usages are given in *The Book of Discipline*. But the spirit of the Friends must be sought in the *Journal of George Fox*, the *Life of Thomas Ellwood*, *John Woolman's Journal*, and to some degree in the biographies of Elizabeth Fry, Lucretia Mott, Isaac T. Hopper, and others. See also many of Whittier's poems. The Evangelical movement within the body is advocated in the works of John Joseph Gurney, and the Hicksite movement in Janney's *History*, vol. iv., and *Journal of Elias Hicks*. See also Fisher, Index, "Quakers;" Schaff, vol. i. pp. 859-874 (the Confession of 1675 is in vol. iii., p. 789). In the United States, see Bancroft, Palfrey, *Memorial History of Boston*, and G. E. Ellis's *The Puritan Commonwealth;* from the Friends' point of view, R. P. Hallowell's *The Quaker Invasion of Massachusetts*.

---

3. THE NEW CHURCH.

To be spiritually minded is life and peace. — ROM. viii. 6.

Name. — The members of this body are commonly called Swedenborgians; but they do not use the name themselves. Their official title is "The Church of the New Jerusalem."

History. — Emanuel Swedenborg, whose theological writings are regarded by this religious body as containing a true and divinely revealed exposition of Christian doctrine, was born at Stockholm, Sweden, in 1688. His father, Jesper Swedberg, was a professor of theology and a bishop in the Lutheran Church, a man of great piety and learning, and a zealous reformer. His son Emanuel was finely educated, and became famous for mechanical and mathematical inventions. He was led by his researches into higher regions of thought, and especially to inquire into the relations of matter and spirit. About the year 1745 he claimed that his spiritual sight was opened. Of this call Swedenborg himself wrote: "I have been called to a holy office by the Lord Himself, who most graciously manifested Himself in person to me His servant in the year 1745, when He opened my sight to the view of the spiritual world, and granted me the privilege of conversing with spirits and angels, which I enjoy to this day (1769). From that time I began to print and publish various *arcana* that have been seen by me or revealed to me, — as respecting heaven and hell, the state of man after death, the true worship of God, the spiritual sense of the Word, with many most important matters conducive to salvation and true wisdom."

He gave himself up entirely to these matters, abandoning his former studies. To his seventy-seven treatises on scientific subjects were now added more than that number upon Biblical and theological subjects, the chief of them being his "Arcana Cœlestia," in eight large volumes. Throughout his long period of spiritual activity, he retained and honorably filled a seat in the Swedish senate, and presented several memorials of importance to his country. He died in 1772. He was a man of iron constitution, of prodigious intellectual activity and power, of simple life, universally respected and loved even by those who ridiculed his claims and his doctrines.

His views were taken up after his death by scholars in Sweden, England, Germany, and the United States. The first public meeting was held in London, 1783; but the first society was organized there in 1787. The first general conference was held there in 1789, and the first convention in this country, at Philadelphia, in 1817.

Doctrines. — The doctrines of the New Church claim to be a revelation of spiritual truth, intended to enable us rightly to understand the sacred Scripture, to unfold its higher wisdom, whereby a purer and more exalted state of life may be attained. For this purpose a human instrument was needed, and such an instrument was provided in the person of Emanuel Swedenborg. By those who are convinced of the truths of his religious system, his mind is believed to have been illumined to an extraordinary degree. His spiritual senses were opened, enabling him to see and converse with beings in the other world and describe the nature of its life, and also to discern the internal, or as it is called, spiritual meaning of the Scripture.

The New Church believes and teaches that God is love itself and wisdom itself; that he is one both in essence and in person; and that the Lord Jesus Christ in His now glorified and Divine Humanity is the perfect embodiment of that God. The Trinity is not a trinity of persons, but of divine *essentials*, consisting of love, wisdom, and their proceeding operation, and called in the Gospels Father, Son, and Holy Spirit. It is like the soul, body, and their resultant energy. The Father is in the Son, as man's soul is within his body; the Holy Spirit proceeds from the Father by the Son, as man's power proceeds into act from his soul by means of his body. The divine trinity in the Lord is, then, of the same nature as the finite trinity in man, — the Father, Son, and Holy Spirit being one Lord in one Person, as the soul, body, and the life of man are one man.

While the Lord was on earth, He had both a human and a divine nature, just as every man has an external and an internal, or what is sometimes called a lower and a higher nature. As to the external nature, which was derived by incarnation, He was frail, finite, liable to temptation, like any other man; but as to His internal or essential being He was infinite, perfect, divine. By His own divine power, He gradually overcame the evil appertaining to the Humanity or nature assumed by birth, conquered all the powers of hell, put off all that was frail and finite, and brought down into every region of that nature the very divine love and wisdom, and so made it one with the essential and indwelling divinity. This is what is understood by the Lord's "glorification" mentioned in the Gospels.

According to the New Church, the Sacred Scripture is inspired. When understood in its true sense, it is seen to treat of things spiritual and eternal, — of God, the soul, immortality, redemption, regeneration, sin, forgiveness. It *appears* to treat of things natural and temporal. But these are believed to be capable of spiritual interpretation. They all have a deeper or more properly a spiritual meaning. So that within or above the apparent meaning of any passage there is a higher meaning called the spiritual. And this spiritual sense is to that of the letter as the soul is to the body.

But Swedenborg, in revealing the law of a divine composition, has disclosed at the same time a means by which the spiritual sense may be unfolded; namely, the law of analogy, or more properly, of correspondences. According to this law, which was known to the ancients, all natural things are seen to bear a relation to spiritual things. A knowledge of this law opens the book of Nature, making every living object a voice to tell us of the spiritual forces from which it springs. It is also found to be the key to the Bible, enabling us to see within a temporary and local clothing principles of universal and eternal application. So definite and systematic is this law of correspondences that a hundred different expositors equally skilled in its use will thereby arrive at substantially the same spiritual sense.

The New Church believes that man is born with hereditary tendencies to evil. But he is not a sinner because he inherits these proclivities, but only when he yields to them in actual evil. This natural or hereditary state is not a heavenly one. Gradually the natural, inordinate love of self and the world must be replaced by a love to the Lord and the neighbor. This takes place in the degree that a man regards the indulgence of any known evil as a sin against God, and shuns it because it is a sin, at the same time conforming his life to all known truth from a sense of religious obligation. So far as he does this, his evils are removed and forgiven, and the opposite good affections are given him in their stead.

The New Church teaches that *man* does not die. The material body alone dies. The spirit, which is the real man, continues to live, but in the spiritual world where all things are homogeneous to itself. The spirit is in the human form, having senses far more acute than those of the body; and these senses are opened as soon as the body dies, so that the spirit sees and hears other spirits as men see and hear one another. During our life on earth the spiritual body is within the natural. But after the death of the latter, the spiritual body still lives on in its own world, and never resumes its material vestment. And the separation of the spirit from the incumbrance of gross matter, which takes place almost immediately after death, is what is understood by the resurrection.

The "Judgment" consists in the revelation of man's real inward character or purpose. By the law of affinity which governs all associations in the other world, spirits go with those whose characters are most congenial to their own. Thus each one goes " to his own place " in perfect freedom.

The happiness of heaven does not consist in idleness or cessation from active employment, nor in continual psalm-singing and oral prayer, nor in feasting sumptuously with the patriarchs, nor in being raised to honors, nor in the exercise of dominion over others, but in the diligent and wise performance of good uses from love to the Lord and the neighbor; in the freest expansion and highest exercise of all one's best faculties, not for the sake of self, but primarily for the good of others.

The New Church believes that the Lord's second coming has actually commenced ; that it is a coming, not in person, but in a new power of the Spirit of Truth, which will lead all who from the heart believe in God and his Word into the way of truth, and into a new power of Christian goodness and love.

Government. — The polity of this religious body is both simple and liberal. Strict uniformity as to liturgical usages or rules of church government is not insisted upon. Each society is free to arrange for its own services and act under its own rules, which, however, are quite similar. Societies geographically near to each other group themselves into an " Association," which then appoints one of its ministers as a " General Pastor," whose duty it is to exercise a general oversight of the spiritual interests of his Association. These Associations are joined together in a general body, known as the " General Convention of the New Jerusalem in the United States of America." This general body meets annually. To this body the several Associations make a report of their work. These meetings, together with a special conference, or meeting of all the ministers, Sunday-school superintendents, and teachers, etc., occupy about a week, and are much enjoyed. The Rev. Chauncey Giles, D.D., of Philadelphia, has been president of the General Convention for many years.

Ministers are introduced into their office by the usual rite of ordination, performed by one of the "General Pastors" above mentioned. The church recognizes and carefully observes two sacraments, Baptism and the Holy Supper.

Statistics. — The "New-Church Almanac" for 1889 sums up in America, including Canada, 11 Associations, 127 active societies, of which 88 have regular ministerial services, and (estimated) 7,028 communicant *members*. To these are added 3,150 not connected with any body, making a total of 10,178. There are 82 houses of worship, 65 "reading circles," 91 Sabbath-schools, and 91 clergy in active service of various kinds. To the membership must be added the usual merely congregational connection. The largest number is in Massachusetts. There is a Theological School in Cambridge, Mass.; and Urbana University, at Urbana, Ohio, is under New Church control.

In England there were, in 1885, 65 societies and 32 ministers, with about a dozen educational and missionary institutions. There are also churches in the colonies, in South Germany, Austria, Norway, and Switzerland.

The influence of the doctrines of the New Church upon those who sincerely and intelligently hold them is very marked and very beautiful. They give very much the same serenity and quiet trust which the primitive Friends had, without their intolerance and proselytism, and especially sweet equanimity and faith in death and bereavement. They have also great power over many thoughtful people in their theory of the Scriptures, and in the wider application of the doctrine of "correspondences" throughout the relations of matter and spirit. There has been much intellectual sympathy between them and the Unitarians of this country, though there has been no formal expression of it. In their exclusion from the fellowship of "Evangelical" Christians, in their dissatisfaction with the doctrine of the literal infallibility of the Bible, in their search for a higher and wider interpretation of sacred history, in their denial of the Trinity and other doctrines held by the popular sects, and in their theories of the future life, we find much to

A STUDY OF THE SECTS. 153

accept. On the other hand, we cannot accede to the claims made
for Swedenborg; and we share with the rest of the world, even
after a century of open and fair discussion, its denial of the
"second sense" of the Scriptures. The latter is an old doctrine,
running back to the Jewish scholars of the time of Jesus, and the
Christian scholars of the third century, but always failing to gain
support. It is but a temporary refuge for those who are driven
from belief in the literal infallibility of the Scriptures; and the
spiritual beauty and elevation which it finds in so many plainly
commonplace passages are evidently first transferred to them out
of the revelations which the Spirit makes to-day. But the arguments which Swedenborg addresses directly to the reason of men
are often of the highest value; and no more beautiful, comforting,
or reasonable ideas of the future life have ever been uttered than
by him. He stands among the great religious teachers of history.

QUESTIONS.

What is the popular name of this sect? its official name? Who was its
founder? Of what nation was he? of what parentage? In what was he
first eminent? When was his attention turned to religious matters? How?
What course did he pursue? What is his chief work? What can you say
of his character? How were his views spread?

What is the New Church view of Swedenborg? of the Trinity? How
does this differ from the popular doctrine? What is said of the relation of
the two natures in Christ? of the inspiration of the Scriptures? of the
double meaning? How is this applied to the world in general? What is
the doctrine of human nature? of salvation? of death? of the relation
between the living and the dead? of the future life? of the judgment? of
the second advent of Christ?

What can you say of the effect of New Church doctrines upon those
believers whom you know? What is the feeling of Unitarians toward the
New Church? What points have they in common? How do we differ
from them as to Swedenborg? as to the "second sense"? What is the
history of this latter doctrine? What use has it served? How do you
account for the satisfaction it gives? What great good has Swedenborg
done?

REFERENCES.

A good summary in Appleton's Encyclopædia. The latest and presumably
best life of Swedenborg is that by Benjamin Worcester, Boston, 1883, though
there are several others. The later and larger biography of White is said
to contain many slanders. See also Emerson's essay in *Representative Men*.
The best brief exposition of the doctrine is James Reed's *Swedenborg and*

the *New Church*, Boston, 1881, of which there is also a very cheap edition. Also good is Chauncey Giles's *Why I am a New Churchman*. Swedenborg's own works are, of course, the standards. The *Arcana Cœlestia*, in eight large volumes, is an exposition of the spiritual sense of Genesis and Exodus. The *True Christian Religion* contains a summary of doctrine, while *Heaven and its Wonders and Hell* goes into detail about the future life. A short summary in Swedenborg's own words is *The New Jerusalem and its Heavenly Doctrine as revealed from Heaven*. The literature of the New Church is remarkably abundant, and may be learned from the catalogues of the publication societies.

4. THE ADVENTISTS.

WHERE is the promise of his coming? for since the fathers fell asleep, all things continue as they were. — 2 PETER iii. 4.

ADVENTISTS are those Christians who believe that the visible, personal second coming or advent of Christ is near at hand, and that at this coming the millennium, or thousand years' reign, will begin. They exist in several organizations, and are often called "Millerites," from their founder, William Miller.

That Christ will soon come back was the belief of the first Christians, as shown by many passages in the Epistles. Though opposed by Jerome and Augustine, it reappeared at times throughout Christian history, being especially strong at the Reformation. The present organizations owe their beginning to William Miller, a native of Massachusetts and a Baptist, who began to preach his new views in the State of New York, in 1831. Followers multiplied, camp-meetings and tent-meetings were held where churches or halls could not be had, and great excitement arose, which reached a climax when Miller set the date of the advent between March 21, 1843, and March 21, 1844. The date of the crucifixion, April 14, was a favorite. The failure of all prophecies was a blow to the cause, which had never been organized; and at Miller's death, in 1849, the number of believers decreased still faster. But an organization had been begun four years before at Albany, around which a new sect gathered.

All Adventists are Evangelical in main points of doctrine, and congregational in church government. They all believe in the visible and speedy personal coming of Christ, though at an uncertain time; in the resurrection of the righteous dead then; in their reign with Christ during the millennium, while the earth is being set in order and the wicked subdued; and in the Judgment to follow. All baptize by immersion.

1. The "Evangelical Adventists" represent the original body. They hold to the natural immortality of the soul, the conscious state of the dead, and the conscious eternal suffering of the wicked. They number about five thousand.

2. The "Advent Christians" broke from the main body, in 1854, on the question of date. They deny that the immortality of the soul is natural, and affirm that it is the gift of Christ, and only to believers; that, therefore, the wicked will be destroyed, and will not suffer eternally. They number about thirty thousand.

3. The Seventh-Day Adventists have their headquarters at Battle Creek, Michigan. They originated in the "visions" of "Sister White," of Palmyra, Maine, which are regarded as spiritual manifestations. They believe that Christ is at work cleansing the heavenly sanctuary "from the presence of our sins, imparted to it through the blood of Christ there ministered in our behalf." When this is finished he will come back, but the time is uncertain. The law of Moses is still valid, including the Sabbath on the seventh day. They practise the washing of feet and the kiss of peace at the Lord's Supper. They number nearly thirty thousand, compactly organized. They are zealous opponents of intoxicating liquor and tobacco.

There are also smaller sects, as "Life and Advent Union" and "Age-to-come Adventists," both of which reject the eternal torture of the wicked, and the "Church of God" in Missouri founded on a very insignificant divergence from the doctrine of the Seventh-Day Adventists. The three have together about nine thousand members.

All these bodies are careless of educational matters, having scarcely any institutions of learning. There is little church property, but much publishing of books, tracts, and periodicals. The ministers usually labor during the week, and so support themselves.

There is also an association called "The Baptist Conference for Bible Study," organized in Chicago in the spring of 1890, which consists of Baptists who look for a second coming of Christ. They set no date, and do not regard it as necessarily near, but make it a sort of third dispensation. What the Old Testament dispensation was to the New Testament, the present stage of revelation is to that of the Advent. Without this the sin and infidelity of the world can never be overcome. At his coming Christ will "set up his kingdom in person, and sway his sceptre over the empires of the world for one thousand years, subduing evil, and crushing out wickedness." Then will come the Judgment. There are also many Presbyterians who hold the same views. In neither case is there any intention or desire to form a separate body, and they must be carefully distinguished from the sectarian Adventists. The "Irvingites" or "Catholic Apostolic Church" in England also look for the coming of Christ to precede the millennium.

The earliest documents of Christianity contain a clear expectation of the return of Jesus before his generation had passed away (1 Thess. iv. 13–18; 1 Cor. vii. 29–31, xv. 51, 52; Phil. iv. 5; James v. 8; 2 Peter iii. 1–13; and the Apocalypse generally). That this expectation was founded upon the words of Jesus or some misunderstanding of them is also clear from many passages in the Gospels (Matt. x. 7, 23; xxiv. 3–51, especially 34, xxv.; xxvi. 29; Luke ix. 27). These limit us to three theories, — either that these passages are to be taken in a figurative sense, or that they have been misreported, or that Jesus himself mistook the time or manner of his return. The first two probably unite in the fact. Jesus may have spoken of the establishment of his cause upon the earth as his own second coming; but there is much of his language that cannot be fairly so understood, and it may be that it has suffered in passing through the minds of those who heard him, and of those who recorded his words. If the Adventists, and indeed most Evangelical Christians, are right in understanding him to have meant a *personal* return to the earth, the assertion of Jesus and his Apostles that this would happen within their generation, and before those who heard it were all dead, remains irreconcilable with historic facts.

The belief formed undoubtedly one of the rallying-points and mainstays of the first Christians, and its gradual and quiet death was a most remarkable result of the earthly success of the new religion. In spite of its many revivals, it has no serious place in practical Christian faith now. Indeed, it seems to many a pessimistic doctrine, as if the Christian revelation and the agencies it has set at work in the world were failures, or sadly insufficient, and a new start were necessary. To the more thoughtful mind the coming of Christ is an inward and gradual fact, — not a failure, but an increasing success, though not as swift as we could wish. "Even so come, Lord Jesus!"

QUESTIONS.

Who are the Adventists? What other name is often given them? How old is their main doctrine? Who revived the belief in this century? Give an account of the circumstances. What doctrines are held by all Adventists in common? Who are the "Evangelical Adventists"? The "Advent Christians"? The "Seventh-Day Adventists"? What other bodies do you recall? What peculiarities have they all? What Adventists exist in other bodies?

Is any belief in the second advent of Christ to be found in the New Testament? What texts of this tenor can you recall? What three theories in regard to these texts may be held? Which seems to you most probable? What did the belief in the second coming of Christ do for primitive Christianity? Has it any use for us? What is the true doctrine?

REFERENCES.

Articles in McClintock, American Cyclopædia, etc.; *The Reign of Christ*, by D. T. Taylor; *History of the Second-Advent Message*, by J. C. Wellcome; *History of the Sabbath and First Day*, by John Nevins Andrews; *Thoughts on Daniel and the Revelation*.

Section III.
THE LIBERAL PROTESTANT SECTS.
1. THE UNIVERSALISTS.

As in Adam all die, even so in Christ shall all be made alive. —1 Cor. xv. 22.

Name. — A Universalist is one who believes in universal salvation; that is, the ultimate perfection and blessedness of all human beings. The name "Restorationist" is older, but has in later times been restricted to those who hold to a probability of future punishment before ultimate salvation, as opposed to those who believe that all men reach heaven at once after death.

History. — Many of the most prominent of the earlier Christians, especially Origen, in Alexandria (185–254), believed that all men would finally be saved. But the great influence of Saint Augustine (354–430) prevailed, and the doctrine sank almost out of sight till after the Reformation. It did not come into prominence till the last century. James Relly, a preacher of Calvinistic Methodism under Whitefield, at last carried his view of predestination so far as to believe that God would see that *all* men were saved. By his writings John Murray was converted, and became the father of American Universalism as a body; though there was a good deal of latent belief in the doctrine, and Mayhew and Chauncy, of Boston, had openly preached it in the middle of the century. Landing in America in 1770, Murray founded the first Universalist Church in Gloucester, Mass., in 1779, becoming minister of the church in Boston in 1793, and dying as such in 1815. Following Relly, he taught election in this life, — that the elect go directly to heaven at death. The non-elect are purified by fire till the Judgment Day, when they find that they too are saved by the atonement of Christ. Elhanan Winchester, of Philadelphia, thought the interval would be about forty-four thousand years. Murray was a Trinitarian of the modal or Sabellian type, maintaining one God in three manifestations, but not divided into three persons. He was thus a thorough Calvinist, except that he widened predestination to include all mankind.

The preaching of Hosea Ballou, which began in 1790, marked a new era. He was practically a Unitarian in all points — though believing Jesus to be divinely sent and endowed — except that he taught that *all* men were saved at death. There would be no future punishment, except for future sins. This doctrine proved more popular than Murray's, and the sect grew more rapidly. A minority, however, still clung to belief in punishment hereafter, and their view seems now to have become the prevailing one. Probably few, if any, Universalists hold to immediate universal salvation at death.

The doctrine of "eternal hope" has also found many advocates in the Church of England, who claim that the omission of the article on eternal penalty in the revision of the Articles under Elizabeth allows this latitude. Stanley, Kingsley, Maurice, Farrar, Robertson, and many others have held to the *hope*, though not to the *certainty* of universal restoration, — a hope which is widely cherished among other Evangelical Christians, though not always openly proclaimed.

Doctrines. — Universalism, as we have seen, has passed through an almost complete transformation. Beginning as Calvinism, it has become Unitarian and liberal. Like many other sects, it has a conservative and a liberal party, in which the transformation is seen in different stages, but the liberal tendency seems to be rapidly gaining ground.

The nominal standard of belief is the "Profession of Faith" adopted at Winchester, N. H., in 1803. Murray was then living, and the creed bears the marks of a compromise between the old and the new phases of belief. It probably does not represent exactly the position of even the majority of the denomination, but as usual, it has been found difficult to make satisfactory changes in a form of faith once settled.

ARTICLE I. — We believe that the Holy Scriptures of the Old and New Testaments contain a revelation of the character of God, and of the duty, interest, and final destination of mankind.

Article II. — We believe that there is one God, whose nature is Love, revealed in one Lord, Jesus Christ, by one Holy Spirit of Grace, who will finally restore the whole family of mankind to holiness and happiness.

Article III — We believe that holiness and true happiness are inseparably connected, and that believers ought to be careful to maintain order and practise good works; for these things are good and profitable unto men.

As to the Bible, great latitude of opinion exists, from those who hold the older view of its textual infallibility to those who see in it the record of a progressive revelation to a people peculiarly fitted to receive it, but a revelation neither perfect nor final. The Trinity is generally rejected, and the essential humanity of Jesus believed, there being some diversity as to the extent to which he was supernaturally endowed and guided. Perhaps more emphasis is laid by the average Universalist upon the official station of Jesus, as in a special sense a son of God and redeemer of men, than by other Liberals. As to the future life, there is general agreement as to the probability of some kind of future discipline for those who are not sufficiently purified by the penalties and sufferings of this life; but the belief in the final restoration of all to "holiness and true happiness" is emphatic and universal. This is their distinctive doctrine.

Their worship is, like that of most Protestants, unliturgical, prayer being extemporaneous, though there is a growing tendency to the antiphonal reading of the Psalms.

Government. — The Universalists have retained from their primitive Calvinism a tendency to a presbyterian form of church polity. They are not strictly congregationalists. The supreme body is the "General Convention," which is made up of delegates from the various "State Conventions." It has established the "Profession of Faith" as the creed of the denomination, and makes it a condition of fellowship in itself or in the State Conventions, of the ordination of ministers, and of admission to membership in the churches. The State Convention is made up of a minister, two delegates, and one additional delegate for every fifty members over the first fifty from each church in its fellowship.

Statistics. — The Universalists are practically an American body, the only churches outside this country being two in Scotland. There are here (1889) 721 churches, containing 38,780 members and holding about $8,000,000 of property, and having 53,000 in their Sunday-schools. They are strongest in Massachusetts, New York, Maine, Vermont, Ohio, and Illinois. They do not increase much, if at all, in numbers, though they are said to be more active than formerly in church and denominational life. They have 3 theological schools, 4 colleges, 5 academies, and 7 periodicals, besides Sunday-school papers. The "Universalist Record," recently established, represents the influential and increasing liberal element.

The Universalists and the Unitarians are commonly called together "Liberal Christians." The differences between them are small and are growing smaller. Both have changed very much since their modern reappearance. The Universalists, beginning as Calvinists, have become Unitarian at almost every point, while the Unitarians, beginning with an aversion to the doctrine of universal restoration, many with an actual belief in eternal punishment, have all come to hold at least the eternal hope. The differences which remain may be summed up as follows: —

1. Universalists lay more stress on *dogmatic belief* than Unitarians, having their common creed, and generally a very vivid and positive opinion on its various points. They have always been fond of textual controversy, as well as of argument on grounds of reason and conscience.

2. They emphasize the *supernatural* element in religion more fully, — the divine mission and endowment of Jesus, the exceptional inspiration of the Bible, the agency of God in bringing all men to goodness in the end; while Unitarians have seen more clearly the moral and spiritual excellencies of Jesus and of the Bible, and the power of man over his own destiny.

3. As to the future life, the Universalist says that all men *will* be saved, while the Unitarian says that he *hopes* they may. The Universalist retains so much of his Calvinism as to emphasize the sovereignty of God even to predestination; while the Unitarian, in his respect for the power of the human will, even for evil, seeing that characters are often still diverging as they go out of this world, feels a certain sad reserve in his trust in their union hereafter.

4. As the Universalist still leans toward Orthodoxy in his love of dogma, so he does in his loyalty to the outward institutions of religion. He is more faithful in attendance at church, more likely to become a "member," more fond of baptism and the communion, more interested in prayer-meetings.

5. But probably the real cause of the separate existence of the two bodies lies in their separate origin and history. The Unitarians were at first simply a section of the old Congregational body, the established church of New England, broken off in controversy, and carrying away bodily most of the oldest church organizations, with their wealth, social prestige, scholarly traditions, and general conservatism of temperament. The Universalists were an entirely new body, raised by earnest though not always well-educated preachers out of sturdy and fearless stock in the middle class. They were the "Roundheads" of the Liberal movement, and have always had more influence upon the mass of people than their Unitarian co-workers. Out of this difference have grown many considerations which kept the two bodies apart in the past. Now those considerations are disappearing, and the two movements keep apart merely because they began so. The union of the two is devoutly to be wished, and must some day be accomplished.

The Universalists have been prominent in social reforms, and are always good fighters. They were active in the anti-slavery movement, and are zealous in temperance and woman suffrage.

QUESTIONS.

What does the name "Universalist" mean? what "Restorationist"? What place had this doctrine among the earlier Christians? Who was its greatest champion? its greatest opponent? Who was its modern reviver? What was his history? How did it influence his belief? Who was the father of American Universalism? What were his doctrines? Who succeeded him as leader? What change did he effect? How far is his view of the future life still held? What advocates has the "eternal hope" elsewhere?

What tendency is gaining ground now? What do you mean by this? What is the nominal standard of faith? What do you see in Article II. of the nature of a compromise? What is the belief about the Bible? about the Trinity? about Jesus? about the future life? What is their worship? What is their form of government? What power has the General Convention? How does all this differ from our own polity?

What are Universalists and Unitarians together called? How have they both changed? What beliefs have they in common now? How do they differ as to dogmatic belief? how as to supernaturalism? how as to the future life? how as to outward religion? What can you say of their origin? Who were the "Roundheads"? How were the Universalists like them? How were the Unitarians like the "Cavaliers"? Have these differences increased, or not? What position have the Universalists taken toward social reforms? Do you know many Universalists? Have you found any difference between them and ourselves? Do you think they are likely to grow? How far do you think their main doctrine is held in other bodies? What effect would this have upon the growth of Universalists? Do you think all men likely to be saved? Why? What influence do you think this belief would have upon people generally? If men resist God here, what reason is there for thinking that they will yield to him hereafter? What does the Bible say?

REFERENCES.

The best exposition of average Universalism is T. B. Thayer's *Theology of Universalism*. The views of the liberal party are given in a recent work, called *Essays Doctrinal and Practical,* by several clergymen. The Lives of John Murray, Hosea Ballou, and T. B. Whittemore are useful in history. See also McClintock and Strong, Fisher's Index, and Encyclopædia Britannica.

---

2. THE UNITARIANS.

One God and Father of all, who is above all, and through all, and in you all. — Eph. iv. 6.

Name. — The word Unitarian is now commonly used to designate those who believe in the unity of the personality of God, as distinct from the Trinitarians, who believe in three divine Persons. The origin of the name is disputed, but it seems to have appeared first in Hungary, in the (new) Latin form of *Unitarius*, about 1570. It was first officially used in Transylvania in 1638, and the English word is now so used by the Associations of England and America also, though it is not found till 1687. The common names for Unitarians were at first *Anti-trinitarians, Arians, Socinians, Racovians,* and others. In this country they are often called *Unitarian Congregationalists*, as being the Unitarian branch of the Congregationalist body since the division at the beginning of this century. In England, for a similar reason, they are often called *Presbyterians*.

History. — Unitarianism, considered as the doctrine of the unity of the Godhead, is older than Christianity. The Jews were in this sense Unitarians, when they had emerged from polytheism. Jesus and his Apostles were therefore brought up in this faith, and nothing but the plainest proof should allow any one to believe that they ever departed from it. That the earliest Christians did not believe in the Trinity is shown not only by the New Testament, but by the fact that the last remnant of the Jewish Christians, the Ebionites, believed in the unity of God, till they vanished in the fifth century. The development of the doctrine of the Trinity (see pp. 24-28) had to fight its way to success; and when the Arians were officially denounced at the Council of Nicæa in 325, they were almost, if not quite, as numerous as their victorious opponents.

Unitarianism, however, reappeared with the Reformation. Its martyrs began with Adam Duff, who was executed in Dublin in 1326, and the last man burned for heresy in England was Edward Wightman, a Unitarian, in 1612. The most celebrated of the Unitarian martyrs was Michael Servetus (Miguel Serveto), a Spaniard, who was burned at Geneva in 1553 at the instigation of John Calvin. Of far greater influence upon Unitarian doctrine and history were Laelio and Fausto Sozzino, better known under their Latin names, Lælius and Faustus Socinus, uncle and nephew. The former had the finer mind; the latter was the more active teacher, and from him came the name *Socinianism*, under which the Unitarianism of the Reformation days was generally known. He taught, however, that Christ, though not pre-existing, became God by his goodness, and is, therefore, now to be worshipped; and held other doctrines which Unitarianism to-day would reject. Under his leadership, Socinianism became the belief of a wealthy, cultivated, and powerful body in Poland, of which the king was a member. But under the Catholic reaction all kinds of Protestantism were swept out of Poland, and Socinianism never has regained a footing there. It had also been brought to Transylvania by Lælius Socinus; and there, though much reduced at one time by Catholic oppression, it still survives with some prosperity. The seed planted in Italy, France, Switzerland, and Holland, though at first seeming to flourish, died out under the combined hostility of Catholic and Protestant enemies.

The most prosperous bodies of Unitarians to-day are in England and the United States. Socinianism was introduced into England by Bernardino Occhino, Faustus Socinus, and others of their generation, and it flickered more or less plainly through the sixteenth century. The first church was established about 1645 by John Bidle, who is called the "Father of English Unitarianism." He died in prison, whither he had been sent on account of his belief; but other churches sprang up, and their doctrine spread quietly but widely in the Church of England. Milton, Newton, Locke, and other famous men were Unitarians of various shades. But more Unitarians came from the Presbyterians than from any other body, nearly half of the churches of this faith now existing in England having been once Presbyterian, many of them still retaining that name.

The founder of the present organized body of English Unitarians was the Rev. Theophilus Lindsey, who left the Church of England and gathered a Unitarian congregation in Essex Street, London, in 1774, which included many noted people. He was followed the next year by Dr. Joseph Priestley, famous as a man of science, and especially as the discoverer of oxygen. The law at that time held the denial of the Trinity to be blasphemy, and it was not until 1813 that Unitarians were placed on a level with other Dissenters. The denomination has continued to flourish, and now holds a respected place among Protestant bodies. There are also some strong churches in the north of Ireland and in Wales, and a few in Scotland.

In the United States Unitarianism began in New England and is still strongest there, though rapidly spreading of late in the West. Its history may be divided into four periods, — *formation*, *separation*, *vocation*, and *organization*. Its *formation* was quiet, gradual, and long. It extends from early New England history down to the year 1819, when the Unitarian churches first assumed a separate existence. The chief events of this time were the "Half-way Covenant" and the "Great Awakening," and the leading liberal was Charles Chauncy, minister of the First Church in Boston. The Half-way Covenant of 1662 set aside the old idea of a converted church membership and admitted to the church those who had been baptized in infancy, who did not deny the doctrines, and were not of scandalous life. They were not, however, allowed to come to the communion; hence the name of the measure. The result was the dilution of the old Calvinistic theology in pew and pulpit, and Arminianism made great strides in New England. To counteract this state of things Jonathan Edwards stimulated a "revival" at Northampton in 1735, which was renewed in 1740 by Whitefield, the great English Methodist preacher, by Gilbert Tennent in New Jersey, and by others. This latter revival was known as "The Great Awakening." It aroused the churches and increased their membership; led to the abolition by most churches of the Half-way Covenant and the restoration of a converted membership and ministry. But by its appeal to the emotions and its obvious inconsistency with predestination, it made the way easier for the very Arminianism it was intended to check, when it came in the form of Methodism. Still further, it forced people to take sides. The revival of Calvinism had reminded New England again of what that grim system really was; the excesses of the revival meetings and the meddlesome disposition of many of the revival preachers awoke an opposition, especially in Eastern New England, among the cultivated and influential classes. From this time Unitarianism began to develop from mere Arminianism. The first minister *known* to have been Unitarian was Ebenezer Gay of Hingham (1695–1787). The first minister whose doubt of the Trinity was *published* was Jonathan Mayhew of Boston, who, in 1755, added a note to that effect to one of his printed sermons. The first *church* to become openly Unitarian was King's Chapel (Episcopal). The congregation, finding in 1787 that their new minister, James Freeman, was Unitarian, ordered all phrases inconsistent with that belief to be expunged from the Prayer Book.

The new doctrines spread fast, but were not openly preached. The reasons for this silence were that the liberals were not yet clear in their own minds, disapproved of controversy, believing the dogmas in question not of as much importance as their opponents claimed, shrank from precipitating a break in the old Congregational body, and were not willing to have the name "Unitarian," which was borne in England by men with whose doctrines they did not agree, thrust unjustly upon them. They therefore emphasized the value of the Christian character, and simply omitted the disputed doctrines from their preaching. The appointment of Henry Ware, to be Hollis Professor of Divinity in Harvard College roused great excitement, as it showed that the College itself had now come under the control of the new faith. At length it became evident to the leaders of the Unitarian party that the evils of controversy would be less than those of silence; and in 1819, at the ordination of Jared Sparks in Baltimore, William Ellery Channing, minister of the Federal Street Church in Boston, preached a sermon defining and defending the Unitarian faith.

This began the period of *separation,* which extends to the Parker controversy, in 1841. Its leader was Dr. Channing, though he was disinclined to close denominational organization. The Baltimore sermon was followed by declarations of belief all over New England; and soon it was found that about one hundred and twenty-five churches, most of them among the oldest and strongest of the Congregational body, were Unitarian. The question whether "church" or "parish" owned the property had been settled by the "Dedham case" in favor of the latter, which, where there was any difference between the two, was usually of the liberal faith. So began the Unitarian body. In social, political, educational, and literary circles it had an influence out of proportion to its numbers; and to a remarkable extent the poets, historians, statesmen, and jurists of that day in this country were Unitarians. The clergy were scholarly; the laity cultivated, honorable, and philanthropic. Partly by temperament, partly by reaction, they shunned controversy, looked askance at anything like sectarianism, and disliked proselyting. The American Unitarian Association was formed in 1825, but not warmly supported.

Into this quiet and happy but unprogressive life of the churches Transcendentalism, or the idea that the soul has private and direct insight into truth, and may set aside all authority, came at first as an intruder. But it was now that Unitarianism first realized its *vocation*, or reason for separate existence. Hitherto it had based its faith, or thought it had, upon Bible texts. Henceforth it was to be the champion of the human reason and conscience, which the best in the Bible nourishes but must not contradict. The leaders of this period were Ralph Waldo Emerson, who touched Unitarianism in his famous " Divinity School Address," in 1838; and Theodore Parker, of West Roxbury, whose sermon on " The Transient and Permanent in Christianity," in 1841, was the beginning of a sad and bitter controversy. In time, however, the two parties came to understand each other better, and to stand together in the "inner light."

The period of *organization* showed the new life which had entered the body. The great events of this period have been the institution of the National Conference of Unitarian and other Christian Churches and of the local Conferences, in 1865, under the lead of Dr. Henry W. Bellows, and in more recent years of many other instrumentalities, such as the Women's Alliance, the Church Building Loan Fund, Unity Clubs, Unitarian Clubs, and others. The American Unitarian Association has come into closer union with the churches by admitting their pastors and delegates to its Annual Meeting, and is supported with a generosity which in earlier days would have seemed impossible. The churches have multiplied, and Unitarianism is fast extending to all parts of the country. The decay of the old beliefs and the quiet leavening of the older sects with Unitarian principles have made the growth of the Unitarian body slower than it would have been if it had met with a more bitter opposition. But it grows at an increasing ratio, especially in the West and on the Pacific coast, while founding new churches still in New England.

Government. — The American Unitarians are all congregational in polity; that is, they maintain the right of each church to regulate its own affairs. There is a strong tendency to independent action on the part of the churches, though of late years there is more inclination to a closer fellowship. The American Unitarian Association is a purely voluntary organization, consisting of life members, who are made such by payment of fifty dollars, and of the delegates of churches which have contributed to its funds for two successive years or more. The Association is practically the missionary and executive arm of the denomination. The National Conference and the local Conferences are also voluntary associations, the former meeting once in two years, the latter from one to three times a year. Their purpose is to awaken interest in the activities of the denomination, and to stimulate sympathy and the sense of fellowship by bringing together those of a common faith. They are not executive, and seldom undertake enterprises of their own.

Doctrine. — Unitarians, being congregational in church government, have no common authoritative creed. The American Unitarian Association declares that its object "shall be to diffuse the knowledge and promote the interests of pure Christianity." What is meant by "pure Christianity," however, it does not define, nor does it claim the right to establish any conditions of fellowship. The constitution of the National Conference of Unitarian and other Christian Churches contains these statements:

"Art. IX. Reaffirming our allegiance to the gospel of Jesus Christ, and desiring to secure the largest unity of the spirit and the widest practical co-operation, we invite to our fellowship all who wish to be followers of Christ.

"Art. X. While we believe that the Preamble and Articles of our Constitution fairly represent the opinions of the majority of our churches, yet we wish distinctly to put on record our declaration that they are no authoritative test of Unitarianism, and are not intended to exclude from our fellowship any who while differing from us in belief are in general sympathy with our purposes and practical aims."

The Western Unitarian Conference thus states its position:

"We declare our fellowship to be conditioned on no doctrinal tests, and welcome all who wish to join us to help establish truth and righteousness and love in the world."

No church, however, holds itself bound by any of these declarations, every church reserving the right to state its own belief, if it cares to do so. Many churches have "covenants" or statements of faith and purpose, generally very simple, which are used with varying interest. More extended and detailed definitions of Unitarianism have been issued by the American Unitarian Association in the form of books or tracts, but with the understanding that they are not to be considered authoritative.

The doctrines of the Unitarians have already been set forth in contrast with those of other sects. But this contrast may give the impression that Unitarianism is a mere negation, whereas in reality it denies and excludes less, affirms and includes more, than any other form of Christian faith.

Unitarianism is rather a tendency than a fixed and definite set of opinions. It may be defined as the tendency to see God in the natural order of the world, material and spiritual, as distinguished from the Orthodox tendency to see Him only in isolated and exceptional phenomena, persons, and experiences. Unitarianism is founded upon law, Orthodoxy upon miracles. Unitarianism believes in the rule, Orthodoxy in the exceptions. Unitarianism sees the beauty and power of what Orthodoxy calls exceptions, but considers them as still under law, parts of the natural and divine order of the world, and as illustrations of what is true or may become true of all. This distinction will become clearer as it is applied to the separate doctrines.

Fundamental to Unitarianism, and following from this tendency, is its trust in the dignity of human nature. It believes that it is neither hopelessly blinded nor helplessly corrupt, but that in spite of much weakness and selfishness it loves at heart both truth and goodness.

Out of this come the two most distinctive principles of Unitarianism, — reliance upon human faculties for the discovery of truth, and appreciation of the common virtues and graces of human life, — or as they are usually called, reason in religion and character before creed.

By reason in religion is meant that the truth necessary for the right conduct of human life is revealed to and received by the faculties which are common to all men, though they may exist in very different strength, and be capable of very different degrees of apprehension in different minds. The inspiration of the Almighty giveth all understanding, though all men are not able to receive the same amount. Orthodoxy denies this broad idea, and confines inspiration to certain individuals and to exceptional faculties in them, isolating these faculties from those common to human nature by a difference not in degree but in kind. To these psalmists, prophets, evangelists, apostles, or other sacred persons is given the power to perform miracles; that is, to do in the physical world what no man could do without divine aid. Revelation is thus made a rare act of God, and involves a change both in Nature and human nature. 'Orthodox Protestantism thus confines revelation to Bible times and personages, though it asserts the continued action of the Holy Spirit in opening the deeper meaning of the Bible to the eyes of faith. The Roman Catholic, while believing the Bible to be a special divine revelation, maintains that revelation continues, but only through the equally divine Church. The Unitarian tends to unite these two views, rejecting their negations. The revelations made through the Bible and through the Church both contain divine truth, but God is not shut within either Bible or Church. He strives everywhere and always to make Himself and His truth known to men; and the science, philosophy, history, poetry, and all other forms of the mental activity of to-day may be the instruments of His revelation. Infallibility is impossible in human life, as is proved most clearly by the errors and sins of those who most proudly claim to have infallible authority for their beliefs. But revelation, the unveiling of truth, is a constant process. Unitarianism, therefore, looks to the natural operation of the human mind for truth, and holds itself in sympathy with all sincere thought, and in readiness for new revelations. Nor does it believe that God must break the laws of Nature to make Himself known. On the contrary, it is in those laws that He is best seen. The real miracle is the order and harmony of the whole, not the disturbance of any part; and the way to a deeper knowledge of God lies not in being startled now and then by some exceptional thing, but by studying reverently and patiently the world as it is.

The other distinctive principle of Unitarianism, and one more generally understood than the first, is the value set upon the virtues and graces which sweeten and strengthen common life. The position of Orthodoxy is that these are not only worthless, but actually abhorrent to God, unless they are the results of certain beliefs and certain experiences. Unitarianism maintains that the fruits are not known by the tree, but the tree by the fruits; and that love, justice, purity, patience, and the other virtues of a manly or womanly character have their value and their evidence in themselves. It declines to consider only certain experiences as the effect of the Holy Spirit,—as the crises of "conversion," "revival" emotions, and the like,—but believes that It is seen in the common joys and sorrows, peace and struggle of humanity, ever urging men upward. And while Orthodoxy tends to emphasize certain "sacred" times, places, and ceremonies as if they were valuable in themselves or the unique channels of divine grace, the Unitarian values these only so far as they are of use to practical life. The sacredness often attributed to them alone he spreads over all earnest human life. Divine service is whatever serves God. Holy ground is wherever holy emotions come. Sacred times are all times when the soul burns with new faith or insight.

These two principles, flowing from the main one, contain the essence of Unitarianism, and explain its minor doctrines.

The Bible it considers as containing words of God, but not His entire Word, or all that He wishes men to know. Moreover, since the truth it contains came through human channels, it is more or less mingled with error. The discernment of the truth is made by the reason and conscience of to-day under the constant enlightenment of the Holy Spirit.

The Church is the association of men for religious purposes, and has no authority but that of the truth it teaches, and no use except to purify and strengthen daily life.

About *Jesus* Unitarians widely differ. There are still some Arians, who hold him to have been a being superior to man though subordinate to God. There are others who look upon him as a man endowed with superhuman powers, entrusted with a mission differing in kind from any other ever given to man, and exercising an authority to which reason and conscience must bow. But the strong tendency of Unitarians generally is to consider him as in all respects a man, though with a spiritual insight and moral power which, while really differing only in degree from those given to all men, are in degree so far above those of all other men as to set him by himself in human history. This inclusion in humanity, however, must not be taken as degrading Jesus, since Unitarians hold a higher conception of human nature than the Orthodox, but as marking the possible elevation of humanity. He is not "mere man," but more man. Unitarians believe that God was in Jesus, but that He is in all men. Jesus at once reveals God to man and man to himself. He glorifies our common human nature. He teaches that love, fidelity, patience, cheerfulness, are divine qualities, and that the line between divine and human, which the ancient councils found it so hard to draw in the nature of Jesus, is as uncertain in every earnest human soul. Jesus is not an exception, save in degree, but a bright illustration of the possibilities of human nature. Unitarians therefore reject the Trinity, and all the doctrines which cluster about the dogma of the Deity of Christ.

The *atonement* is considered by Unitarians as a natural process. By his imperfections and sins man removes himself from God; and all good influences, including those which flow from the life and character of Jesus, bring him back into the divine likeness, and into harmony with the divine will. The office of Jesus lies in no arbitrary arrangement with God by which the innocent is substituted for the guilty. All the conceptions of the atonement held by the Orthodox seem to the Unitarian to subvert the fundamental principles of justice, to confuse the conscience, and to dishonor God. The life and death of Jesus have had a powerful influence upon the minds, hearts, and souls of men, but this has come by the natural working of moral and spiritual laws, and in ways which all truth and goodness follow when they affect human life. *Salvation* is not rescue from any external peril, but from sin and weakness within. Holiness is wholeness and healthiness, and is accomplished not by means outside of practical life, but by doing justly, loving mercy, and walking humbly with God every day. *Conversion* may be hastened by special influences or experiences, but is more likely to come gradually. Not believing in the essential depravity of human nature, Unitarians do not look for that complete revolution which the Orthodox logically must aim at, but for a quiet and steady evolution of the germs of truth and goodness into such development as is possible in this life. They therefore distrust "revivals."

The future life Unitarians consider a natural continuance of the earthly life. Death is not a moral crisis, but an event common to all living things, a purely physical change. Unitarians are very reluctant to indulge the imagination in depicting the details of the future life, holding that life freed from the body and from the circumstances of the earth is beyond our power to conceive with certainty. But they maintain with great firmness that the character begins there as it ends here, and that the laws of the moral nature, not being conditioned by space or time, continue in force after death. The Orthodox division of all men into saints and sinners, "fixed in an eternal state," they reject as most unjust as well as unwarranted in reason. The moral life will be as varied, as capable of progression and change, as here. Whether all men will reach perfect happiness and holiness, is a question which the Unitarian refuses to decide. The mystery of human freedom must always veil its future results. Nor can the Unitarian believe in the "Judgment" so often pictured by the Orthodox, an arbitrary decree by which men are sent to the right or the left according to some other standard than that of character. Each soul will gravitate to its place according to its real condition.

In worship, Unitarians commonly preserve the simplicity and directness of the Congregationalists, from whom they have in this country descended. Prayer is extemporaneous, though a very few congregations have a liturgy. There is an increase in the use of antiphonal psalms; and an attempt is making, under the auspices of the American Unitarian Association, to compile a book which shall be acceptable to those who wish a liturgical service.

The faults most frequently attributed to Unitarians, — their neglect of stated worship and their ignorance of theology, — while they are to be admitted and deplored in some measure, follow naturally from that very breadth of faith which has been described as their characteristic, and which it is their privilege to hold and their mission to teach. As all life is seen to have possibilities of sacredness, and all duty to be divine service, "sacred" times and places must seem less important than to those who tend to concentrate sacredness upon them. And as all truth takes on a divine aspect, opinions about historical and speculative matters, most of which seem to be of little real use even to those who have most definite views about them, must retire more into the background. While, therefore, the Unitarian cannot afford to neglect any means of spiritual culture, or any truth that concerns the spiritual welfare of mankind, he must rejoice in that sympathy with all truth, with all goodness, and with all earnest life which his faith makes possible to him. The Orthodox, so the Unitarian thinks, buys his devotion to sect and church and definite creed at the cost of breadth in love and hospitality to truth.

Statistics. — ("Year-Book" of 1891). There are in this country 424 churches and 459 ministers. There are 24 local Conferences, and the National Alliance of Unitarian and other Liberal Christian Women has 75 branches.

There are also a Sunday-School Society, besides three local societies for the same purpose, a Temperance Society, a National Bureau of Unity Clubs, several associations of ministers, etc. The American Unitarian Association received in 1890-1891 $54,440, the Women's Alliance $3,110, and the Sunday-School Society $3,700. The Church Building Loan Fund has $18,400 with which it aids societies in the erection of churches. A Unitarian mission is sustained in Japan. There is one nominally Unitarian theological school, at Meadville, Pa., besides the Divinity School of Harvard University, which has been made unsectarian, and devoted to the study of theology as a science. Another school is contemplated on the Pacific coast. There are five Unitarian periodicals, — the "Christian Register," of Boston, and "Unity," of Chicago (weekly), "Every Other Sunday," of Boston (fortnightly), the "Unitarian" and the "Unitarian Review," both of Boston (monthly).

In England, there are 273 churches, in Ireland 41, in Wales 31, in Scotland 10, and in Australia 3. There are three theological schools in the British dominions, — the largest, Manchester New

College, being in Oxford, England; and three periodicals, — "The Christian Life," and "The Unitarian Herald" (weekly), and "The Christian Reformer" (monthly). The denomination is represented by "The British and Foreign Unitarian Association."

In Transylvania there are 165 churches, with 107 pastors and about 60,000 adherents. They are governed by a bishop, eight rural deans, and an ecclesiastical council of 350 members. They have a college at Kolosvár, with a theological school, and two middle schools.

There are also thousands of professed or virtual Unitarians in Austria, Germany, Holland, France, Sweden, and Switzerland, and many even in Spain.

QUESTIONS.

What is the origin of the name "Unitarian"? How is it now applied? What other names have been given to Unitarians? What are they often called in this country? in England? Why?

How old is Unitarianism? What is its relation to Judaism? to the early training of Jesus and the Apostles? What right have we to believe that they retained it? that the early Christians held it? What was its greatest contest with Trinitarianism? What was its subsequent fate? When did it reappear? What martyrs to it can you name? Who were its chief leaders at the Reformation? What views did they hold? Where did Unitarianism flourish then? Where else did it take root? Where is it most prosperous to-day?

Who brought Unitarianism to England? Who founded its first church? Who were famous English Unitarians? From what body did many come? Who founded the denomination in England? Who deserves mention next after him? What was the position of Unitarianism before the law? What is the condition of the body now? Where else in British dominions has it churches?

Where did Unitarianism begin in the United States? Into what four periods may it be divided? What years does the first period cover? What were its chief events? Who was the leading spirit? What was the "Half-way Covenant"? the "Great Awakening"? What was their effect? What influence had Jonathan Edwards in preparing the way for Unitarianism? What faith was the stepping-stone to it? Who was the first minister known to be Unitarian? Who first published his Unitarianism? What was the first Unitarian church? Why were Unitarian views not avowed at first? What brought about the break with the old faith? Who led it?

A STUDY OF THE SECTS.

When and how did it begin? What was the second period? What was the "Dedham case"? What was the character of the first Unitarians? What was the third period? Who were its leaders? What works proclaimed their views? What has been their effect? What was the fourth period? Who was its leader? What were its chief events? What is the condition of Unitarianism in this country to-day?

What is the polity of the American Unitarians? Into what bodies are they organized? What is the difference between the Association and the National Conference? How do they differ from a Presbyterian synod? Have Unitarians any common creed? Why? What is the declaration of the American Unitarian Association? of the National Conference? of the Western Conference? What are the "covenants" of many churches?

What can you say to the charge that Unitarianism is a mere negation? Why should the Orthodox think it is? Must not all belief deny something? How may Unitarianism be broadly defined? How does it differ in this from Orthodoxy? What fundamental principle follows from this? What two principles does this involve? How are they commonly stated? What is meant by "reason in religion"? What are the Unitarian and Orthodox ideas of revelation? Which is the broader? Which honors God the more? Compare the Roman Catholic, Orthodox Protestant, and Unitarian ideas on this point; on physical miracles. Where does Unitarianism find God in the universe? What is meant by "character before creed"? Compare the Evangelical and the Liberal views of human nature; of "sacred" times and places.

What is the Unitarian view of the Bible? of the Church? of Jesus? What is Arianism? Humanitarianism? What view lies between these? To which view does Unitarianism tend? Does this view degrade Jesus? Why is it more repugnant to the Evangelical view of man than to ours? How does Jesus elevate our idea of humanity? Does the Unitarian believe that God was in Jesus? In what sense? What is the Unitarian view of the atonement? of the Evangelical doctrines about it? How have the life and death of Jesus affected humanity? What is the Unitarian view of *predestination?* of conversion? of the future life? of death? of the future state? of the variety of character hereafter? of the ultimate fate of all souls? of the "Judgment"? What is the common form of worship among Unitarians? What exceptions do you know?

What are the faults most frequently charged upon Unitarians? What answer can you give?

REFERENCES.

The best summary of the general history of Unitarianism is the American Unitarian Association tract by Rev. R. R. Shippen. E. H. Hall's scholarly *Orthodoxy and Heresy in the Christian Church* gives a fuller account. The best short history of American Unitarianism may be found in the opening chapters of W. C. Gannett's *Life of Ezra Stiles Gannett*. For longer accounts, see *Unitarianism: Its Origin and History* (Channing Hall Lectures, 1888-89), J. H. Allen's admirable *Our Liberal Movement*; George E. Ellis's *Half Century of the Unitarian Controversy*; O. B. Frothingham's *Boston Unitarianism, 1820 to 1850*, and his *Transcendentalism in New England*; the Unity Club lectures of 1890-91. *A History of Religious Thought and Life in New England*, edited by George W. Cooke, the Lives of Channing, Dewey, the Buckminsters, Parker, J. F. Clarke, etc.; Sprague's *Annals of the American Pulpit* (Unitarian Congregationalists); Dorchester's *Christianity in the United States*; Brooke Herford's *The Story of Religion in England*; and references in ecclesiastical histories and histories of doctrine.

As to the doctrines of Unitarians, good summaries are to be found in the tracts of the American Unitarian Association; but no more beautiful account exists, especially to those who can see what is involved in it, than Dr. Channing's sermon, *Unitarian Christianity*. See also J. F. Clarke's *Manual of Unitarian Belief, Essentials and Non-Essentials in Religion, Common Sense in Religion, The Ideas of the Apostle Paul, Vexed Questions in Theology*, and *Orthodoxy: Its Truths and Errors*. The tendency of the denomination is seen in Dr. Hedge's *Reason in Religion* and his *Ways of the Spirit*, and still more fully and clearly in Martineau's *Seat of Authority in Religion*. The works of Channing, Parker, and Dewey, and the sermons of A. P. Peabody, J. H. Allen, J. W. Chadwick, and M. J. Savage represent various schools of thought within Unitarianism. English Unitarianism is stated in *Unitarian Christianity*, a volume of sermons by several preachers. Controversial books are Norton's *Statement of Reasons for not believing the Doctrines of Trinitarians concerning the Nature of God and the Person of Christ*, Wilson's *Unitarian Principles confirmed by Trinitarian Testimonies*, and Priestley's *History of the Corruptions of Christianity*. For books on special doctrines, see references in part ii. chap. i. Mr. Wendte's tract *What do Unitarians believe?* has an appendix containing a valuable list of celebrated men and women who have been Unitarians.

Part III.

SECTS NOT CALLING THEMSELVES CHRISTIAN.

1. THE SOCIETY FOR ETHICAL CULTURE.

YEA, a man will say, Thou hast faith and I have works: shew me thy faith apart from thy works, and I by my works will shew thee my faith. — JAMES ii. 18.

What is known as the "Ethical Movement" began with the formation of "The Society for Ethical Culture" in New York city, in 1876. Felix Adler, the son of a Jewish Rabbi in New York, and lecturer for a time on the Oriental languages and literature in Cornell University, was the founder of this society. In 1883 a similar society was founded in Chicago; and others arose in Philadelphia and St. Louis in 1885 and 1886. In 1887 the "South Place Religious Society" of London became the "South Place Ethical Society." The same year witnessed the formation of the "Union of the Societies for Ethical Culture." The aim of the movement was declared in the constitution of this Union to be "to elevate the moral life of its members and that of the community;" and it "cordially welcomes to its fellowship all persons who sympathize with this aim, whatever may be their theological or philosophical opinions." The movement has no creed, and does not teach religion, if by religion is meant a conception of God. At the same time, it is not opposed to religion; and its members and lecturers are free to take whatever religious standing-point seems reasonable to them. Some maintain that ethics *is* religion, by which is meant that genuine moral action is the means of connecting the finite soul with the Infinite. Others are complete secularists. The bond of fellowship does not lie in a special theological view or theory, but in a practical moral aim. Each society has a lecturer, or lecturers, and holds Sunday meetings for at least seven or eight months during the year. Supreme attention is given to various phases of personal and social morality. The movement has been distinguished from the outset by devotion, both theoretic and practical, to social reform. A workingman's school, district nursing, improved tenement houses, neighborhood guilds, a bureau of justice, economic conferences between business men and working men, workingmen's self-culture clubs, are outgrowths and illustrations of its spirit.

The literature of the movement is for the most part in the form of pamphlet lectures; two books have appeared, *Creed and Deed*, by Felix Adler, 1877, and *Ethical Religion*, by William M. Salter, 1889. Besides these are *Die Religion der Moral*, by Salter, 1885, *Moralische Reden*, by same, 1889, and *Die Ethische Bewegung in der Religion*, by Stanton Coit, lecturer of the London Society, 1890, — all published in Germany. The movement published "The Ethical Record," Philadelphia, from April, 1888, to July, 1890; this quarterly has now been enlarged into "The International Journal of Ethics" (Philadelphia and London), has European as well as American editors and contributors, and ceases to be the organ of the Ethical Movement.

At their roots, the Ethical Movement and rational Unitarianism are one. Both are based upon faith in the supreme authority of the sense of duty, and both aim at the production of moral life. The main difference between them is that Unitarianism emphasizes certain other doctrines, corollaries of faith in the moral law, especially a personal God as the source of righteousness and immortality as its quality or consequence, while the Ethical Movement is silent upon these points. The Ethical Societies, therefore, omit prayer and praise from their public exercises, retaining only the sermon or "lecture," adding sometimes music and reading from ethical writings, including the Bible; and the lecture itself differs from a Unitarian sermon chiefly in the absence of reference to God and the future life, as well as to historical Christianity. The Ethical teaching seems to us, therefore, bare and undeveloped, if not weak, like an unsprouted root, — having real religious life, but not furnishing food enough for the practical needs of the soul. Belief in God and in an immortal opportunity have been considered necessary to man's highest spiritual life. To cut the vision of the present down to humanity, and the vision of the future to a merely human though developed career would impoverish human life. Nor can we forget in our admiration of the devotion of the Ethical Societies to "good works" that the Christian Church, both originally and now, cannot be said to have overlooked them. It no doubt deserves this rebuke to its many idle speculations, and to its frequent absorption in merely contemplative worship; but it has also undertaken just as good and successful works as these. The practical energy of the new movement is itself the result of a general awakening of the conscience of the age, which is showing itself quite as plainly in the churches. Since, however, there are many earnest people in the world who cannot receive what are commonly called religious doctrines, and are not interested in historical Christianity, there is a sphere for the Ethical Societies which we wish them to occupy, and in which we bid them "Godspeed," — all the more because our knowledge of their leaders convinces us that in the deepest and purest sense they too are religious, in *so far*, as the text above says, as they hold that "ethics *is* religion, by which is meant that genuine moral action is the means of connecting the finite soul with the Infinite." So far as the command of duty is seen to come from a source deeper than human experience or knowledge, it is a command of what we call "God."

QUESTIONS.

What is meant by the word *ethical?* What is the difference between it and *moral?* How did the Ethical Movement begin? What societies now exist? How are they combined? What is their object? What is their relation to religion? What are their leaders called? What public exercises have the societies? What good works have they undertaken? What is the main objection to them from our standing-point? What beliefs have commonly been held of value to human action? What have we in place of them here? Does the Ethical Movement undertake anything which churches may not do? What faults in the churches does it practically rebuke? What room has it in the world? How far *is* it religious? What good does religion do to you?

---

2. THE SPIRITUALISTS.

In this rejoice not, that the spirits are subject unto you; but rather rejoice because your names are written in heaven. — LUKE x. 20.

In the widest sense of the word a spiritualist is the opposite of a materialist; that is, he is one who believes that spirit, not matter, is reality. In a more restricted sense it was once used to denote those who claimed to be under the direct guidance of the Holy Spirit. In the modern popular sense it means those who believe that the spirits of the dead can hold communication with the living through their senses.

This belief is as old as man; for hardly a tribe of savages or a stage of human history has been found in which there has not been a belief in the presence of the souls of the departed and in their action upon the living. Some have claimed that this was the beginning of religion; that is, of any belief in the supernatural. Instances of alleged communication are found throughout sacred and secular history. But the belief has found especial acceptance in the United States, and in the present century.

It gained its most powerful stimulus from the experiences of Margaret and Kate Fox, children of twelve and nine years of age, at Hydeville, Wayne County, New York, in March, 1848. Hearing strange rappings, they established by them communication with alleged spirits, by whose aid the skeleton of a murdered man was found in the cellar of their house. The two girls went about the country giving exhibitions of the strange phenomena, and arousing great excitement. In 1850 Daniel Dunglas Home appeared with mysterious powers, which attracted great attention in Europe as well as in this country. Since then great numbers of "mediums" have sprung up, who have done many different kinds of strange things by the aid, as they claimed, of spirits. In 1875 Messrs. Crookes and Varley, well-known English men of science, and later the still more celebrated Alfred Russell Wallace, proclaimed their belief in spiritual manifestations. In one form or another Spiritualism has a very large following; but due partly to the fact that it must be a private and not a public affair, as ordinary religious worship is, and partly to the reluctance of many to confess their belief, no estimate of the numbers of its adherents can be made. They are probably very large. It cannot be said that the confessed believers are commonly from the more intelligent classes. The world of science is almost solid against them, though it has generally refused to investigate.

As Spiritualists are not organized, rarely even in congregations, they have no authoritative creed, and differ more or less in their belief. There is, beyond doubt, a large number of impostors, who play upon the credulity of the ignorant for selfish purposes. This is admitted and deplored by Spiritualists as well as by others. But that there is also a large number of quiet and sincere believers in the reality and value of communication with departed spirits must not be overlooked by the fair-minded.

These believe that our spirits, when they leave our bodies, do not undergo any essential change. Their characters and tendencies remain the same; and there is therefore among them the same great variety of goodness and wickedness, wisdom and ignorance, as when they were in the flesh. They are not separated, as the old theology maintained, into the perfectly good and the perfectly wicked. Nor is their condition fixed. Progress is open to them under the new influences, as well as under the continued influence of the better spirits; and the occupations and duties entrusted to them in the "spirit-land" correspond to their fitness for them. But they retain their interest in the affairs of earth, and seek to take part in them, especially in those of the persons whom they knew in the body. The good spirits wish them well, and try to warn, console, advise, and guide them. The evil spirits maliciously misinform, misdirect, and corrupt them, if they can.

There is a state, called "sensitiveness," in which it is possible for mortals to perceive the presence of the spirits, and to communicate with them. It is, as it were, a new sense, — "the heritage of all, yet manifested only at rare intervals by favored individuals. . . . It is a faculty pertaining to the spiritual nature, and is acute in proportion as that spiritual nature dominates the physical senses. . . . It is variable in the same individual; is often the result of drugs, of fatigue, of sleep; and may be induced or intensified by hypnotism or mesmerism. . . . It may have all degrees of acuteness, from impressibility scarcely distinguishable from the individual's own thoughts to the purest independent clairvoyance." Those who are "sensitive" to an unusual degree are called "mediums," as having an intermediate relation between the dead and the living.

The character of the spirits thus communicating will vary, partly according to the personal character of the medium, and partly according to his sensitiveness. Spirits, out of the body as in it, seek their like. The evil spirits are also fond of playing tricks. Others are innocently roguish. Not all communications, therefore, are valuable, any more than all words of mortals. The closeness of relationship with the spirits has also increased with the increasing sensitiveness of the mediums, which grows, like any other endowment, by cultivation and practice. Beginning with crude forms, as rappings and table-tippings, it has gone on through writing, the direct touch, speech, clairvoyance, clairaudience, "materialization" or the assumption of human and other physical forms, to the seeming presence of the dead in their former shape, in broad daylight, and in every respect as real as when in the flesh, yet with added powers of appearance and disappearance which belong only to incorporeal beings. Spiritualists believe that only the development of sensitiveness is needed to make the spirit world capable of immense service to mankind, bringing ever higher classes of beings to its aid.

Spiritualists vary very much in other points of belief. Some make their confidence in spirit communications an addition to and explanation of much of Christianity, though they adopt a liberal form of that religion. To them Spiritualism explains much that seems strange in the Bible and in the history of religion,—the appearance of angels; the inspiration of prophets, psalmists, and other writers of Scripture; the miracles; the evil spirits of the New Testament; the vision of Moses and Elias in the Transfiguration; the saints coming from their graves at the Crucifixion; the re-appearance of Jesus; the alleged visions of the saints in Church history, etc. The strange facts of mesmerism, trances, hypnotism, dreams, the visions of the dying, premonitions, telepathy, and many such phenomena, which have long puzzled the minds of men, to them come under the head of "spiritual" action. Some interpret prayer as communion not with God directly, but with spirits who bear the message to Him. Others, however, begin and end their real religion with the alleged facts of spiritualism. The spirits are the only superhuman beings they believe in or have anything to do with. All else is unreal or unpractical.

The difficulty with Spiritualism is that, like all miracles, visions, etc., it rests upon individual testimony. If a fact at all, it is a fact usually of individual experience. But all scientific investigation of human testimony has shown that it is never so unreliable as when dealing with the alleged supernatural. So far from the senses being trustworthy ("seeing is believing" etc.), they are at times, especially when strange things are expected or feared, exceedingly treacherous. The history of religion shows this. In such circumstances it is not the senses which give information to the mind, but the mind which dictates to the senses what they shall see, feel, etc. The more ignorant and uncritical the age, the more abundant are its "miracles;" and the same may be said of the mind. However well informed and critical on other points, if inexperienced in dealing with the "supernatural," it is utterly untrustworthy; and it often happens that the most intellectual and sceptical are most easily deceived or self-deceived.

This consideration must be added to the universally admitted mass of imposture and gross delusion. The honesty of no man is necessarily impugned by doubting that he has seen or heard what he is firmly convinced he has. Let him read the scientific works named below. There is an admitted body of facts which have not yet been reduced to the categories either of imposture or of illusion. Their causes are not known; and the wise man is slow to pronounce judgment upon them. But the hypothesis of "spiritual" influence has not been established; and by the laws of evidence no such hypothesis is admissible till all natural causes, such as strange powers of the human mind, have been definitely set aside. Such facts belong to the realm of mystery.

As to the direct value of Spiritualism, its most ardent believer must admit that it is rather hoped for from future developments than realized from anything yet attained. It has added nothing reliable as to the future world, and nothing valuable as to the practical affairs of the present world. Whatever the "spirits" know of either, they have told nothing yet which the unaided human intellect or imagination could not have attained. On the contrary, Spiritualism has often done great harm. It would be unfair to quote the immoralities which have been stimulated by impostors or even by ignorant and coarse believers. But it is not uncommon to see that Spiritualism so inflames the imagination that it dulls interest in the affairs of this world, and leads to a restless and useless idleness, for which nothing but a feverish curiosity as to the uncanny phenomena of the "séance" seems to have any attraction. And where Spiritualism is the sole religion, it is generally a low one, tending to the "animism" of the savage state, lacking in height, breadth, or grandeur of any kind. Spirits but a little above the human condition cannot be so exclusively dealt with to any great benefit of the soul.

Yet on the other hand it may be said that Spiritualism, where it exists as a part of a wider and higher religion, has often brought inexpressible comfort to its believers. It has assured them of the continued existence of their dead, and has seemed to prolong pure and elevating intercourse with them. In an age when the historic proofs of immortality have become to many incredible, this has taken their place. Moreover, it has allied itself with more rational phases of theology in profoundly changing the popular ideas of the future life. That the dead are "fixed in an eternal state" or "done with all below," that the good cannot be better themselves or exercise that pity and love which were their marks here in helping the sinful and miserable hereafter, that the evil are tormented with a useless eternal punishment, — are beliefs destined to pass away; and in this blessed change Spiritualism has played an important part.

QUESTIONS.

What is a Spiritualist? How old is the belief in spirits? Where and how did it revive in our day? How has it continued? Who have been distinguished adherents of it? What sort of a following has it? Have they a formal creed? Why? Are they all sincere? What do they hold as to the condition of spirits after death? How do they differ here from the popular theology? Are the spirits fixed or changeable? What is their relation to men? What is "sensitiveness"? a "medium"? What affects the character of communications? Are they all reliable? What progress has been made in them? What varieties have you ever heard of? What is the hope of Spiritualism? What is its attitude toward religion? How does it interpret Christian history?

What is the main difficulty with Spiritualism? What has experience shown as to the testimony of the senses? What kind of an age or mind sees most "miracles"? What of the educated mind? Does this impugn the honesty of testimony? Are all such facts known to be delusions? What has Spiritualism done for man directly? What has been its effect often upon the ignorant? As a man's only religion, what is its grade? What good has it done?

REFERENCES.

The history is minutely given in Emma Hardinge's *Modern American Spiritualism*. The higher doctrine is set forth in *Spirit Teachings*, by M. A. Oxon. The testimony of scientists may be found in A. R. Wallace's *On Miracles and Modern Spiritualism* and Crookes' *Researches in the Phenomena of Spiritualism*. Robert Dale Owen in the Introduction to *The Debatable Land between this World and the Next* has an interesting appeal to the Protestant clergy, and in this book and *Footfalls on the Boundary of Another World* masses many strange testimonies. Other noted books are

D. D. Home's *Incidents in my Life;* Hudson Tuttle's *Studies in Psychical Science;* and *Light on the Hidden Way,* with Introduction by James Freeman Clarke.

Against Spiritualism, see W. A. Hammond's *Spiritualism and Nervous Derangement;* Edward H. Clarke's *Visions;* W. B. Carpenter's *Mental Physiology;* Lecky's *History of Rationalism in Europe,* chap. i. ; and C. W. Upham's *Salem Witchcraft.* Interesting are Howells's novel, *The Undiscovered Country;* Besant's *Herr Paulus;* Quincy's *Peckster Professorship;* and Browning's poem, *Sludge, the Medium.*

---

3. THE MORMONS.

THE name adopted by the Mormons themselves is "The Church of Jesus Christ of Latter-Day Saints." The name "Mormon" was transferred in popular speech from the ancient author or compiler of the sacred books. The claim is that in 600 B. C. a colony from Jerusalem landed on the coast of Chili. A division as to the leadership caused the rebellious elder brothers and their adherents to have dark skins and to be an idle and worthless race. Hence the North American Indians. Between them and the descendants of the divinely appointed younger son raged perpetual war, in which at last the former were victorious in 384 A. D. in New York State. Mormon, one of the survivors, collected the records in sixteen volumes and buried them. They were found by one Joseph Smith in 1823 under angelic guidance, and became the foundation of the new religion. It is now known that they were written by a half-crazy preacher, in 1812, as an historical romance.

The new sect was organized in 1830 at Fayette, New York, but soon transferred to Ohio. Here Brigham Young, a man of power and genius, became their elder in 1832. Driven away by their scandalized neighbors, who had to call in the aid of the State, they founded the city of Nauvoo, in Illinois. Here in 1843 a revelation enjoined the practice of polygamy, and a most toilsome and perilous emigration to Utah followed, where Salt Lake City was founded in 1847, and a State soon after named "Deseret." Conflict arose at once between the Mormons and the United States authorities, which has continued, often with bloodshed, to the present time. It is now hoped that by the increase in the "Gentile" population and the active efforts of the Christian missionaries the sect may be shorn of its political power, if not driven out of the country, and perhaps gradually obliterated. They are, however, still numerous and powerful, numbering in Utah 110,000, and in Idaho, Colorado, Montana, Wyoming, Washington, and England to 140,000 more. They threaten to control Nevada. They are very active in missionary work, especially among the poorer classes of England and Scandinavia. A secession took place, in 1851, of the "Reorganized Church of Jesus Christ of Latter-Day Saints," in the old temple in Ohio. They repudiated Young, vested the presidency in Joseph Smith's descendants, and threw off polygamy and some minor tenets. They also have been active missionaries.

The belief of the Mormons is a singular product of modern superstition and fanaticism, working on certain texts of the Scriptures. They hold to the Bible as authority, but believe in a continual process of revelation through the prophet, who is the head of the Church. Additional revelations are embodied in the "Book of Mormon" and the "Book of Doctrine." The Mormans are in a sense polytheists, believing in a system of gods, all of whom were at one time men. Their belief about them is in confusion, and no satisfactory statement can be made from conflicting accounts and sermons. The most characteristic features are the doctrines that all men may rise to be gods, but will retain their human forms and functions, and that the polygamous relation is carried throughout the divine hierarchy. From the gods and their numerous wives are born innumerable spirits who take possession of human bodies at the birth of the latter and begin thus their ascent to divinity. The father of these children becomes the head of this family of spirits hereafter, and his power will depend upon their number. Hence polygamy, though not an original, becomes a natural part of the system. The welfare of woman hereafter also depends upon her union with some one of the "saints."

There is also a sort of Trinity, — God and Christ being clothed with human bodies, but the Holy Spirit being omnipresent, though a material substance. Men are saved through the atonement made by Christ, on condition of their faith in the Church, repentance, baptism, and having the hands of the apostles laid on them to give the Holy Spirit. Baptism is by immersion, but only after the eighth year of age. Water is used at the communion in place of wine. In the future state, not only the body, but the habits, occupations, and necessities of the human state will be continued. Unbelievers will be burned with fire; but departed saints have preached the true faith in Hades, and any believer here may be baptized for any of his dead family or friends. The gifts of Apostolic days are continued, — as prophecy, miracles, tongues, etc. Christ is to return in person, gather Israel, including the lost Ten Tribes, to a Zion on this continent, reign for a thousand years, and then hold final judgment. The Mormons are strenuous for total abstinence from fermented liquors and tobacco; restore the Hebrew custom of paying tithes or tenths of all produce and profit to the priesthood; and believe in dancing, as of old, as a religious rite.

Their organization is firm and complete. At its head are three presidents, of whom one is supreme, and the others his counsellors; a patriarch who gives blessings; the twelve apostles, under whom the seventies act as missionaries and preachers; high-priests, bishops or secular overseers, etc. The subjection of the people to these officers is complete, and they evidently believe, as they are taught, that this government is divinely established, and that all other governments are illegal and rebellious. Their self-sacrifice and devotion to their religion have often been pathetic.

QUESTIONS.

Whence came the name Mormon ? What is the legal name ? What is the story of Mormon ? What was the real origin of the sacred records ? When and where was the sect organized ? Who has been their greatest leader ? What has been the bearing of the world toward them ? Where do they now live ? What has been the relation between them and the United States government ? Has that government the right to prohibit a religious practice ? Why has it the right to interfere with the Mormons ? How numerous are they ? Where do they abound ? Where do they get their recruits? What other body of Mormons is there, and how do they differ from the main sect?

What are their standards of doctrine? Did any prominent characters of the Bible practice polygamy (Gen xvi. 3; xxv. 1; xxviii. 9; xxix. 27, 28; 1 Chron. xi. 3)? Why, then, should it be condemned in the Mormons? Was it an original doctrine among them? What advantage has polygamy to men according to Mormonism? To women? What do they believe concerning God? What does Gen. i. 27 mean? Were not many of the classic gods once men? What is the Mormon Trinity? How are men saved? How do Mormons baptize? What do they believe concerning the future state? Where did they get their idea of baptizing for the dead (1 Cor. xv. 29)? Are they Adventists? What other peculiarities can you recall? What is their organization? What is the spirit of the laity toward the Church? Do you see anything to approve in the Mormon system? What truth is there in their idea of a continued revelation? In men growing to be gods? How far is God human? How far is the custom of taking isolated texts from the Bible as a basis of doctrine to blame for their vagaries? Or taking texts literally? Why is not the Mormon justified in taking Luke xviii. 29 so? Do you think Mormonism likely to increase? Why?

REFERENCES.

A bibliography may be found in the *History of Utah*, by H. H. Bancroft; *Book of Mormon*, Orson Pratt's edition, 1881; *Book of Doctrine and Covenant*, Orson Pratt's edition, 1880. A long and impartial account in McClintock; T. B. H. Stenhouse (once a Mormon), *Rocky Mountain Saints; New America*, by W. Hepworth Dixon.

INDEX.

A.

ABRAM, 1, 2.
Abyssinian Church, 64, 65.
Adam's Sin, 29, 31, 55, 132. (See *Human Nature, Total Depravity.*)
Adler, Felix, 179, 180.
Adventists: classified, 11; excitement, 138; peculiar belief, 154; evangelicism, 154, 155; pastors and sectarian divisions, 155; Scriptural support, 156, 157; questions and books, 157.
Agape, 49. (See *Love-feasts.*)
Albrights, 130.
Alexandrian Council, 26.
Altar: ornamented, 56; rejected, 97. (See *Worship.*)
America: discovered, 70; Lutheranism, 78; religion, 129. (See *United States.*)
American Revolution: rebellious Hessians, 78; affected by Congregationalism, 116.
American Unitarian Association: organized, 167; work, 169, 174, 175.
Anabaptists, 119. (See *Baptists.*)
Andover Seminary: doctrinal liberality, 40, 117; established, 112.
Anglican Church: view of atonement, 35; leaders, 43; part of Catholic, 95; struggle with Covenanters, 101; first step, 109; opposed by Puritans, 111; revival party, 128, 129; ritualism, 128; Universalist element, 159; Unitarian, 165. (See *England, Episcopal.*)
Antiburghers, 101.
Anti-effort Baptists, 5, 122.
Antinomianism, 37.
Anti-sectarian Sects: condition and history, 137-157; questions, 139.
Antislavery, 162. (See *Slavery.*)
Anti-Trinitarians, 163. (See *Trinity, Unitarianism.*)
Antwerp Synod, 83. (See *Holland.*)
Apocalypse, 42.
Apocrypha, 73.
Apollinaris, 26.
Apostles, relation to the Church, 45.
Apostles' Creed: cited, 14; not Trinitarian, 22, 23; teaching bodily resurrection, 43; used by Lutherans, 79; by Episcopalians, 93, 96, 97; by Congregationalists, 115.
Apostolic Succession, 63, 73, 74. (See *Bishops, Church, Episcopal.*)
Archbishops, 91, 92. (See *Bishops.*)
Arianism: modern, 27, 137; name, 163, 164; in New England, 166.
Arius, 26.
Armenian Church, 68.
Arminianism: view of atonement, 34, 35; conversion, 37, 41, 42; controversy, 83; in English Church, 90; in New England, 112; among Baptists, 122; espoused by Methodists, 131, 132. (See *Free.*)
Arminius, 31, 32.
Arnold, Thomas, 86.
Asbury, Francis, 129.
Assurance in Religion, 132.
Athanasian Creed: cited, 16; origin, 22, 23; Lutheran use, 79; discarded by American Episcopalians, 88.
Athanasius, 26.

Atonement: common views stated, 33–37; objections, 34, 35; Lutheran opinions, 80; particular efficacy, 105; views of Methodists, 132, 134; of Christian Baptists, 138; of Universalists, 160; of Unitarians, 173, 174; of Moravians, 189. (See *Jesus*.)
Augsburg Confession, 77–79.
Augustine: on human depravity, 31, 32; on salvation, 158.
Austin, missionary to England, 85.
Australian Liberals, 175.
Austria: religion, 77; Unitarianism, 176.
Authority in Religion: general reliance on, 17; rational and ecclesiastical limits, 17, 18; Scriptural, 19, 20; questions and books, 21. (See *Bible, Church*.)

B.

BALLOU, HOSEA, 159, 163.
Baltimore, settled by Catholics, 53.
Baptism: a condition of salvation, 37, 58; efficacy, 47, 74, 89; origin, 48; change of form, 48, 49; books on, 51; Catholic rite, 55; Oriental customs, 67; supernatural element, 80; among Reformed Episcopalians, 96–98; Presbyterians, 103, 104; Methodists, 132; Christian Baptists, 138; Campbellites, 138, 139; Mormons, 189. (See *Immersion, Infant, Regeneration, Sacraments*.)
Baptists: literary help, iv; classified, 11; creeds, 13; Calvinistic, 32, 71, 121, 122; opinions about atonement, 35; churches, 46, 47, 130; rites, 48; communion, 50; numbers, 75; rise in England, 86, 119, 120; congregational polity, 109, 121, 123; name, 119; history, 119–121; antiquity of opinions, 119; in America, 120; middle classes, 120, 121; government, 121; doctrines and rites, 121, 122, sects, 122, 137; statistics, 122, 123; maintenance of religious freedom, 123; ceremonial narrowness, 123, 124; questions, 124; books, 125.
Barrowism, 110, 111.
Belgic Confession, 83.
Bellows, Henry W., 168.
Bennett, Justice, 140.
Bible: infallible authority, 17–20, 54, 55, 74; books anonymous, 20; reading disapproved, 54, 73; Catholic view, 54, 58, 59; divinely inspired, 66; Eastern language, 68; versions, only standard, 73; generally trusted, 74; opinions of Liberals, 75; German criticism, 77; among Episcopalians, 90, 97; Presbyterians, 103, 107; Congregationalists, 114, 117; Baptists, 121; Methodists, 132, 134; basis of churches, 137; among Christian Baptists, 139; Quakers, 142, 143; Swedenborgians, 148–150, 153; Society for Study, 156; among Universalists, 159–161; theological texts, 168; among Unitarians, 171, 172; Spiritualists, 184; Mormons, 188. (See *Infallibility*).
Bidle, John, 165.
Bishops: Roman Catholic, 58, 59; Old Catholic, 62, 63; Greek, 67; Lutheran, 80; American Episcopal, 87–89, 92; English, 89–92; outspoken, 93; Reformed Episcopal, 97, 98; rejected by Congregationalists, 109; Moravian, 127; Methodist, 129–133; opposed, 137. (See *Archbishops, Clergy*.)
Boniface VIII., 53.
Book of Common Prayer: early revision, 86; proposed American change, 88; relied upon, 90; official use, 91; errors, dignity, and beauty, 93, 94; in Reformed Episcopal Church, 96–98; in Scotland, 101, 102; phrases changed, 166. (See *Liturgies*.)
Booth, General, 135, 136.
Brahminism, 11.
Brewster, Elder, 111.

Broad Church: scholarship, 86, 90, 91; liberality, 89.
Brownists, 119.
Brown, Robert, 110.
Buddhists, 11.
Burghers, 101.
Burial, Greek rite, 144. (See *Death*.)

C.

CALVINISM: dying, 32; atonement theories, 34–36; doctrine of election, 41, 42; sacraments, 47–50, 71; clergy, 47; baptism, 48; Lutheran variations, 79, 80; Reformed Church, 82–84; in English Church, 90; Five Points, 104, 105; among Congregationalists, 114; Baptists, 121; sway broken, 126; antagonized by Methodism, 131–134; among Universalists, 159–161; diluted, 166. (See *Arminianism*.)
Calvinists: European leaders, 71; opposed by Luther, 77; in Hungary, 78.
Calvin, John: views of Scripture, 18, 101; adherence to Augustine, 31; theories of infantile guilt, 32; books, 33; opinion of the eucharist, 50, 79; liturgy, 84; Institutes, 100; church-government, 102, 103; Sabbatarianism, 104; on predestination, 107; a persecutor, 164.
Cambridge Synod, 111, 114.
Campbellites, 138.
Camp-meetings, 129.
Candles, in worship, 56.
Cardinals, 58.
Carey, William, 123.
Carver, John, 111.
Cathedrals: English, 91; American, 92.
Catholic Apostolic Church, 156.
Catholic Church, breadth and name, 71. (See *Episcopal, Old, Roman*.)
Celibacy of Clergy, 58.
Chalcedon Council, 26, 65.

Chalmers, Thomas, 101.
Channing, William Ellery: on Jesus, 19; on the Trinity, 27; on the Church, 46; on Calvinism, 117, 167; on human nature, 133; works, 178.
Character, all-important, 170–172.
Charles I., 100.
Charles II, 101, 110, 111, 141.
Charles V., 69, 83.
Chauncy, Charles, 158, 165.
Christendom, a race divison, 71. (See *Teutonic*.)
Christening, 49. (See *Baptism, Sacraments*.)
Christian Baptists: doctrines, 122; protest, 139.
Christian Connection, 137.
Christian Denomination: classified, 11; creedless, 13; denial of Trinity, 22; names and unsectarianism, 137; history, growth, and belief, 137, 138; statistics, 138; books, 138, 139; questions, 140.
Christian Doctrines: books on, 13; essays on, 13–51. (See separate headings, such as *Total Depravity, Trinity*.)
Christianity: Jewish and Gentile, 3; early converts, 4; indebtedness to Hebrews, 6; books on, 9; name, 9, 11; Mosaic tendencies, 10; origin, history, and divisions, 10, 11; four ecclesiastical systems, statistics, 11; questions, 12; creeds, 13–16; sources of authority, 17–21; separation from Judaism, 25, 26; divinely revealed, 66; spirituality, 72; return to primitive, 137.
Christian Mission, 135. (See *Salvation Army*.)
Christians: earliest, 10; sects and numbers, 11; right to the title, 11, 12; in presence of death, 39, 40; the name, 77.
Christian Unionists: no creed, 13; sect and history, 139.
Church: authoritative establishment, 17, 18; subordination to Scripture,

194 INDEX.

18; early formation, 45; visible institution, 45, 46, 73; invisibility, 46, 73; varying forms, 46; membership, 46–48; pastors, 47 (see *Clergy*); ceremonies, 47–50 (see *Sacraments*); questions, 50, 51; books, 51, 95; superior to Scripture, 66; Eastern idea, 67; property, 70; to be obeyed, 72; liberal view of, 75, 172; authority in England, 90; not one only, 97; relations to state, 103; Presbyterian theory, 103; Congregational, 110; Methodist, 130, 131; Christian Baptist, 139; Quaker, 142, 143, 145.

Churches: in New Testament, 112, 113; distinct from societies, 113; Universalist polity, 160. (See *Congregationalism*.)

Church-membership: terms, 46, 48; among Quakers, 143. (See *Baptism, Confirmation, Sacraments*.)

Church of England, history, 85, 86. (See *Anglican, England, Episcopal*.)

Church Party, 71, 72.

Circumcision, 5.

Classes, Methodist, 130.

Clergy: rank, 47; papal, 58; Eastern, 67; authority, 73; Anglican, 91; American Episcopal, 92, 93; Presbyterian, 99, 100; Congregational, 113; Moravian, 126; Methodist, 130-133; Campbellite, 138; Christian Unionist, 139; Quaker, 142, 143; Swedenborgian, 152; Universalist. 161; Moravian, 189; Unitarian, 175. (See *Bishops, Cardinals, Education, Popes, Priesthood, Sacraments*.)

Close Communion, 121, 122.

Coke, Thomas, 129.

Colet, John, 86.

Communion: Protestant view, 47–50; name, 49; Methodist, 132; Christian Baptist, 138. (See *Consubstantiation, Eucharist, Sacraments, Transubstantiation*.)

Concord: Form of, 77; Book of, 79.

Conferences: Orthodox, 113, 114; Methodist, 130; Christian Baptist, 138; Unitarian, 168, 169, 175.

Confessional: Roman Catholic, 56, 57; Greek, 67.

Confirmation: rite, 49, 55, 56; replaced, 74. (See *Church-membership*.)

Confucians, 11.

Congregationalism: rise in England, 36, 86, 101; in Reformed Episcopal Church, 98; anti-Presbyterian, 100, 106, 107, 109; history, 109–115; founders, 110; established church of New England, 111, 112; the great defection, 112; among Baptists, 121, 123, 138, 139; relation to Methodism, 130; among Universalists, 160; Unitarians, 163–170; church-government, 112, 113; ancient town system, 113; catechisms, 114; Statement of Doctrine, 114, 115; relation to liberalism, 116, 117; books on, 118. (See *Church*.)

Congregationalists: literary aid; iv; classification, 11; creed, 13; Calvinistic, 32, 71; views of atonement, 35; future probation, 40; churches, 46, 47; clergy, 47, 113; numbers, 75; name, 109; independent principle, 109, 110, 113; early English societies, 110, 111; Holland exiles, 111; compromises, 111, 112; Western missionary work, 112; officers and membership, 113; conferences, 113, 114; synods, 114; doctrines, 114, 115; statistics, 115, 116: questions, 117, 118; education, 120, 121. (See *Unitarians*.)

Constantine: authority, 26; Donation, 53.

Constantinople Council, 26, 65.

Consubstantiation: theory, 50, 79; denied, 103, 104. (See *Eucharist, Sacraments, Transubstantiation*.)

Conversion: process, 36, 37; Methodist view, 132. (See *Human Nature*.)

Conviction of Sin, 132.

Coptic Church, 65.

INDEX. 195

Correspondence of Scripture, 149, 150, 153.
Councils of the Church: great, 52, 63–65; failure, 53; Eastern, 67, 68. (See special names, such as *Trent*.)
Covenanters: theology, 71; established, 100, 101.
Covenants of Churches, 13, 169.
Creeds: the word, 13; prevalence, 13, 14; earliest, 14; three general, 14–16; Baptist, 121; Moravian, 127; Christian Baptist, 138; Universalist, 160; below character, 170; ethical, 179. (See special names, such as *Athanasian, Nicene*.)
Cromwell, Oliver, 101, 110.
Crookes, Professor, 183, 186.
Crucifix, 67.
Crusades, 70.
Cumberland Presbyterians, 102, 106.
Cummins, Bishop David, 96, 98, 99.

D.

DARWINISM, 11, 12.
Deacons, 67. (See *Clergy*.)
Death: how met, 39, 40; prayers, 67.
Decalogue, 2.
Dedham Case, 167.
Denmark: religion, 78; churches, 80.
Dioceses, 131. (See *Bishops*.)
Disciples of Christ: creedless, 13; numbers, 75; sectarian names and facts, 128.
Dissenters in England, 92.
Divorce, 58. (See *Marriage*.)
Döllinger, Dr., 53, 62.
Dort Synod, 83, 84.
Douay Bible, 73.
Dress, among Quakers, 144. (See *Vestments*.)
Duff, Adam, 164.
Dyer, Mary, 141.

E.

EASTERN CHURCH: first great schism, 11; sects, 26; view of sin, 31; name, philosophy, and extent, 64; history, 64, 65; patriarchs, 64, 68; doctrinal secession from Latin Church, enemies and defeats, 65; doctrines, 65–68; councils, 64–66; estimate of tradition, Scripture, deity, and human nature, 66; means of salvation, value of rites, 66, 67; ecclesiastical authority and pastors, 67; ceremonies, 67, 68; liturgies, government, and statistics, 68; questions, 68, 69; books, 69. (See *Greek*.)
Ebionites, 25.
Education: among Baptists, 120, 121; Congregationalists, 116; Quakers, 142, 145; Adventists, 155. (See *Harvard*.)
Edwards, Jonathan, 112, 166.
Edward VI., 86.
Elders: Presbyterian, 106; Methodist, 130–132 (See *Clergy*.)
Election: doctrine affirmed, 35; denied, 80; unconditional, 104, 105; of infants, 105. (See *Free Will, Predestination*.)
Elizabeth, Queen, 159.
Emerson, Ralph Waldo: poem, 17; influence, 19, 168.
Emotional Religion, 126, 133, 134. 152.
England: Calvinism, 71; independence of Rome, 86; liberal scholarship, 86, 87; prelates and lords, 91; ecclesiastical property, 91, 92; religious changes, 100, 101; emigration to America, 102; the Independents, 107; Baptists, 123; Moravians, 126; Quakers, 140, 141; Swedenborgians, 148, 152; Unitarians, 163–166, 175, 176; Mormons, 188. (See *Anglican*.)
Eparchies, 68.
Ephesian Council, 26, 65.
Episcopal Church: literary aid, iv; classification, 11; creeds, 15, 16; Pelagianism, 32; free grace, 36; conversion, 37, 38; hell, 43; bishops, 46; sacraments, 47–50; baptism, 48, 49; eucharist, 49, 50, 74; Calvi-

nism, 71; denial of Protestantism, 71; apostolic succession, 74; numbers, 75; names and foundation, 85; history, 85-88; relation to Rome, 85, 86, 89, 95; prayer-book, 86; laxity and reaction, 86, 87; in United States, 87, 88; doctrines, 88-91; forms of worship, 88, 93; three parties, 88-90; church unity, 89; apostolic succession, 89, 90; evangelicism, 90; High, Low, and Broad divisions, 90; organization, 91, 92; bishops, 91; statistics, 92; in United States, 92, 93; claims, 93, 94; questions, 94; books on, 95, 96; Reformed, 96-99; contest with Presbyterianism, 103, 107; Sabbatarianism, 104; distinction from Congregationalism, 109, 112, 113; Toryism, 116; persecution of Baptists, 120. (See *Anglican* and *Reformed*.)

Erasmus, 86.
Erskine, Ebenezer, 101, 130.
Eternal Hope, 159. (See *Universalism*.)
Eternal Punishment: believed, 40, 41; English views, 90; denials, 91; belief of Presbyterians, 105; of Methodists, 132, 134; rejected by Adventists, 155; by Universalists, 158, 159; by Unitarians, 174. (See *Future Life*.)
Ethical Culture: literary aid, iv; history of the movement, 179; methods, 179, 180; literature and moral basis, 180; place and questions, 181.
Etiquette, 145.
Eucharist: a help to salvation, 37, 47-50; name, 49; books on, 51; a sacrificial offering, 55, 67, 74; differing opinions among the Reformers, 71; Luther's view, 71, 79, 80; later Protestant opinions, 88; English view, 89, 90; in Reformed Church, 97; among Presbyterians, 103, 104. (See *Communion, Lord's Supper, Sacraments*.)
Eutyches, 26.

Evangelical Alliance, 71.
Evangelical Association, 130.
Evangelical Christianity: name, iv, 71; theory of conversion, 36; dread of death, 40, modified views of hell, 43; adherence to Scriptures, 72; agreement among Methodists, 132; Christian Baptists 138, 139; Quakers, 142, 143; Adventists, 154-156.
Experimental Religion, 132-134.
Extreme Unction: practised, 56; set aside, 67, 74.

F.

FAITH: a supreme spiritual act, 72; opinions of Reformed Episcopal Church, 97; limited to the elect, 105; among Methodists, 132.
Fall of Man, 29-31, 66, 74. (See *Human Nature, Total Depravity*.)
Farrar, Archdeacon, 42, 90, 159.
Fashions, 145, 146. (See *Dress* and *Vestments*.)
Fenwicke, John, 141.
First Churches in New England, 112. (See *Congregationalism*.)
Fisher, Mary, 140.
Flowers, used in worship, 56.
Forgiveness, priestly, 56, 57. (See *Atonement*.)
Fox Children, 182.
Fox, George: life, 140, 141, 146; books, 147.
France: Calvinism, 71; liberality, 164, 177.
Freedom in Religion: three steps, 109; defended by Baptists, 122, 123.
Free Grace, 36, 133, 136, 137.
Free Methodists, 130.
Freen, James, 166.
Free Seats, 93.
Free (Will) Baptists: name, 120; numbers, 122; secessions, 137.
Free Will: doctrine, 31-33; Unitarian view, 174. (See *Arminianism*.)
Friends: literary aid, iv; silence, 10; classified, 11; creedless, 13; views

of Trinity, 22; rejection of sacraments, 48; exclusion, 71; opposed to Calvinism, 71, 141, 142; rationalism developed, 72; rise in England, 86; names, 140; history, 140-143; tolerated, 141; in the American colonies 141, 142; inferences from doctrine of the inner light, 142, 143; common ceremonies rejected, organization, 143; discipline and customs, 144; philanthropy, 144, 145; statistics, 145; criticism, first liberals, questions, 146; books, 147; serene trust, 152.
Fry, Elizabeth, 142, 144.
Funerals, 143. (See *Burial* and *Death*.)
Furness, W. H., poem, 33.
Future Life: general belief, 39; hopes and fears, 39, 40; drama in four acts, 40, 41; early Christian belief, 41; two ultimate conditions, 42, 43; modern protest, 43; questions, 43, 44; books, 44; general agreement, 74; Swedenborg's view, 151; opinions of Universalists, 158-161; Unitarians, 174; Mormons, 188, 189. (See *Eternal*.)

G.

Gay, Ebenezer, 166.
General Baptists, 120.
Genesis: not inspired, 20; teachings about sin 29, 30.
Genevan Church, 103. (See *Calvin*.)
Gentiles: religion, 3; intermarriage, 4.
German Methodists, 130.
Germany: emigration, 53; Biblical criticism, 77, 81, 86, 87; general religion, 78; Lutheranism, 80; emigration to America, 102; Baptists, 120, 122; Moravians, 126; Swedenborgians, 148; Unitarians, 176. (See *Lutheranism*.)
Giles, Chauncey, 152.
God: general Christian belief, 22; divergencies, 22, 23; questions, 23;

salvation compact, 34; view of Swedenborgians, 149; Universalists, 160; Unitarians, 163-167; relation of Ethical Movement to deity, 179. (See *Atonement, Holy Spirit, Jesus, Trinity*.)
Good Hope, discovery of Cape, 70.
Gospel Truth, considered a monopoly, 71.
Grace, effectual, 105. (See *Free*.)
Great Assize, 41.
Great Awakening, 112, 165, 166.
Greek Church: classification and numbers, 11; creeds, 14, 15; clergy and sacraments, 47; future progress, 64; language, 64, 68; errors, 71; branch of one great church, 89. (See *Eastern* and *Russia*.)
Greenwood, John, 110.
Gregory the Great, 52, 85.
Guilt, 32. (See *Adam, Eternal, Human Nature, Total Depravity*.)
Gurneyites, 142.

H.

Half-way Covenant, 111, 112, 165, 166.
Harvard College, 112, 167, 175.
Heaven, a condition, 151. (See *Eternal, Future Life*.)
Hebrews, 1. (See *Jews*.)
Hebrews, Book of, 34, 35.
Heck, Barbara, 129.
Hegel, 11, 12.
Hell, 42, 43. (See *Eternal, Future,* and *Judgment*.)
Henry VIII., 86, 92.
Heredity, 35, 107. (See *Election, Predestination*.)
Hicks, Elias: career, 142; books, 147.
Hicksites: tenets, 22; numbers, 145.
High Church: proper place, 72; in England, 86, 88, 90; in America, 96; baptism, 124; Wesley, 128. (See *Episcopal* and *Low*.)
Hildebrand, 53.
Holland: Calvinism, 71, 100; Luth-

eranism; 78; tenets, 78; connection with America, 78, 102; churches, 83; ecclesiastical history, 84; Congregationalism, 110, 111; sects, 119, 122; liberalism, 164, 165, 176.

Holy Spirit: deity, 23, 90; converting work, 37; in creeds, 65–67; in councils, 67; response to faith, 72; connection with Scripture, 73; in Westminster Confession, 104, 105; views of Congregationalists, 114, 115; Methodists, 133, 134; Quakers, 142, 143, 145; Swedenborgians, 149, 150. (See *God, Jesus, Trinity*.)

Home, David Dunglas, 182.

Hubmaier, Balthazar, 119.

Huguenots: Calvinistic, 71, 100; connection with America, 102.

Human Nature: innocence and fall, 29–33, 66; corruption and guilt, 31; three views, 31, 32; questions, 32; books, 33; soundness, 33, 34; restoration, 67; Swedenborg's view, 149. (See *Guilt* and *Total Depravity*.)

Hungary: religion, 78; Unitarians, 163.

Huss, John, 126.

Hyacinthe, Father, 53, 63.

I.

IMAGE-WORSHIP, 67, 74.

Immersion: Greek rite, 67; reasons stated, 121–124; among minor sects, 138, 139; Mormon practice, 189. (See *Baptism, Sacraments*.)

Immortality, lost, 66. (See *Eternal* and *Future*.)

Incense, 56.

Independents: rise in England, 86, 101; church-government, 109; persecution and emigration, 110, 111; in Holland, 119; Baptist relationship, 120. (See *Congregationalism*.)

Indians: Lutheranism, 78; origin, 187.

Indulgences, theory explained, 57.

Infallibility: not taught in Scriptures, 20; papal, 53, 54; impossible, 60; decreed, 53, 62; rejected, 53, 62, 63, 171. (See *Bible* and *Pope*.)

Infants: perdition, 32, 43, 105; baptism, 48, 49, 58, 89, 93, 96, 97, 119, 121, 123, 124. (See *Baptism* and *Regeneration*.)

Inner Light, 140, 142. (See *Friends* and *Holy Spirit*.)

Inquisition, 58.

Inspiration, 17–20, 58. (See *Bible, Holy Spirit, Infallibility*.)

Ireland: emigration, 53, 102; ecclesiastical history, 85; disestablishment, 91; Presbyterianism, 138; Unitarianism, 165, 175.

Irvingites, 156.

Isidorean Decretals, 52, 53.

Italy: emigration, 53; liberalism, 164.

J.

JACOB, HENRY, 110.

Jacobites, 65, 68.

James, Saint, liturgy, 68.

Jerusalem: a centre, 64; capture, 65; synod, 66; patriarchate, 68.

Jesuits, 53.

Jesus: nationality, 3, 5, 24; preaching and life, 10; church founded, 17; no writer, 20; rank and office, 24; deified, 24, 25, 27, 58, 74, 90, 118, 132, 134; textual discussion, 24, 25; earthly appearance and gospel pictures, 25; Greek and Latin ideas, 26; early doctrinal controversies, 25–27; modern dissent, 26, 27; questions, 28; books on, 28, 29; view of human nature, 30; influence in salvation, 33–36; second coming, 40, 41, 151, 154–157; on the judgment seat, 41, 42; relation to the Church, 45, 54, 89; communion, 49; two natures, 65; in creeds, 66, 67; opinions of Congregationalists, 114, 115; of Baptists, 121; devotion of believers, 126; ancient heretical theories, 137, 138; rites, 143; opinions of Swedenborgians, 149, 151;

INDEX.
199

of Universalists, 158, 159, 161; of Unitarians, 164–175. (See *God, Holy Spirit, Trinity*.)

Jews: suggestions from Dr. Lasker, iv; name and origin, 1; history, 1–4; three periods and formation, 2; affirmation, 2, 3; exile and changes in belief, 2, 3; Scriptures, 3; denial of Christianity, 3, 5, 6; reformation, 3, 4; creeds, authority, marriage, 4; doctrines and Sabbath, 4, 5; ceremonies, 5; persecution and theological influence, 6; occupations and statistics, 7; questions, 7, 8; books on, 8; numbers, 11; Messianic opinions, 24; ideas of deity, 24, 25; rites discarded, 72; ritualistic spirit, 123; secondary sense of Scripture, 153; Unitarianism, 164, 172, 173.

John's Gospel, doubtful authenticity, 24, 25.

Jones, Abner, 137.

Jowett, Professor, 86.

Judgment Day: general view, 39–43; opinions of Swedenborgians, 151; Universalists, 158; Unitarians, 174. (See *Eternal* and *Future*.)

Justification: theories, 37, 38, 58, 72; ancient opinion, 83. (See *Faith*.)

K.

KEBLE, JOHN, 86.

King's Chapel, 166.

Kingsley, Charles, 43, 86, 90, 159.

Knox, John, 100.

L.

LATIN CHURCH: philosophy, 25 : language, 56. (See *Eastern, Greek, Roman*.)

Leo the Great, 52.

Letters of Church-fellowship, 113. (See *Church-membership*.)

Liberal Christians: the epithet, iv; views of human nature, 33, 34; of predestination, 35; of conversion, 36; of sanctification and justification, 37, 38; not afraid of death, 40; sacramental opinions, 49, 50; anti-Calvinistic, 71; rationalistic, 72; in English Church, 89. (See *Arminianism, New Church, Unitarianism, Universalism*.)

Liberal Protestant Sects, 158–179.

Lindsey, Theophilus, 27, 165.

Litany, 88, 91, 93, 94.

Liturgies: ancient, 68; American, 88; dignity, 93; Methodist, 132. (See *Book*.)

Locke, John, 165.

Logos, 26, 49.

Longfellow, Samuel, poetry, 45.

Lord's Supper: name, 49; terms, 112; kiss, 155. (See *Communion, Eucharist, Sacraments*.)

Love-feasts, 49, 132.

Low Church, 86, 88–90. (See *Episcopal* and *High*.)

Lutheranism: sacraments, 47–50: not tolerated, 69; in Holland, 71, 83; history, 77–79; creeds, 79; differences from Calvinism, 79, 80, 100; questions, 82; books on, 82; formulas of belief, 88; relation to Presbyterianism, 103; view of Scriptural inspiration, 107.

Lutherans: classified, 11; baptism, 48; eucharist, 50, 71, 74; divisions, 71, 78, 79, 122; numbers, 75; name, 77; location, 78; doctrines and rites, 79, 80; organization and polity, 80, 81; old guard, statistics, 81; Sabbath-observance, 104; Moravian element, 126.

Luther, Martin: views of Scripture, 18; outlawry, 69, 70; advent, 70, 71; limiting truth, 81; stirring efforts, 86, 119.

M.

MARONITES, 65.

Marriage: sacrament, 47, 56, 58; of

Greek priests, 67; restrictions, 74; English, 92; Quaker strictness, 142, 143; ceremony, 144.
Mass, 49, 50, 55. (See *Eucharist*.)
Massachusetts: parish taxes remitted, 111; churches, 113; Congregationalists, 115; Baptists, 120; Universalists, 161; Unitarians, 165-168.
Maurice, F. D., 43, 86, 90, 159.
Mayhew, Jonathan, 158, 166.
Meadville School, 175.
Melanchthon, 77, 79.
Mennonites, 119, 122.
Messiahship: claim and meaning, 6; denied, 24. (See *Jesus*.)
Methodism: creed, 13; Pelagianism, 32; views of atonement, 35; free grace, 36; conversion, 37, 38; anti-Calvinistic, 71, 133, 134; Moravian influence, 126; history, 127-130; revival influence, 128; expansion, 128, 129; doctrinal theories and three theological characteristics, 131, 132; books on, 131, 135; evangelicism, 132; questions, 134. (See *Arminianism*.)
Methodists: literary aid, iv; classified, 11; church-government, 46; reaction, 86; numbers, 75; in the South, 119, 120; name, 127; in America, 129, 130; divisions, 129, 130, 131; warmth, 129, 133; organization, 130, 131; literature and standards, 131; liturgy, 132; statistics, 132, 133; popular devotion, 133; in New England, 166.
Millennium, 40, 156, 157. (See *Adventists* and *Second*.)
Millerites, 41, 138, 154.
Milton, John, 165.
Miracles, 171, 184, 185, 189.
Missions: Lutheran, 84; Congregational, 115, 116; opposition, 122; Baptist, 122, 123; leaders, 123; Moravian, 126; Methodist, 132, 133; Salvation Army, 135, 136; Campbellite, 138; Quaker, 140.
Missourians, 78, 155.

Mohammedans: numbers, 11; success, 65.
Monophysites, 26, 65, 68.
Monothelites, 26.
Moravians: classified, 11; name, 125; history and customs, 126; statistics, questions, and books, 127; influence on Methodism, 128.
More, Sir Thomas, 86.
Mormonism: name and foundation, 187; history, 187, 188; literature, 188; theology, 188, 189; ceremonies and organization, 189; questions, 189, 190; books, 190.
Mosaic Law, 4, 5.
Muhlenberg, Henry Melchior, 78.
Murray, John, 158, 159, 163.

N.

NATIONAL CONFERENCE, 168, 169.
Negroes, 129, 133.
Nestorian Church, 65, 68.
Nestorius, 65, 68.
New Church. (See *New Jerusalem*.)
New Connection, 120.
New England: Calvinism, 71; Episcopacy, 87; Congregationalism, 106; established church, 111; revivals, 112; creeds and textbooks, 114; settlement, 116; Baptists, 125; Universalists, 158-161; Unitarians, 165-160; Arminianism, 166. (See *Massachusetts* and *United States*.)
New Hampshire Confession, 121, 125.
New Jerusalem Church: literary aid, iv; theory of the judgment, 42, 43; exclusion, 71; rationalism 72; name, 147; history, 147, 148; founder, 147-149; doctrines, 148-151; the Lord, 149; correspondence of Scriptures, 149,150; human nature, 150; continuity of life, 150, 151; second coming of Christ, 151; organization, 151, 152; pastors, statistics, and influence, 152; books on, 152-154; claims denied, 153; questions, 153. (See *Swedenborg*.)

INDEX. 201

Newman, Cardinal: quoted, 18, 95; submission, 63; leadership, 86.
New School Presbyterians, 102, 106.
Newton, Sir Isaac, 165.
New York: Dutch Church, 83; Universalists, 161.
Nicæa, Council of, 26, 64, 164.
Nicene Creed: cited, 15, 16; changed, 23, 65; Lutheran use, 79; Anglican, 90; Reformed Episcopal, 96, 97; Congregational, 114. (See *Apostles, Athanasian,* and *Creeds.*)
Non-Christian Societies, 179-190.
Non-conformists, 128, 129. (See *Dissenters.*)
Norway: religion, 78; churches, 80.

O.

OCCHINO, BERNARDINO, 165.
O'Kelly, James, 137.
Old Catholics: leaders and movement, 53; origin and purpose, 62, 63; stagnation, questions, and books, 63. (See *Döllinger.*)
Old Connection of Baptists, 120.
Old Lutherans, 78.
Old School Presbyterians, 102, 106.
Ordination: sacramental, 56; by people, 74. (See *Clergy* and *Sacraments.*)
Oriental Missions, 140.
Origen, 158.
Original Sin, 29. (See *Adam* and *Human Nature.*)
Orthodox Protestants: photographed, iii; literary aid, iv; dread of death, 40; views of communion, 50; in New England, 109; Universalist leaning toward, 162; relation to Unitarians, 171-175.

P.

PAPAS, in Greek Church, 67.
Parker, Theodore, 19, 167, 168.
Particular Baptists, 120.

Patriarchs, 64, 67, 68. (See *Clergy.*)
Paul: denials, 10; opinions not fully accepted, 12; spiritualizing Jesus, 25; views of sin, 30, 31; epistles, 31; relation to Christianity, 72.
Pauline Tendencies, 10, 72, 97, 145.
Pelagius and his Doctrine, 31, 32. (See *Human Nature.*)
Penances: Romanist, 56; Greek, 67.
Penn, William: position, 141, 146; books, 147.
Pepin's Gift, 52, 53.
Perfection, as a doctrine, 132.
Permission to Sin, 57.
Perseverance of the Saints, 35, 105.
Peter: in Rome, 52; the rock, 54; relation to Christianity, 72.
Petrine Tendencies, 10, 72, 97, 123.
Philadelphia: a Presbyterian centre, 102; Confession, 121, 125.
Pictures in Church, 67. (See *Image-worship*).
Pietists: sect, 77; missions, 123.
Pilgrims: Calvinistic, 83; leaders from Holland, 111; unlike the Puritans, 117.
Plymouth, settled, 111.
Poland: Unitarianism, 27, 164; churches, 77; Calvinism, 100; Catholic reaction, 164. (See *Hungary* and *Transylvania*.)
Polygamy, 187-189. (See *Marriage*).
Polytheism, 188.
Popes: prominent, 52, 53; position, 58; power, 59; authority rejected, 62; corruption, 70. (See *Clergy, Infallibility,* and personal names of different pontiffs.)
Prayer: to the saints for friends, 57; among Methodists, 132; among Unitarians, 174.
Prayer-meetings, political example, 116.
Predestination: doctrine, 35, 36; Presbyterian views, 107; disregarded in New England, 112; and by certain Baptists, 122. (See *Election, Eternal, Human Nature.*)

202 INDEX.

Presbyterian Churches, becoming Unitarian, 106, 107, 163, 165.
Presbyterianism: Calvinistic 71, 102, 103; rise in England, 86; established in Scotland, 91; name, 99, 100; polity, 100; history, 100-102; in United States, 102; Confessions, 102, 103; doctrines, 102-105; Scriptural reliance, 103; peculiar tenets in Five Points, 104, 105; theories of perdition, 105; questions, 107, 108; books on, 108, 109; second step toward religious liberty, 109; withdrawals, 110; among Baptists, 122.
Presbyterians: classified, 11; views of atonement, 35; ecclesiastical government, 46, 47, 103, 106, 109, 130; clergy, 47; numbers, 75; kinship with Reformed Episcopacy, 98; discipline, 100, 101; liturgy, 101, 102; two schools, 102, 106; schisms, 102, 106, 110, 137; originators of Puritan Sabbath, 104; evangelicism, 105; statistics, 106; Protestant colorguard, 107; Plan of Union, 113, 114; relation to Christian Baptists, 137; second-advent views, 156.
Preterition, akin to predestination, 35, 105.
Priesthood: corrupt, 70; universal, 73, 97, 98.
Priestley, Joseph, 165.
Priest, name omitted, 96. (See *Clergy.*)
Printing, 70.
Probation: earthly, 35, 36; future, 112; Methodist custom, 132. (See *Eternal* and *Future.*)
Propaganda at Rome, 58.
Prophets, 2.
Protestantism: appearance in Christendom, 10, 11; appeal to authority, 17, 18; views of free grace, 36; sanctification, 37; hell, 42, 43; race division, 63, 71; differences from Greek Church, 66, 67; revival of Christianity, 72; name, 69, 70; history, 70-74; causes of protest, 70, 71; three main parties, 71, 72; doctrines, 72-74; importance and impartation of faith, 72, 73; divergence from Romanism, 73; church and ministry, 73, 74; two sacraments and minor differences, 74; questions, 75, 76; books on, 76; opposed in Scotland, 100; indebtedness to Presbyterianism, 107; Calvinistic, 133.
Protestant Reformation: adherence to Scripture and rejection of ecclesiastical authority, 18-20; unchanged views of the Trinity, 26; human nature, 31, 32; atonement, 34; changed views of the Church, 46; clergy, 47; sacraments, 47, 48; long preparation, 70; first aim, 70, 71; literature, 108, 109; development of Universalism, 158; of Unitarianism, 164.
Protestant Sects: evangelical, 77-136; anti-sectarian, 137-157; liberal, 158-179.
Protestants: numbers, 11; creeds, 14; denial of sacramental grace, 37; dread of death, 39-41; drift toward belief in future probation, 40; retracing steps, 50; friendly prayers, 57; schisms and sects, 71; proper classification, 71, 72; statistics, 75; use of Catholic creeds, 88; Episcopal differences, 90.
Prussian Church, 77.
Purgatory, 40, 57, 67, 74.
Puritans: adherence to Bible, 18; atonement, 35; Calvinistic, 71; rise, 86; in New England, 87; rigidity, 93; "belated," 97; Sabbath observance, 104; origin, 107; name, 109, 110; emigration, 111; education, 116; not identical with Pilgrims, 117.
Pusey, Edward Bouverie, 86.

Q.

QUAKERS. (See *Friends.*)

INDEX.

R.

RACOVIANS, 163.
Radbert, Paschasius, 49, 50.
Rationalism, 81.
Rationalists, 170, 171
Rational Party, 72, 77. (See *Liberal* and *Unitarian*.)
Reformed Dutch Church: classification, 11; numbers, 75, 106; title, history, controversies, American establishment and language, 83; doctrines, 83, 84; organization, statistics, questions, books, 84.
Reformed Episcopal Church: name and formation, 96; history, 96, 97; principles, 97; belated Puritan tendencies, 97, 98; organization, statistics, and protest, 98; questions, 98, 99; books, 99.
Regeneration: a divine work, 35 - 39, 66; baptismal, 80, 89, 93, 96, 97; Methodist view, 132. (See *Conversion, Human Nature*.)
Reinkens, Bishop, 53, 62.
Relics, 57, 74.
Religious Freedom: three steps, 109; Baptist maintenance, 122, 123.
Relly, James, 158.
Remission of Sin, 57.
Renaissance, 70.
Reprobation, 105. (See *Predestination* and *Preterition*.)
Restorationists, 158, 161. (See *Universalism*.)
Resurrection of Body, 43, 90.
Revelation, Book of, lurid pictures, 42.
Revelation, not rare, 171. (See *Bible, Holy Spirit*.)
Revivals: Methodist, 128, 129; Salvation Army, 135.
Robertson, F. W., 43, 159.
Robinson, John, 110.
Roman Catholic Church: steadfast faith, iii; literary aid, iv; ritual 10, 55–57, 72; classification, 11; statistics, 11, 59; creeds, 14-16; final authority, 17, 18; Pelagianism, 32; theory of atonement, 34; predestination, 35; free grace and conversion, 36; justification and sanctification, 37; inspiring dread of death, 39-41; pictures of hell; 42, 43; ecclesiastical foundation, 45; clergy, 47; sacraments, 47-50, 55, 56; Scripture-reading discouraged, 54, 73; name, 52, 64; historic formation, 52, 53; chief events and temporal power, 53; in America, 53, 54; doctrines, 54 - 59; one infallible body, 54, 60, 73; authoritative decisions, 54, 55; centre of worship, 55; admission, 55; language, vestments, candles, and incense, 56; remission of sin, 56, 57; treasury of merits, aids to devotion, 57; future state, 57, 67; divorce, 58; polity and government, 58, 59; doctrinal liberality, 59, 60; fundamental claim, 60; questions, 60, 61; books, 61, 62; rebellious German scholars, 62; firmer union, 64, 65, divergence from Greek Church, 66–68; landed property, 70; English schism, 71, 85, 86; works and faith, 72; unity, 73; relation to Lutheranism, 77, 79; formulas in Protestant use, 88; in Anglican Church, 89; 90; favorable reaction, 95; Calvinistic opposition, 100; Presbyterian conflict, 103, 107; Sunday-observance, 104; errors rejected 109, 110; missionary zeal, 123; trust in baptism, 124; persecution of Hussites, 126; ecclesiastical system partially adopted by Protestants, 130; zeal, 133; sweeping Poland, 164; estimate of Bible, 171.
Rome: empire, 52, 60; city, 58.
Roundheads of Liberalism, 162.
Russia: Greek Church, 64, 65; elaborate ritual, 68; Protestantism, 78.

S.

SABBATH: Jewish observance, 4, 5; Presbyterian influence, 104; or Saturday, 122.
Sacraments: differing opinions, 47-50; definition, 55, 56; in Greek Church, 66, 67; a channel of faith, 72; priestly ministration, 73; number, 74; Episcopal, 89, 90; Presbyterian, 103, 104; not essential to parish-membership, 113; Methodist, 132; Quaker rejection, 143; Swedenborgian, 152. (See *Baptism* and *Eucharist*.)
Saint-worship, 57, 74.
Salter, William M., iv, 180.
Salvation Army: names, 135; development, 135, 136; growth and literature, 136.
Salvation: two theories, 34; Scriptural support, 34, 35; extent and foreordination, 35, 36; personal crisis, channels of grace, attainment, 37; questions, 38; books, 39; universal, 42; Calvinistic view, 104, 105; Methodist, 132. (See *Atonement, Conversion, Eternal, Universalism*.)
Sanctification, 37, 38.
Satan and Sin, 29.
Savoy Confession, 110.
Scotland: early missionaries, 85; bishops, 87; established church, 91; Calvinism, 100; religious revolution, 100, 101; leaders, 101; emigration, 102; Genevan ideal, 103; churches, 106; Universalist element, 161; Unitarian, 175.
Scriptural Party, 72.
Scriptures. (See *Bible*.)
Scrooby Church, 110.
Seabury, Bishop, 87.
Second Advent of Jesus, 40, 41. (See *Adventists*.)
Semitic Race, 1, 2.
Servetus, 23, 26, 164.
Seventh Day Adventists, 155.

Seventh Day Baptists, 122.
Shinto Sect, 11.
Sin: beginning, 29, 30; consequences, 57. (See *Adam, Atonement, Eternal, Guilt, Human Nature*.)
Six-Principle Baptists, 122.
Smith, Joseph, 187, 188.
Smyth, John, 119, 120.
Socinianism, 163.
Socinus, Laelius and Faustus: rejection of the Trinity, 23, 27; Pelagianism, 31, 32; early influence, 164, 165.
Southern States: Baptists, 120, 121; Methodists, 133; Romanists, 57.
Spain, liberalism in, 176.
Sparks, Jared, 167.
Spiritualism: literary aid, iv; wide definition, 181; ancient and modern, 182; creedless, 182, 183; main belief, 183, 184; sensitiveness, 183; variations in opinion, Biblical incidents, 184; difficulties in supernaturalism, 184, 185; influence and service, 185, 186; questions, 106; literature, 186, 187.
Stanley, Dean, 43, 86, 159.
Sunday-schools: Baptist, 122; Christian Baptist and Campbellite, 138; Congregationalist, 115; Episcopal, 93; Methodist, 132, 133; Quaker, 145; Reformed Episcopal, 98; Swedenborgian, 151, 152; Unitarian, 175; Universalist, 161; summary, 75.
Swedenborg: career and works, 147-154.
Swedenborgians. (See *New Jerusalem Church*.)
Sweden: religion, 78; bishops converted, 80; liberalism, 176.
Switzerland: Calvinism, 71, 100; liberalism, 164, 176.
Syllabus of Errors, 53.
Synods, Greek, 68. (See *Dort*, and other special names.)

T.

TALMUD, 3.
Taxation for Churches: in England, 92; in New England, 111.
Temperance: among Universalists, 162; Mormons, 189.
Temple, Dr., 86.
Temple: rebuilt, 2; and synagogue, 5; sacrifices, 35.
Tennent, Gilbert, 166.
Tertullian, 23.
Teutonic Race, 63, 71.
Thirty-nine Articles: adopted, 86, 88; reduced, 86, 96, 97.
Tithes, Mormon, 189.
Titles, disused, 144.
Tobacco, 189.
Toledo Council, 65.
Toryism, 116.
Total Depravity: general belief, 29, 30; Calvinistic, 104; Methodist, 132, 134. (See *Human Nature* and *Sin*.)
Tractarianism: movement, 86, 87; leaders, 87, 95.
Transcendentalism, 167, 168.
Transubstantiation, 50, 55, 74, 79, 86, 97, 103. (See *Consubstantiation, Eucharist*.)
Transylvania, 78, 163, 164, 176.
Trent Council, 31, 53, 87.
Trinity: not stated in the Bible, 22; word, doctrinal history, questions, 22, 23; Catholic view, 58; true form, 65; in creeds, 66; sectarian agreement, 74; Anglican view, 90; Calvinistic, 105; Congregational, 114, 115, 117; Methodist, 132, 134; denials, 122, 137, 138; opinions of Swedenborgians, 149. 152; Universalists, 158, 160; Unitarians, 163–175; Mormons, 188; Sabellian theory, 158, 159; disbelief punishable as blasphemy, 165. (See *God, Holy Spirit, Jesus*.)
Tunkers, 122.

U.

UNITARIAN BOOKS: on doctrinal differences, 13; on creeds, 17; on authority, 21; on Trinity, and deity of Jesus, 28, 29; on human nature, 33; on salvation, atonement, and kindred topics, 39; on future life, 44, 109; on church and sacraments, 51, 125; on Christian history, 61, 62, 82; on Episcopal Church, 96; on Calvinism, 117; on Congregationalism, 118, 125, 147; on Quakerism, 147; on Swedenborgianism, 153; on Unitarian history and doctrines, 177, 178.
Unitarian Churches: creeds, 13, 14; congregational organization, 46, 109, 116, 172; Presbyterian, 106, 107, 163, 165; New England schism, 112; original parishes, 116; Old Connection, 120; first, 165; denominational formation, 165–167; polity, 168, 169; covenants and conferences, 169, 170; American, 175; English, 175, 176; European, 176.
Unitarianism: difficulty of statement, v; Jewish ideas, 7, 8; teachers, 19; relation to Biblical authority, 21, 171, 172, 177; views of incarnation, 27; of human nature, 28–33; origin of modern, 28; view of the atonement, 34, 38, 173; rejection of predestination, 35; theory of heredity, 35; conversion, 36, 173, 174; justification and sanctification, 37, 38; divine judgment, 42, 177; future punishment, 43, 44, 174; relation to Romanism, 59–62, 63; relation to the Greek Church, 69; swiftly moving tendencies, 71; rationalism, 72; Protestantism, 75, 76; relations with Lutheranism, 81, 82; with Congregationalism, 109, 112, 116, 117, 168, 169; the great defection, 112; relations with Methodism, 133; with Campbellites, and similar minor sects, 139; with Quakerism, 145,

146; Swedenborgianism, 152, 153; Universalism, 159–163; age, 164, 176; historic reappearance, 164; prosperity, 165; English founders, 165, 176; in New England, 165–167, 176; relation to Arminianism, 166; separation, 167, 168; vocation, 168; tendencies rather than opinions, 170; two distinctive ideas, 170–172; reason, 170, 171; miracles, 171; virtues and graces of common life, 171, 172; future life, 174; negations, 170, 177; questions, 176, 177; doctrines, 170, 177.

Unitarians: criticised, iii; literary aid, iv; classified, 11, 12; creedless, 13; rejection of authority, 18–21; belief in inspiration, 19, 20; views as to the godhead, 22, 23; ancient and modern, 23; Polish, 27; Pelagianism, 32; calmness in death, 40; disbelief in endless misery, 43; ecclesiastical forms, 46, 47, 49–51, 174; sympathy with Catholicism, 59, 60; the only true Protestants, 75; excluded, 71; dread of insincerity, 107; indebtedness to Baptists, 123; to Methodists, 133; Quaker adherents, 142; compared with Universalists, 161, 163; martyrs, 164; organizations, 168; platforms, 169; rationalism, 171; opinions about Jesus, 172, 173; character above creed, 171–173; faults, worship, and theological ignorance, 174, 175; non-attendance at church, 175; statistics, 175, 176; policy, 177; radical unity with the Ethical Movement, 180, 181; views of Spiritualism, 185, 186. (See *Liberal*.)

United Brethren, 125–130.

United States: Jews, 7; liberal theology, 27; sacramental differences, 50; Roman Catholics, 53, 54, 59; denominational numbers, 75; Lutherans, 80, 81; Dutch Reformed Church, 82–84; Episcopalians, 87, 88, 92, 93; Presbyterians, 102, 103, 106; Reformed Churches, 106; Independents, 110; Congregationalists, 115, 116; Moravians, 126; Methodists, 129, 133; Quakers, 140–142; Swedenborgians, 148; Universalists, 159–161; Unitarians, 163–178; Ethical Movement, 179, 180; Mormons, 188.

Unity of God: consensus of belief, 22; ancient doctrine, 164. (See *God, Trinity*.)

Universalism: grand protest, 43; name and early advocates, 158; history and American preachers, 158, 159; eternal hope, 159; doctrines, 159, 160; use of Scriptures, 160; relation to Unitarianism, 161, 162; questions, 162, 163; books, 163.

Universalists: literary aid, iv; denial of Trinity, 22; believe in Judgment, 42; church basis, 47; excluded, 71; platform, 159, 160; worship and organization, 160; statistics, 161; conservatism, democracy, and philanthropy, 162.

Utah, 187, 188.

V.

VATICAN COUNCIL, 62, 63.
Vestments, 56, 84, 109.
Vicarious Atonement, 34. (See *Atonement*.)
Virginia Baptists, 120.
Virgin Mary: Mother of God, 26, 65; adored in place of Jesus, 27; immaculately conceived, 53; homage paid, 57, 66; and withheld, 74.
Vulgate, 73.

W.

WALDENSES, 119.
Wales: church-history, 85; establishment, 91; Congregationalism, 109; Unitarianism, 165, 175.
Wallace, Alfred Russell, 182, 186.

INDEX.

Ware, Henry, 167.
Watch-meetings, 132.
Wesley, Charles, 128.
Wesley, John: career and opinions, 126–131; works, 135.
Western Church, 31. (See *Eastern, Latin, Roman.*)
Western Conference, 105, 106.
Western States: Methodists, 133; Christian Baptists, 138, 139; liberalism, 168, 169, 175.
Westminster Catechism, 103, 114.
Westminster Confession: on the Bible, 18; on salvation, 46; adopted by Reformed Church, 84; by Presbyterians, 102, 103; on the Sabbath, 104; used by Congregationalists, 110; in New England, 114.
Whateley, Archbishop, 86.
Whewell, William, v.
Whitefield, George, 112, 127, 128, 158, 166.
Whittier, John Greenleaf, poetry, 29, 39.

Wigglesworth's Poem, 109, 114.
Wightman, Edward, 164.
Wilbur, John, 142.
Williams, Roger, 120.
Winchester Profession of Faith, 159, 160.
Witebrennarians, 122.
Women Preachers, 144.
Worship: Catholic, 56, 57; not connected with the Ethical Movement, 180. (See *Prayer, Sacraments.*)

Y.

Young, Brigham, 187.

Z.

Zinzendorf, Count, 126.
Zurich, Baptist doctrine, 119.
Zwingli: view of sacraments, 50; differing from Luther, 71.

www.ingramcontent.com/pod-product-compliance
Lightning Source LLC
Chambersburg PA
CBHW020822230426
43666CB00007B/1064